SUPPORT AND PROTECTION ACROSS THE LIFECOURSE
A Practical Approach for Social Workers

Caroline McGregor and Pat Dolan

T0385605

P

First published in Great Britain in 2021 by

Policy Press, an imprint of
Bristol University Press
University of Bristol
1-9 Old Park Hill
Bristol
BS2 8BB
UK
t: +44 (0)117 954 5940
e: bup-info@bristol.ac.uk

Details of international sales and distribution partners are available at
policy.bristoluniversitypress.co.uk

British Library Cataloguing in Publication Data
A catalogue record for this book is available from the British Library

ISBN 978-1-4473-6054-4 paperback
ISBN 978-1-4473-6055-1 ePub
ISBN 978-1-4473-6056-8 ePdf

Cover design: Andrew Corbett
Front cover image: Shutterstock 1855853806

Bristol University Press and Policy Press use environmentally responsible
print partners

Printed and bound in Great Britain by CMP, Poole

This book is dedicated to
Amy, Sam, Jack
And in memory of
Seamus Dolan (1940–2021)

Contents

List of tables and figures

Tables

Figures

Acknowledgements

The content of this book has been informed by the many critical dialogues created through exchange, reflections, partnership working, debate and shared learning. We thank in particular all of our past, present and future students whose critical engagement, dialogue and enquiry-based approach has informed how we have developed the framework presented in this book over a number of years. We thank our many colleagues who have contributed to our module including academics, practitioners, policy-makers and people who use services or support those engaged with services. Thanks also to our colleagues within the social work team and programme board for their commitment to human rights and social justice within our social work education programme.

As reflected in the book, our approach to teaching is critical, specific and research-informed. We wish to acknowledge our colleagues at the UNESCO Child and Family Centre within our School of Political Science and Sociology and our Institute for Lifecourse and Society. Being part of this vibrant research community has enabled us to draw significantly and learn from the immense range of research and publications from our esteemed colleagues. We also benefit from excellent partnerships with colleagues within wider academia, policy and practice settings locally and globally, and we have been able to draw significantly on learning from their work to inform this book. We have come to know so many new authors and perspectives through writing this book, and are aware that for all of the papers we have included from different perspectives, there are so many more that could have been availed of. Preparing this book has reinforced our critical awareness of the strengths and challenges in social work globally and the importance of lifelong learning to keep pace with the dynamic, varied and inspiring work available to us from all corners of the globe.

Importantly, we wish to acknowledge all those directly involved with social work services, past, present and future. This book promotes a civic engagement approach that emphasises the urgency for greater partnerships and collaborations with citizens in order to improve and enhance social work and the wider systems it operates within. We need greater collaboration and critical engagement with those closest to the experience of social work services. We fully acknowledge that we still have a long way to go before we can claim to be working from a position of shared power and partnership. We hope the book goes some way towards advancing both our and other people's capacity to move further towards this urgent necessity within the profession.

Working with colleagues in Policy Press has been a pleasure, and we thank everyone involved in the production of this book, from initial proposal stage to final proofing, marketing and publication. The professionalism, support, constructive critical review and encouragement shown by colleagues has been exemplary.

Finally, we sincerely thank all of our family and close friends for their tenacious and constant support to us in our academic endeavours and our professional lives.

Introduction

Social work is a complex activity and there is no simple or singular way to learn how to understand, do, critique and improve it. It takes an array of approaches, theories, skills, knowledge and practice experience built up from the beginning of our education and training and throughout our professional careers. Theoretical, methodological, practical and experiential knowledge all play a role in shaping our understandings, critiques and practices of social work. Students and new graduates in particular need a set of parameters and frameworks around which they can begin to develop a sense of what social work is and how it can be carried out, supporting and protecting children, families and adults through individual, group and community work. Experienced practitioners also need to refresh their learning and keep up to date in their practice teaching and supervision. While it is important to avoid over-simplification of a complex and sometimes contradictory strategy, identifiable 'scaffolding' is necessary. The unique contribution of our work is to bring together in a dynamic way the dual role of support and protection across the *lifecourse* within an *ecological context*. By doing this, we are offering some scaffolding to help students integrate the complex range of intersectional and diverse themes that inform social work practice. Scaffolding means that we have clear theories, ideas or knowledge around which to develop our critical analysis, reflection and thinking.

About us and our learning approach

We are academic professors based in the West of Ireland. We work at an international UNESCO Child and Family Research Centre within the Institute for Lifecourse and Society (ILAS) and School of Political Science and Sociology in the College of Arts, Social Sciences and Celtic Studies, National University of Ireland (NUI), Galway. (Caroline McGregor worked under the name of Caroline Skehill up to 2012.) While our main experience resides in practice in Ireland and the UK, and many of the research examples we use come from work in this domain, including our own and our colleagues' work, work from the US, Australia and Europe also has a significant influence on our fields of practice. In addition, we have some experience of research and policy work in various Eastern European, African and Asian contexts. While we give a range of examples from different perspectives, we do not stray beyond what we consider to be our own expertise drawn from our collective work. So, for each theme covered, we provide illustrations and examples that can be developed, adapted and replaced by other relevant materials from your own experiences and contexts.

The learning approach that informs this book has four main elements:

- specific and research informed;
- enquiry-based;

- critical ART (analysis, reflection and thinking);
- recognising expertise by experience.

Specific and research informed

We encourage the use of evidence from specific research and literature to explore and critique different aspects of support and protection practice. We have selected themes that you can use to look deeply and more specifically at particular issues with a view to adapting this learning to other relevant themes. Our view is that it is neither desirable nor indeed possible to cover every aspect of a topic when teaching students. Rather, by going deep into illustrative examples, we can identify the broad learning, which can then be adapted to research other relevant areas. This is a key feature of an enquiry-based approach to learning.

Enquiry-based learning

We use the enquiry-based learning approach that encourages raising questions rather than seeking answers too quickly. To engage successfully in enquiry-based learning, it is useful, especially for those who are less experienced, to draw from the taxonomy of learning delivered by Benjamin Bloom (1956), which enables you to build up your knowledge and critical skills in a systematic way. Bloom identified six levels of learning as follows: knowledge, understanding, application, analysis, synthesis and evaluation. This implies that, first, we seek to know and understand the subject, and then apply and test it in practice. From this, we then develop our analysis. This then loops back to synthesising the critical learning with practice action and evaluating the benefits and limits on an ongoing basis, which can be done through individual study as well as formal agreed review and evaluation processes, such as an assessment in a college setting or an evaluation of service delivery in an organisational setting.

Enquiry-based learning is a problem-solving and solution-sourcing approach associated with the work of John Dewey (1938). As Hothersall (2019) argues with reference to Dewey: 'Any problem of scientific inquiry that does not grow out of actual (or "practical") social conditions is factitious; it is arbitrarily set by the inquirer' (Dewey, 1938: 499, cited in Hothersall, 2019: 862). It is a widely adapted approach used in schools across all levels. It has international resonance across a range of disciplinary domains. Enquiry-based learning implies that everyone brings some expertise to the table and no knowledge is without further questioning and investigation. It supports a commitment to the democratisation of knowledge and a breaking down of the power differentials of expertise between the educators, researchers, authors and learners, through being critically aware of power differences and taking action to reduce these where possible. We encourage you to bring your own resources to supplement and back up the content of this book, and to engage in critical ART in reading the chapters and associated learning resources and exercises given throughout the book.

Critical ART (analysis, reflection and thinking)

Critical thinking is essential in enquiry-based learning. There are important distinctions to be made between critical 'analysis', 'reflection' and 'thinking', and there is also some overlap, so we suggest that they are best considered in relation to each other. For this book, we use 'critical ART', which stands for 'critical analysis, critical reflection and critical thinking'. The distinction we find helpful is as follows.

Critical 'analysis' means a detailed examination of an issue, question, case, dilemma and so on, weighing up the different elements with a focus on their application and evaluation. Take the example of the impact of extreme poverty on a father's ability to care well enough for his young child. Critical analysis will seek to find out what impact poverty is having on the child. The analysis may break this down to consider the child's wellbeing, development, health and education. Questions will be raised, such as:

- Is the issue mostly related to individual circumstances or social factors, and how should it be addressed?
- What evidence and research relating to family poverty can support assessment and decision-making about intervention?

Critical 'reflection' focuses on the processes of reasoning we apply to and how we respond to a situation. A critical reflective approach adds questioning to the thoughts, values and feelings that come to the fore when we 'think' about a case. A worker may reflect, for example, about how difficult it would be for the father to lose their child to care from the point of view of intergenerational relations. Critical reflection may lead to questions such as:

- Is the child in need of removal? Is the father failing as a parent, or being judged unfairly?
- Does the level of poverty warrant concern, or is it a values issue of judging a way of living?
- Does your own experience or view of poverty impact on this assessment?

Critical 'thinking' is made possible from a set of knowledge and understanding about a particular theory, for example. This theoretical knowledge can be used as 'scaffolding' around which to think about an issue arising in a particular case scenario, practice dilemma or organisational issue. When we think critically, we need to be clear what knowledge is informing this thinking. Keeping with the same example of the impact of poverty on a father caring for his child:

- Is the scaffolding for this thinking based on knowledge about parent capacity – the 'potential to parent'?
- Is it about society and inequality?
- Or is it about the civic disengagement of the family?

It is likely that many types of knowledge will scaffold the thinking. A mapping of this theory, as your scaffold, is a good way to evidence and justify the basis for your 'critical thinking'. In this book, we use the framework presented as the 'scaffolding' to be able to state the knowledge base for the critical thinking posing questions related to what you are basing your assumptions on:

- Is it based on your past experience?
- Is it based on your attitude and value judgements?
- What other ethical and value concerns are influential?
- Has your reading of a brief article in the media about poverty and child welfare affected your assumptions?
- What else?

You can see how this links back again to critical analysis and reflection. In sum, critical ART is an ongoing cyclical rather than a linear process. It takes place within a set of scaffolds, which, in this instance, derive from the framework presented in this book. The more explicit you can be about your critical ART, the better you can justify, evidence and inform your practices of decision-making, assessment, interventions and overall contribution to delivering quality social work. Your own contribution and that of the people you work with should be central in your critical ART.

Recognising expertise by experience

To maximise the benefits of experiential and enquiry-based learning, informed by critical ART, you should draw from your own expertise by experience and pass this into your understanding of service users to find ways, through partnership, to maximise the democratisation of knowledge. This will help you to avoid the 'thinker-expert' position in favour of a more equal view of knowledge from a range of perspectives while remaining critically aware of power–knowledge differences and influences. It is important that you engage reflexively with the material and connect it with your own experiences and lifecourse. A welcome feature of contemporary social work has been the mainstreaming of service user, carer and public participation in their own direct practice experiences as well as service and education development. This issue is not benign, however. Simple involvement of or attention to service user perspectives is insufficient; approaches need to be critically informed in relation to power and power relations. The role of service users in shaping policy and wider system change, as well as being involved in collaborative leadership and partnership in relation to their own personal matters, is crucial.

Sometimes social work can be presented as too objective and removed from service users' lives and experiences. Yet many social workers are also themselves experts by experience. In many ways, social work mirrors life and the lifecourse. An important contribution we wish to make, through emphasising civic engagement, is to maximise the potential for social work to carry out its core support and protection role within an ecological and lifecourse perspective, to continue to strive to promote human rights and social justice. An important starting point for this is for us to make clear how we understand social work, its underpinning assumptions and the current challenges the profession is facing, which we address in Part I.

Our framework and contribution to existing resources

The book's contents have been developed from a double module (10 European Credit Transfers) on a Master's in Social Work Programme, which emphasises the importance of enquiry-based learning and working with students to connect their own experiences to their practice and professional development. The framework we have developed derives from a range of evidence sources including published research studies, student-led investigations, service user and carer perspectives and dialogue about the connections between theory, research and practice.

Our framework brings together different families of theories, including those relating to:

• understanding and engaging with people in their environments (commonly referred to as theories of human behaviour or development and the social environment);
• family and social support (including resilience, empathy, civic engagement and partnership);
• individual and social protection (including theories of power and mediation in the social).

We apply Bronfenbrenner's ecological framework to situate social work practice across the lifecourse to build an approach for support and protection around five main themes:

• duality of protection and support;
• life transitions and life events;
• intergenerational relations;
• civic partnership and engagement;
• health and wellbeing.

Readers will have access to an array of literature on child protection, children and care, family support and adult services relating to areas including disability, older people and mental health. These fields of study are often compartmentalised, even though, in most instances, they involve complex lifecourse relationships, transitions and events. While we fully acknowledge the need for an in-depth specific focus on the vast array of practice domains, we also believe that there is a need for more opportunities to recognise the common and holistic features across practice. We present a focus on the duality of support and protection, using our five themes, as one such example.

Our aim is that this book will complement your learning resources while offering unique and valuable learning that will influence your professional learning and development. The book is aimed at a global audience, valuing local context and diversity. It is designed to promote enquiry and self-directed guided study. We encourage you to actively and critically engage with the content, taking into account your own local context of practice, policy, law, culture, personal prior learning and own experience. We offer recommendations for additional learning resources for illustration at the end of each chapter. We also propose an approach called 'critical ART' (analysis, reflection and thinking), with sections at the end of each chapter to facilitate this.

Structure of the book

In Part I, we introduce our perspective on social work and the overarching framework to be developed throughout. In Part II, the most substantial part of the book, we apply and develop themes within our framework to discuss an illustrative range of practice domains with children, families and adults. Themes covered include: protecting, safeguarding and risk management across the lifecourse; enlisting family support for care and protection; resilience, empathy and social support; supporting and protecting people in transition across the lifecourse; disrupted development across the lifecourse; and social ecologies and networks. Chapters 9 and 10 make up Part III, where we bring together our overall approach and reflect back on the learning approach used in the book. We also provide signposts for ongoing and continuous learning to inform practice.

Who this book is for

This book is primarily for students of social work. It is particularly relevant for modules such as Human Development and the Social Environment; Theories for Social Work Across the Lifecourse; Social Work with Children, Families and Adults in Need of Protection and/or Support; and Person-in-Environment Approaches. It is also written with new graduates and experienced practitioners in mind who wish to refresh their thinking and access some of the newer theories and sources relating to the topics covered. We hope that our colleagues in related social professions, including social care, social pedagogy, youth and community work and social education, will also find it relevant.

Notes on terminology

Children/youth

While the United Nations Convention on the Rights of the Child (UNCRC) defines a 'child' as being up to the age of 18, we encourage sensitivity in how to use the word depending on context. For example, in some societies there is a lower age for marriage, children and teenagers may be expected to work, and children can be recruited to armies at the age of 13 and younger. In addition, developmentally, while the legal definition of a child in many countries is up to the age of 18, we need to make a clear distinction when referring to young children and adolescents. 'Young people' is a more suitable term for teenagers especially, and in many instances, even for reference to the very young. It should also span the legal age of childhood to recognise the transitional phase of young adulthood, and services for young people are often designed to respond to needs up to the early to mid-20s and often beyond this. As we discuss at various points in this book, there is a balance to be made between the importance of recognising the distinctiveness of childhood, especially for child protection reasons, while being consciously critical of an overly paternalistic and adultist approach.

Client/service user/customer/consumer

The way we refer to people with whom we work remains a complicated issue. We mainly use the word 'service user' as this is currently the most common in our context, but we do so with caution. For example, learning from colleagues in a local advocacy service (www.brothersofcharity.ie/galway/advocacy) the term 'persons supported by services' is preferential for those who may use or experience services. We also use 'citizen' to promote a critical perspective on citizenship-based social work. See also the section on 'Words and language' below.

Ecological context

We consider social work in the context of Urie Bronfenbrenner's ecological model with an emphasis on the bio-ecological model. This means considering practice at the micro, meso, exo, macro and chrono levels, and considering it from the point of view of person, process, context and time. We suggest further development of the use of an ecological approach to enable more critical and reflective practice, especially in relation to culture and to emphasising not only social ecology, but also the physical, material and environmental factors that shape and influence people's ecological systems.

Family

Like childhood, family is a social construct that carries different meanings and norms in different societies and at different times, as reflected in the range of sociological and social policy analyses of 'the family' social work students will be exposed to in their studies. When we use the term 'family', we are referring to all globally recognised family and kinship forms. At times, we may refer to specific family forms for illustration, such as 'lone parent', 'gay couple' or 'teen parent'.

Lifecourse perspective

While acknowledging the specific challenges and approaches to working with children and adults, the book starts from the premise that the divide between 'children' and 'adult' services can be too fixed. Most practice requires a more holistic approach that incorporates an individual's lifecourse (such as impact of childhood experience on adult life) and context (for example, the individual in the context of their wider family and community). A lifecourse perspective encourages a dynamic viewpoint that recognises life events, transitions and trajectories as interplayed between past, present and future.

Mental health/mental illness

While it is generally more acceptable to use the term 'mental health', in some contexts 'mental illness' is commonly used. Also, there is a distinction made in some literature between 'mental health' and 'severe and enduring mental illness'.

Social work

When we refer to social work, we are mainly referring to public social work delivered through state or voluntary/third sector/not-for-profit bodies, although we also include reference to for-profit private social work where relevant. Social workers are employed in many different settings and organisations, and this is a strength of the professional qualification. Again, while by no means excluding the diversity of social workers as an audience and concern for the book, we focus on practices that specifically designate 'social work' as the qualification to deliver a service; we also recognise that in some areas the clarification of social work, vis-à-vis other related social practices, remains underdeveloped. Also, in some jurisdictions, while there is a recognised title of 'social work', it is not a registered profession.

The public

This refers to everyone in society, including those who use services and those who don't, those who work for social services and those who know little about this aspect of society. It is more accurate to refer to a range of public spheres, as Fraser (2008) argues, to recognise the diversity therein (see also McGregor and Millar, 2020). Given the centrality of social work in societies, even if often hidden from many who do not come into direct contact with it in their own lives, it is important in our work to create better public awareness and understanding of the discipline and profession of social work, because the relationship between social work and the public has a major influence on how people perceive the experience and engage at an individual, family, group or community level.

Theory

This is a widely used word that covers many domains and which is discussed in detail throughout the book. A theory attempts to explain something. We suggest there are at least four dimensions to the ubiquitous term 'theory for social work'. These are not mutually exclusive, but thinking about the distinction is important to help us get beyond over-simplified discussions about social work and theory.

We argue that, as a social worker, you should not see theory as driving your practice. Rather, you should look to theory using critical ART to steer how it is used and applied in your practice. We argue that *all* dimensions of your theories, methods and skills are underpinned by the core values for social work, which derive from different ethical positions:

- *Social work theory* relates to theories that help us to understand *and* respond to issues arising in practice, such as theories about assessments, interventions and outcomes. Often influenced by wider social or psychological theory, different social work theories imply a set of values, *a position and a particular belief system*. All methods are derived from a particular theoretical starting point. We recommend David Howe's explanation of methods that derive from social work theory as a core guide (Howe, 1987, 2008, 2017).
- *Knowledge theories* relate to theories about certain aspects of society, social problems or individual behaviour that inform our understanding. For example, theories about the nature of grief, human development, attachment, disability and mental illnesses are all 'knowledge theories'. In this book, we specifically focus on knowledge relating to human behaviour and the social environment, family and social support and individual and social protection.
- *Practice theories* relate to theories about how to *do* social work, such as theories about communication, assertiveness, language and listening. Practice theories focus in particular on the skills involved in working as a social worker. These relate to specific actions involved in social work practice that are both generic and specific to the methods being used. We recommend Pamela Trevithick's (2012) *Social Work Skills and Knowledge: A Practice Handbook* as a core guide in this regard.
- *Wider discipline theories* relate to the many theories that come from the core disciplines that inform social work, such as psychology, sociology, social policy, philosophy, education, ethics, health and social care, critical social theory and political studies.

Vulnerable adult

This term is often used to denote adults who need services, but it should be used with caution as it may be interpreted to imply powerlessness – not all adults who seek services are vulnerable, and conversely, all adults are likely to experience vulnerability at some point in their lives. Since social work is sometimes about working with vulnerable adults, we will use the word at times, but with care and specificity. Generally, we use the term 'adults', which, for the purposes of this book, relates to those who seek or receive services at a moment in time or throughout the duration of their lives.

Words and language

These are the basic core tools of social work, and they are powerful and complex, as our colleague Marguerita McGovern (2016) narrates in the first of her seven e-book series, *Social Work Placement: New Approaches. New Thinking.* Through time, words and concepts in social work change and transform. While once 'clients' was an acceptable term, this later became 'service user', 'consumer' and sometimes 'customer', even though few people who use services get to choose from a menu of services as one would expect as a customer. It is important to be aware of the 'correct' or 'acceptable' terminology in use at any one time, and to be critically aware of the same words and meanings.

PART I

Introduction to the framework and our approach

In this first part of the book, we will introduce you to our perspective on social work and the overarching framework, which we will develop throughout the book. We offer Part I as a broad introduction to social work for those of you coming new to the profession, and as a form of recap for the more experienced student and/or practitioner.

In Chapter 1, we introduce you to our rationale for this book and the approach we have taken. We discuss the main assumptions underpinning social work regarding how it has developed over time and in relation to other social professions. We provide an overview of 'person-in-environment' theories and learning from the history of social work that has influenced this book. We also provide a commentary on some of the challenges for global social professions, within local contexts, for the 21st century.

Chapter 2 introduces our framework for support and protection framed within an ecological and lifecourse perspective. We discuss lifecourse and ecological theory and how this is used in the book. We set out the five interrelated themes that are used throughout the book to consider how the framework can be activated to enhance critical ART in practice. We provide illustrative diagrams to depict the framework, and encourage you to develop your own visual and conceptual applications, as most relevant to your own particular context.

1

Setting the scene

Introduction

In this chapter, we outline our own assumptions about social work, with the interrelated themes of:

- defining social work;
- social work values and ethics;
- the role of history to inform present-day social work;
- social work as a strategy focused on person–in–environment;
- balancing care and control;
- mediator in the social;
- social work knowledge.

Following this, we comment on some of the global challenges of social work to acknowledge its complexity from the outset, and to contextualise the content that follows. The interrelated contemporary global challenges and opportunities for social work that we discuss are:

- neoliberalism and managerialism;
- personalisation and marketisation;
- 'cultural practices';
- the global pandemic;
- power imbalances in social work knowledge.

Our own assumptions about social work

Defining social work

Social work may be difficult to define succinctly, but it is not impossible, and students may struggle to explain what it is because it is so diverse. The International Federation of Social Workers' (IFSW) definition, however, offers a useful starting point:

> Social work is a practice-based profession and an academic discipline
> that promotes social change and development, social cohesion, and
> the empowerment and liberation of people. Principles of social justice,
> human rights, collective responsibility and respect for diversities are

central to social work. Underpinned by theories of social work, social sciences, humanities and indigenous knowledge, social work engages people and structures to address life challenges and enhance wellbeing. The above definition may be amplified at national and/or regional levels. (IFSW, 2014)

We suggest that, while useful, this definition fails to capture the sociolegal dimension of social work, which we argue is one of its core identifying features. Sociolegal practice implies mediation between the individual and the policy and legal system in many fields of practice, including child protection, mental health, adult safeguarding, safeguarding and disability, medical social work, youth justice and probation. This mediation needs to be done in a partnership manner, alongside service users, to negotiate, mediate, support and challenge different social, organisational and societal pressures that impact on service users' health, wellbeing, protection and support. Our understanding of social work as 'mediation in the social', discussed below, derives from this position. It also aligns with our proposition of social work as a practice of *both* support *and* protection within an ecological context. Individual and social protection and individual and social support take place through some lifecourses or at points of transition and disruption in others. This is discussed further later in this chapter, in relation to historical continuities in social work.

So, to clarify the definition of social work as discussed in this book, we describe it as a sociolegal strategy that involves practices of mediating support and protection within an ecological context, taking into account both individual and societal factors. These practices include:

- balancing care and control in order to support and protect children and adults;
- supporting and protecting families, and enhancing the combined role of formal and informal interventions to do this;
- promoting social change in individuals, groups and society;
- supporting people to overcome individual problems, and defending their human rights;
- supporting people and working with them to challenge discrimination and to highlight inequalities and social injustice.

Within this broad definition, we recognise diversity within social work, and emphasise the importance of learning from both long-established professions and newly emerging ones. In many countries, social work and related social professions have emerged from a shared history of philanthropy and voluntary religious-based practice. Some practices have emerged from governmental regimes while others have evolved from volunteering and the formalisation of community kinship support systems. There are many overlaps between social work and related social professions. In some countries, professional social work is a registered and/or accredited profession, with governance and recognition of title that distinguishes it from other social professions. In other countries, social work is less defined and regulated, and for some, the quest for the professionalisation of social work is ongoing. There is also critical debate about the very nature of 'professionalisation', with some arguing that social work has gone too far to seek 'professional standing', distancing it from those it aims to serve, including a call by some for the 'end of social work' (see Maylea, 2020, in relation to Australia). In the UK context, there is much debate about the deprofessionalisation of social work through the development of fast-track and shorter educational programmes. Our position is that we need to keep building and sustaining the professional standing of social work to ensure it is a discipline that can achieve its complex goals.

Social work values and ethics

Social work is a relational discipline based on individual and societal values, ethics, human rights and social justice. Social work practice is informed by a complex body of knowledge. It involves engagement with theories about social work, knowledge theories, practice theories and wider social theories to inform practice. In between 'theory' and 'practice', other important knowledge exists including experiential, tacit and intuitive forms. Theory should not drive practice, but rather, practice drives towards and in search of theory that can inform value-based, ethical and rights-oriented practices.

Social work distinctively operates from a set of values based on ethics, principles of social justice and human rights. It is essentially a moral activity, influenced in different times and places by personal values, religion, ethics, philosophy, political perspectives, rights-based theories and social justice ideologies. One of the challenges of practice is to manage ethical dilemmas that arise. As summarised by McCauliffe and Chenoweth (2019), ethical theories can be very complex given that they derive from various established philosophies. Internationally, as Zavirsek et al (2010) show, ethics and ethical dilemmas in social work include a multitude of issues, such as:

- dilemmas of universalism vs pluralism and contextualism;
- justice vs care dilemmas, pragmatics and social ethics;
- ethics, secularism and Christianisation;
- ethics of disability;
- social justice and ethics;
- professional ethics and ethics of professional life;
- morals and ethics in different societal contexts;
- language and ethics, and ethics in social work research;
- ethics in social work management.

McCauliffe and Chenoweth (2019) argue that rather than ethics being taught as a separate subject in social work, it should be an integrated part of social work theory and seen as core to professional identity. Banks (2010: 124) summarises an ethics of professional life as involving:

- commitment (value positions that motivate the worker and the work);
- character (moral qualities);
- context (which 'entails a holistic approach, situating the practitioner in webs of relationships and responsibilities, taking into account the importance of moral orientation, perception, imagination and emotions').

In this book, we refer to ethics of professional life (Banks, 2010), emphasising values of respect, promotion of independence, empathy, honesty, openness, care ethics and a commitment to equality.

The role of history to inform present-day social work

Understanding the history of social work generally, and then the history of your own country specifically, is essential (Skehill, 2008). It helps in being able to appreciate the scope and limits of social work in a specific context. It also informs how you develop your own social work professional identity. Without knowing the lifecourse of the profession and how it has developed, a full critical understanding of present and future dilemmas is not possible. For example, a 'history of the present' approach, informed by the work of Michel Foucault, helps us to understand both the continuities and discontinuities in the development of social work as a strategy (see Skehill, 2003, 2007; McGregor, 2015). In some histories of social work, the path for development has been progressive; in others, it has been disruptive and discontinuous. Since social work itself is by nature a paradoxical activity and has its own 'horrible history' (Ferguson et al, 2018), there are few jurisdictions where it is not possible to identify both transformative and regressive practice 'amid social contradictions' (Hauss and Schulte, 2009) at different moments in time. It is important that you engage critically with the evidence from histories of social work worldwide that show that social work has sometimes been part of the problem, other times the solution, and has often vacillated between the two. As Lorenz (2007: 599) has argued: 'There is little gain in celebrating our profession as one happy family, growing steadily and harmoniously, if we do not listen to the incredible diversity that characterises our profession and face up to the discrepancies, the discontinuities and the disharmony which are also part of this history.'

The following four sections continue a focus on some historical continuities that have shaped present-day social work.

Social work as a strategy focused on 'person-in-environment'

A starting concern for theories of human behaviour and the social environment is the matter of *nature vs nurture*. This raises the question: To what extent are our behaviours, attributes and characteristics a product of our nature, and to what extent are we shaped by nurture, such as our family, community and wider social environment? In other words, how much is it about the 'person', and how much is it about the 'environment'? When we talk about nature, we are referring to what we are born with, including genes, biological and neurological traits that shape our behaviour and our development. A focus on nature assumes there is something 'constant' and 'fixed' about our human traits, behaviours and tendencies, such as a predisposition towards certain mental illnesses or to alcoholism, for example. Nurture, on the other hand, relates to the environment that we grow up in, and assumes that this shapes our behaviour and development. It implies that it is not the 'trait' but the 'socialisation of the trait' that shapes our behaviour, such as gendered socialisation. It assumes 'fluidity' and an 'openness to change'. From a 'nurture' perspective, even if predisposed to certain 'genetic' conditions, it is the environment that has the greatest influence on how this develops. The short answer to this question, then, is that it is both nature *and* nurture.

There has always been an expectation that social workers understand and intervene in a way that takes account of the relationship between the individual and what is affecting them in their immediate and wider social environment. For example, in 1917 Mary Richmond wrote a book called *Social Diagnosis*. She outlined the relationship between individuals and their environment, and the powers workers had to engage in these relations. This approach went on to influence various systems approaches to social work in an attempt to take a unitary approach (Goldstein, 1973) and to develop systems thinking during the 1970s (see, for example, Pincus and Minahan, 1973). One of the most commonly applied systemic frameworks in social work today is the ecological model (or various versions of the model) derived by Urie Bronfenbrenner in 1979. This was written from a human development perspective, but has gone on to be applied in a number of different fields, including social work, social care, nursing, health promotion and, more recently, it has extended into the field of research impact (Dolan, 2019). As discussed next in Chapter 2, we discuss the ecological model more generally, but use Bronfenbrenner's bio-ecological model in particular (see Bronfenbrenner and Morris, 2006) in our illustrations. We offer our own framework to enable more in-depth questioning to identify the impact of what we can call intrinsic (internal) and extrinsic (external) factors on a certain situation or experience. We encourage you to consider the 'person' in the context of their lifecourse and the 'environment' in an ecological frame. 'Environment' itself needs to be understood as a complex interplay between social, economic, physical and material ecologies that impact on people's day-to-day lives. We also need to be cognisant of how day-to-day lives impact on the environment, emphasising not only social but also physical and spatial ecologies.

Balancing care and control

An historical continuity in social work is that it is a practice embedded in support alongside a regulatory and legislative role. Traditionally, this defining feature of social work is referred to as balancing *care and control*. Much of social work can be framed within associated dualities. Philp (1979) suggests that social work emerged during the 19th century to occupy a space between two discourses: 'the discourse of wealth and that of poverty, the powerful and the weak' (1979: 93–4). Whatever example of social work you choose, you can observe that it has this dual mandate around care and control, albeit more subtle in some contexts than others. In child protection and welfare, the mandate for care and control relates to supporting families but also regulating families if children are being harmed or at risk of harm. Working with people who are disabled, the balance can be articulated as mediating between the individual's rights to freedom and independence and the need to manage personal risks. In working to support families where parents have substance abuse problems, interventions seek to support and regulate those parents while protecting and supporting the children who are affected. In relation to adult protection, the care–control dilemma is typified in the challenge of promoting independence and rights on the one hand, and managing risk on the other. This care–control duality should not be depicted as a simple linear one, but rather as a continuum. It is complex and systemic, involving adults with disability, mental health issues or problems associated with ageing, their families, local contexts and communities and their wider social systems. There are arguments that some strands of social work have been specifically constructed as a form of social control in the past to quieten discontent among the poor, for example in the development of the Charitable Organisation Society (COS) in the 19th century in the UK and US. Such arguments persist, for example, in arguments about the colonisation of social work in Africa, as expressed by Mathebane (2020).

While a continuity for social work, the nature of this relationship between care and control is much contested in social work debates, and we need to challenge the tendencies to define it as one or the other. For example, McGregor, in a response to Jones (2014), argues that:

> We can't write out our more complex and troublesome history that also shows within the complexity continuity. Rather than rejecting this, we need to engage and embrace it and, in so doing, contribute to the articulation of what is indeed continuous about social work – a practice of mediating between "dualisms in diversity". (McGregor, 2015: 1635)

Social work as mediator within the space of the 'social'

Following on from this, the mediation of the duality of care and control takes place within the space of the 'social'. In this regard, we develop further the work of Skehill (1999, 2000, 2003, 2004) with an emphasis on the work of Philp (1979), Parton (1991, 2014a, b), Hyslop (2013) and Hyslop and Keddell (2018). We assert that social work is a practice of mediation between individuals and 'systems' at different levels. This implies that a core feature of social work is that it mediates between individual subjectivity and potential (for example, to reform, recover and refrain from abuse) and objective laws, policies and procedures. As Philp put it: social work operates between 'internal subjective states' (for example pain, want, suffering) and 'objective characteristics' (for example old age, crime, debt, illness) (1979: 92), and 'the social worker cannot help but try to create people, subjects, where everyone else is seeing cold, hard, objective fact' (1979: 99). Hyslop (2013), with reference to New Zealand, uses Philp's work in his empirical research with practising social workers. He argues that 'social workers, in their role as mediators in the social, develop insight, and apply knowledge, which is informed by experientially generated understandings of the social nature of knowledge in a particular social and economic context' (2013: 201). The impact of the social, economic and political context of social work enables and constrains the scope of this mediation and the complexity of this role, not only between countries, but also within countries (see, for example, Yi-Bing et al, 2020, with reference to social work in China). Mediation in the social necessarily involves sociolegal practice. While not exclusive to 'social work', it is a core function of the strategy, as suggested earlier. Through critical attention to the ecological context from a lifecourse perspective, the scope and range of sociolegal practice and mediation in the social is elucidated.

Social work knowledge

Another related historical continuity in social work is that social work knowledge, by implication, must include a mix of knowledge about people and knowledge about society. This derives from sociology, psychology, philosophy and social policy, education, criminal justice, health, child protection, social services, social welfare, housing welfare, education, social geography, and so on. The form and source of theoretical knowledge that informs practice is often contested. Throughout the history of social work, we have vacillated between an emphasis on the individual and collective strategies. The orientation of social work, best seen as a continuum, influences different methods of social work, from strategies for maintenance and coping to strategies for transformation at individual and/or collective levels (McGregor, 2019). One of the main historical features of social work is its paradoxical purpose in relation to the person-in-environment with regard to reform vs transform or maintenance vs radical change (McGregor, 2019). This duality of social work can be traced throughout most histories, such as the dual development of the COS and the Settlement Movement in the UK and US during the 19th century, the former more associated with casework (maintenance) and the latter with social reform (radical change). The radical movement of social work in the 1970s – influenced by wider societal change at the time in light of the impact of socialism and feminism – called into question the mostly individualist nature of social work, and promoted a more overt egalitarian and social action stance. Philp (1979: 84) described the debate as it stood over

40 years ago as being that: 'Each argues that the other has failed to grasp what social work should really be about. In doing so their stance is essentially idealist for not only do they fail to question their own objectivity, but they also fail to ask what social work actually is.'

Things have moved on a lot since the 1970s, and many of the novel and new ideas from then – such as listening to service users' views – have now found common place in contemporary social work. We owe a great deal to those who promoted radical social work during this time (see, for example, Bailey and Brake, 1975). While in modern paradigms of social work there was a tendency to divide individual social work methods into more traditional maintenance and reform approaches, and collective methods into more radical and emancipatory approaches, postmodern and current paradigms recognise a greater depth of complexity (McGregor, 2019). This requires consideration of a wider range of knowledge, including that derived from experts by experience (MacDermott and Harkin-MacDermott, 2020). In addition, different societal contexts have resulted in different pathways and scope for social work. For example, relatively recently derived histories of social work in Eastern Europe during communism show that much of social work took on a strong social action dimension, reflecting the challenges in society at that time (Schilde and Schulte, 2005; Hering and Waaldijk, 2006; Hauss and Schulte, 2009). Yi–Bing et al (2020) show how social work in China follows three distinct pathways, each reflecting a different set of relations with local stakeholders and wider sociopolitical goals and institutions. It is clear that different social contexts make certain types of social work more feasible than others. Ferguson et al (2018) give the example of community action to protest against state cuts and service limits that social workers may use extensively in some jurisdictions, which could result in criminal prosecution for a social worker in another part of the world. The stark and challenging reality for social work, as we discuss in more detail throughout the book, is that we continue to face historically persistent challenges, such as:

- persistent inequality supported by capitalism, poverty and deprivation;
- persistent concerns about racism, discrimination and marginalisation;
- regressive social policies and contested views on entitlements and rights, and threats to international treaties;
- the effects of colonisation and a movement towards decolonisation in social work knowledge and practice (see, for example Mathebane, 2020, in relation to social work in Africa);
- the impact of political conflict in many parts of the world for practice during and after conflicts, where the legacy can persist for generations (see Campbell et al, 2013; Duffy et al, 2018, 2020; Campbell and Pinkerton, 2020).

In the next section, we illustrate some of the current global challenges of social work in order to highlight, from the outset, the complexity of social work as a strategy.

Contemporary global challenges and opportunities for social work

Overview of challenges and opportunities

In every era of social work, there are unique challenges and opportunities for social work, both locally and globally. These will vary depending on the specific political, policy, social, cultural and organisational context you find yourself within, but it seems that there are also many universal themes to consider (see Harrikari and Pirkko-Liisa, 2019). The Global Agenda for Social Work, launched in 2010 by the three global social work organisations – the International Association of Schools of Social Work (IASSW), the International Council on Social Welfare (ICSW) and the International Federation of Social Workers (IFSW) – summarises the current global priorities for social work as:

• promoting social and economic equalities;
• promoting people's dignity and worth;
• working towards environmental sustainability;
• strengthening human relationships (see Jones and Truell, 2012).

Following this, the 2020–30 Agenda emphasises the importance of Ubuntu philosophy, global cooperation and collaboration within social work. Its core themes are:

• valuing social work as an essential service;
• co-building inclusive social transformation;
• Ubunta: 'I am because we are';
• transforming social protection systems;
• promoting diversity and joint social action.

These global challenges are occurring in the context of the United Nations' (UN) 17 Sustainable Development Goals (SDGs) and an increased awareness and emphasis on the importance of attention to both individual micro-level relationships alongside wider macro-level ecological and environmental themes (Dominelli, 2012, 2020). The Global Agendas remind us that we cannot separate out the individual experience, the material, economic, practical and emotional, from the wider ecological context. Instead, we need to find ways to appreciate the complex interconnections and diversity through a lens of human rights, social justice and a commitment to social change. Throughout this book, we identify further significant themes and connect them with our framework. For now, based on many of the themes arising in our own conversations with students and practitioners, we briefly discus the following themes as illustrative: neoliberalism, marketisation, cultural competence, the impact of the global pandemic and power imbalances in social work knowledge. We acknowledge that there are many other challenges, but they remain beyond our scope in this book. In the 'Recommended resources' at the end of the chapter, we refer you to the Global Agenda for Social Work and the UN's SDGs, to help you to continue to explore a further range of challenges and to connect them to your own specific contexts and practices.

Neoliberalism and managerialism

Neoliberalism features greatly in current social work debates. It implies a challenge to the assumption of solidarity that underpinned the notion of a social welfare state and welfare rights and entitlements. It has created further divides and inequalities globally and within national states, and contradicts many of the core principles of participatory and community-oriented social work practice (Sewpaul, 2013). Marthinsen (2019), reflecting on neoliberalism from a European perspective, explains one of its main challenges, that 'all investments in people, such as social policy, education and health services, become areas of investment with expectations of return, in line with economic investments as such' (2019: 352). This puts workers and the discipline in a paradoxical and contradictory position of having to align quality of and rights to service with costs and efficiencies, as expected within market welfare conditions. Marthinsen connects neoliberalism with managerialism. He reminds us that 'social work is one of the expert areas concerned with governing the family, the child and the "social" in general', and finds itself in an ambivalent position because, on the one hand, its importance is emphasised, while on the other hand, it does not have the 'requisite conditions to perform best practices' within a managerial context (2019: 359).

Linked to critiques of neoliberalism and new management, Munro (2004) warns about the destructive nature of an audit culture within social work, especially in the UK. She emphasises the importance of using audit for research that can constructively produce evidence on effectiveness of services (see also Frost, 2021). Cree et al (2019: 608) also highlight this tension that is often expressed when it comes to measuring effectiveness between the new public management imperative and an agency's own needs for reflecting on their services.

Critical awareness of the increased emphasis on procedure, paperwork and audit that comes with greater managerialism in social work is essential for the 21st-century practitioner. A concern with measuring investment and outputs from these investments is often at odds with the goals of social work. However, we should also be cautious about critiquing outright features associated with increased proceduralisation, risk management, audit and managerialism, because their absence also causes problems. As McGregor has argued in a discussion about UK social work, we need to avoid reference to this challenge of social work in terms of 'unhelpfully simplistic and binary ways: the "Good R (Relationship) and the Bad R (Risk)"' (2015: 1638). For example, procedure and inspection can be overly focused on social control, but are also about ensuring standards and demanding accountability from those who have power over people's lives. Failures to protect and support in the past were often associated with systems that were not properly regulated, leaving those in power to practice without accountability. This led to abuse, harm and exploitation. In these instances, greater social control of these practices, rather than socially controlling those who were subject to them, was required. This is evidenced in histories of institutional care for children and unmarried mothers in Ireland, for example (Commission to Inquire into Child Abuse, 2009; Commission of Investigation into Mother and Baby Homes and certain related matters, 2020). Likewise, a West of Ireland case relating to Áras Attracta brought to the fore concerns about abuse and neglect of adults (Áras Attracta Swinford Review Group, 2016). This led to the development in Ireland of the Health Service Executive's *Safeguarding Vulnerable Persons at Risk of Abuse Policy* in 2014 (HSE, 2014).

Personalisation and marketisation

While social work started in many contexts as a strategy within a welfare state context, it currently resides in a much more complex mix of state, voluntary, third sector and private services. In many instances, too much responsibility is being put onto families through a current emphasis on personalisation (Lymbery, 2012, 2014; Spicker, 2013) and community-based care in the name of autonomy and justice (Owens et al, 2017). As Scourfield (2005: 107) argued a few decades ago, 'what were once public responsibilities are being transferred to the individual', and this trend persists. Critical studies of personalisation agendas in relation to mental health highlight this. For example, Southall et al (2019), referring to England, show how the principles of autonomy, personal responsibility and self-determination reflected in policy do not always take into account the realities of implementing this for the individuals and families involved. A challenge for social work, they argue, is 'to reconcile the gap between the profile of the service user in policy and the reality of the people that social workers are supporting in practice' (Southall et al, 2019: 1). Fraser (2019) highlights how concepts such as choice and empowerment have been taken from the critical left and used in neoliberalism to reinforce individualism (and limited state support) rather than address structural inequality.

Cummins (2020) discusses Fraser's model of progressive liberalism that argues that neoliberalism has 'colonised progressive discourses' (2020: 77). He illustrates this with reference to the UK Coalition Government, 2010–15, that 'introduced new mental health policies such as "No decision about me without me"'. This emphasised 'inclusive approaches to service organisation and delivery', but 'at the same time, it followed social and economic policies that increased inequality, reduced welfare payments and entitlements, and cut services' (Cummins, 2020: 77). A related theme is the privatisation of care. With reference to Korea, for example, Chon (2019) argues that the marketisation of care can be associated with institutional ageism. Meagher et al (2016), in relation to the privatisation of residential care in Sweden, highlight the complexity of the privatisation of services for 'care' in what they describe as a 'big business in a thin market'. The impact of this global trend in exo- and macro-level policy that associates care with business needs further and ongoing critical interrogation.

'Cultural practices'

There are a plethora of models and approaches to guide you in relation to 'cultural practices' that include cultural competence, awareness and consciousness. While useful, many still fall short in terms of sufficient attention to wider structural issues, complex cultural considerations and analysis of power and power relations (Käkelä, 2019). Azzopardi and McNeill (2016: 287–8) argue for an approach where 'cultural consciousness is conceptualized not only at the level of the individual social worker, but also at the broader level of the organization, recognizing that systemic support is crucial to delivering culturally responsive services'. Linked to this, more critical approaches to anti-oppressive and anti-discriminatory practice are required (Larson, 2008; Pon, 2009; de Montigny, 2011; Flynn, 2017), along with more nuanced and critical consideration of issues of race and ethnicity.

With regard to race, there is an ongoing need to reflect on McIntosh's (1988) critical discussion on 'white privilege' (Hall and Jones, 2019) and an intersectional approach that 'moves away from monolithic views of culture and binary social categories' (Azzopardi, 2020: 472; see also Hall and Jones, 2019). Zimba (2020) calls for 'cultural complexity' thinking, referring to the context of South Africa, to address diversity and complexity of culture. She argues that working within the context of the SDGs can offer a framework for this. Gottlieb (2020: 1) argues for 'A cultural humility framework', drawing from the medical and nursing field that 'aligns with collaborative, intersubjective, and anti-oppressive models of social work practice'. Generally, the message is that while 'aware' to some extent of race and culture, social work often falls short in terms of engaging in a way that takes account of rights and justice within the wider ecological system, the complexities, and the dynamics between person, process, context and time. This is referred to as 'PPCT' and discussed further in Chapter 2. As one way forward, we argue for the need to imbue attention to culture throughout the ecological context. We also argue that it is not just about models or frameworks, but also about our own ethics of professional life. We need to:

- pay constant attention to our own awareness of othering;
- be critical and mindful of the language we use;
- have open and critical dialogue;
- be open to learning and not afraid to make a mistake or say the wrong thing;
- ask people directly about issues of race, ethnicity, identity and personal experiences, and then listen attentively in response;
- call out subtle and overt racism and discrimination with colleagues, other professionals and in our organisations;
- engage with our professional association and/or our organisation in relation to developing and implementing anti-racist strategies;
- develop a perspective based on intersectionality and superdiversity;

- develop confidence in leadership in relation to ensuring social work practice does not reinforce othering, stereotyping or denial of difference and diversity, and actively seeks strategies to combat racism, discrimination and oppression;
- critically analyse, reflect and think about the causes, effects and responses to racism and oppression through ongoing continuing professional development.

The global pandemic

The COVID-19 pandemic that occurred from late 2019 onwards poses another contemporary challenge. This global event required the rapid development of transformative approaches in social work practice and education. Evidence from responses to the pandemic by social workers and educators highlights many proactive, creative and energetic responses to the literal transformation of practices, and open sharing and development of resources, in solidarity. This happened in the context of enormous concerns for the less powerful and less protected members of society, and the ways social workers can positively contribute to social justice and human rights practices. As Dominelli et al (2020: 1) express, '(t)he pandemic and our local and global responses to it have significantly impacted our way of life, how we interact with each other and our environment, and how we help and care for those most vulnerable on the margins of our societies'. They discuss the impact of the pandemic on the 'socio-ecological fabric' of society (Dominelli et al, 2020: 2). Key concerns for social work include: the digital divide and a lack of access to education for many; increased dangers for adults and children experiencing or at risk of experiencing violence in the home; enhanced poverty through loss of employment; and the devastating lack of regard shown for those least able to socially distance and most in need of protection and support. Dominelli et al (2020) and Lavalette et al (2020) consider how different nations have responded to COVID-19, highlighting how the pandemic has intensified inequality and injustice globally. The pandemic reinforces the importance of a human rights approach to practice at an individual level as well as a wider ecological level. It also reinforces the value and importance of an enquiry-based learning approach, where the learner must now, perhaps more than ever before, be self-directed and proactive in practice and in education.

Power imbalances in social work knowledge

Ongoing power imbalances in the knowledge base of the discipline are a recurrent challenge. We have a thoroughly unbalanced discipline in that 'knowledge' underpinning theories and practices is more oriented towards 'First World'/'Euro-centric'/'Western world' concepts. This creates major challenges for those within contexts such as Africa, as expressed by Mathebane (2020), who attributes the dominance of 'Euro-North American systems of psychosocial care' to the detriment of indigenous ways of problem-solving to "work and research back" to the African roots' (2020: 77). Over-simplified assumptions are often made about indigenous knowledge approaches that fail to recognise the complex internal and local constructions of social work within different social, historical and political settings, as shown, for example, by Yi–Bing et al (2020) in relation to social work in China. It is imperative that we continue to build on progress that has been made worldwide in raising awareness about indigenous social work, diversity of practice in different cultural contexts and the need to challenge over-reliance on dominant discourses alone (see, for example, Ferguson et al, 2018; Munford and O'Donoghue, 2019). We have many global examples of transformative social work focused on the democratisation of knowledge, a mainstreaming of partnership approaches and a surge in patient and service user-led momentum for change and self-governance (see, for example, Munford and O'Donoghue, 2019). Helpful concepts such as 'superdiversity' (Grzymala-Kazlowska and Phillimore, 2018; Hendriks and van Ewijk, 2019; Phillimore, 2019) and 'intersectionality' (Mattsson, 2013; Collins and Bilge, 2016) encourage us to avoid linear explanations and be prepared to engage in complex, intersecting themes that affect social work in different contexts. As well as needing to give more space to diverse and global perspectives with a focus on human rights and culture (see, for example, Sewpaul, 2021), we also need to recognise the power of learning from a range of different practices, especially those connected to indigenous populations and drawn from a mix of formal and informal systems.

We acknowledge that, as authors, we are ourselves limited by the hegemony of 'Western' discourses in our own experiences and knowledge, despite our commitment to critical awareness regarding this in how we have written this book. We also acknowledge that no one book could identify, let alone address, the range of challenges and opportunities facing social work worldwide. However, what we hope to provide in this book is a set of scaffolds to critically analyse, reflect on and think about social work as a holistic and global strategy. In this context, for jurisdictions where the focus is more on micro- and meso-level practices, it can help to extend workers to engage more proactively with the wider exo and macro levels. Conversely, for jurisdictions where community and social development is more dominant, this book may be particularly useful for complementing this work with a focus on integration of practice from micro- and meso-level practices to these exo- and macro-level practices. Whatever the 'orientation', we need to recognise that social work is always, to some extent, a political activity defined by the context in which it resides. It has a role to *both* act within this context *and* call or keep it to account. For example, radical and critical social work approaches are commonly identified as more politically oriented, and distinguished helpfully by Mulally (2007) in terms of practices 'inside' the system and practices 'outside' the system. This book, and our approach, is focused on social work inside the system, and the political stance taken is based on a commitment to civic and political engagement with citizens who are service users now, in the past, or in the future. Our approach focuses on material, practical and therapeutic support and protection within a framework that recognises and critiques the dynamic interaction between the person and their ecological environment throughout the lifecourse. For example, as well as critiquing the dynamics of poverty at a socioeconomic level, we must attend to the practical and actual needs of individuals in day-to-day life. Bi-locating ecological environment and the lifecourse acts as an 'anchor' to understanding and responding to families in policy and practice, and in our view, as expressed in our framework which is foundational to social work.

Concluding thoughts on challenges for social work

In this book, we emphasise the importance of taking a holistic approach, where you engage critically in the debates but avoid polarisations – such as traditional versus radical practice – that can over-simplify the complexity and contradictions that are part and parcel of what social work is about. One of the major opportunities that we see in present-day social work is the potential for social work to develop a transformative approach that builds on scholarship focused on partnership, civic engagement, collaboration and public engagement. We need to think about how social work can engage from a social justice perspective that takes account of intersectionality and superdiversity, and is able to mediate contradictory positions. This requires critical attention to the marginalisation of many individuals, groups and populations at an individual and wider social context. It also requires an in-depth understanding of the multidimensionality of the 'person' and their 'environment' – in other words, constantly thinking about the person and the environment with a focus on proactive collaboration with citizens who used, are using, or will use services in the future (Ferguson et al, 2018; Munford and O'Donoghue, 2019), and cooperation with other relevant disciplines, services, networks and agencies. Clients, service users, patients and consumers all become, within this frame, fellow citizens. This potentially transforms how we understand, deliver and critique supportive and protective services. Development of the related concept of citizenship in social work, with a focus on civic engagement and partnership in this book, is an opportunity for social work globally to align with commitments to work *alongside*, rather than *with* or *to*, people.

Summary

The discussion in this chapter should remind you that social work is complex and open to challenge and debate. Linking back to social work 'in the social', the following statement from *The British Journal of Social Work* captures the current challenge of balancing the orientations and intentions of social work, which resonates with the messages throughout this book:

> To be sure, social work is committed to social justice and empowerment of marginalised and disadvantaged persons and protection of those made vulnerable through, age, disability or ill-health. It is tempting

to proclaim that we are engaged in the "fight against poverty" and the "elimination of child abuse", for example. In truth, neither is within our remit or capacity. But walking alongside, lending our strength to the vulnerable, facilitating a voice for the voiceless, fostering resilience and strengths in others, speaking truth to power – these are all core to the essential job of social work across the globe. (Golightley and Holloway, 2020: 303)

Hyslop, drawing from Philp's work (1979), makes a similar point:

Social work practice knowledge involves an analysis of social and material context in structuring the lives of clients. However, it is also cognisant (and respectful) of an underlying "possibility" that characterises human "being". The social work knowledge form can be described as paradoxical. It resists discourses that deny human potential but simultaneously acknowledges that social circumstances may prevent human form being realised. (Hyslop, 2013: 199–200)

In this book, we encourage you to critically engage with theories of the relationship between the individual and society by considering this in relation to the lifecourse and the ecological perspective. In so doing, we incorporate knowledge about support and protection, lifecourse, family and social support, intergenerational relations, civic engagement, health and wellbeing. We have set out in this chapter our view of social work by way of a 'recap' for the reader, as well as clarification of the assumptions that inform our approach. In Chapter 2, we present our knowledge and understanding of social work as a mediation between a person's lifecourse and the ecological environment by using five interrelated themes to advance social work as a practice of support and protection, as shown in Figure 1.1.

Figure 1.1: Snapshot overview of a framework for support and protection across the lifecourse – an advanced perspective on the 'person-in-environment'

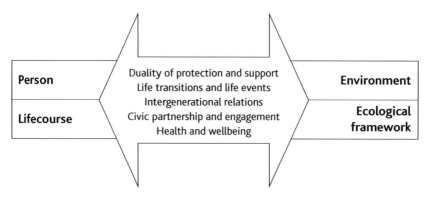

Recommended resources

Global Agenda for Social Work, 2010–20 and 2020–30

To complement the discussion in this chapter, especially about the challenges of current social work, we recommend reading the Global Agenda for Social Work 2010–20 and the Global Agenda for Social Work and Social Development 2020–30 to gain a fuller understanding of the current challenges and opportunities for the profession (see www.ifsw.org/social-work-action/the-global-agenda).

Ethics and values

You need to be familiar with your own association's code of values and ethics, your professional accreditation body's code of values and ethics and the global ethics statements from the various international organisations (see the Ethical Principles from the IFSW and IASSW below). These should inform your critical ART. The codes and statements should not be seen as simple guides or lists, but as core and central to whatever theory or method you are using and that is connected to your professional identity and professional life. The historical development of core ethics and values is also important in understanding the impact of wider societal values, ethical positions and culture on practices, as discussed in this chapter.

- The IFSW Global Social Work Statement of Ethical Principles: www.ifsw. org/global-social-work-statement-of-ethical-principles
- The IASSW Global Social Work Statement of Ethical Principles: www.iassw-aiets.org/Global-Social-Work-Statement-of-Ethical-Principles-IASSW

UN's Sustainable Development Goals (SDGs)

No matter where you work, you should have a view of yourself as a global as well as a local practitioner. The UN's SDGs (https://sdgs.un.org/goals) provide a framework for placing your work within this wider critical context. The SDGs have different implications depending on your context.

Tips for critical ART in practice

Understand the 'scope' of social work in your context

To help clarify your own perspective on the scope and limits of social work practice, Table 1.1 captures the position of social work vis-à-vis other forms of knowledge and disciplines to help visualise the scaffolding around which knowledge for social work practice lies in relation to other disciplines and activities. Adapt this to your own context to help develop a sense of social work

Table 1.1: Knowledge and practices within and around social work

Related disciplines and strategies drawing from psychological and psychosocial perspectives	Core to social work Social policy and legal context			Related disciplines and strategies drawing from sociological and social policy perspectives
For example, psychology, specialist therapeutic practice, counselling	More psychologically oriented social work Social work oriented towards counselling, therapies and psychology	Social work mediation in the social between the individual and society or social policy Majority of core social work with individuals, groups and communities	More sociologically oriented social work Social work oriented towards social and community development	For example, social development, community development, social policy, social action

in relation to related disciplines in order to help you articulate clearly the specific role and function of social work in practice alongside its associated disciplines.

Use history to inform your present analysis and understanding of social work

Every student and practitioner should have a strong sense of the history of their profession in context to help forge their own identities as members of the profession and to more fully appreciate the debates current at any particular moment in time (see Table 1.2). You can do this by:

- Reading published books and articles on the history of social work in your country and local region.
- Asking experienced practitioners and practice teachers about their history; be interested to listen and learn.
- If you are experienced, take time to tell your story of the profession to your students and newer professional colleagues.
- If you find there is a limited knowledge of the history, consider doing a project or use your dissertation to collect oral histories or research in your local archives.
- Draw a map of the development of social work based on this work to include a training and education programme, key people, the role of religion, philanthropy, and the state, other societal influences, big debates (such as individual versus the collective), cultural norms that inform individual training and significant environmental factors that influence the social work context.
- Use this exercise to start to develop your own approach to critical ART.

Table 1.2: Using history to inform present understandings

Critical ART	Your notes
Analyse the history of your context	
How does this history impact on present-day practices of social work with regard to its strengths and its limits?	
Reflect on your own views (or position) in relation to social work	
How have you developed your understanding?	
What aspects of the discussion on the nature of social work make most sense to you?	
What areas are unclear and do not connect for you at present?	
Think about how you can develop your social work approach as a practice of human rights and social justice based on this understanding noting potential and limitations	

Consider how global challenges impact on your practice

From the discussion in this chapter, create a table of your own record of global challenges directly affecting your practice. Use this to record each challenge and specifically how it affects your practice and/or the people you are working with. Be specific and concrete in your examples to avoid becoming overwhelmed by the range of issues you may have on your list when you finish. Other global challenges are discussed throughout this book, so keep this exercise to guide further critical ART as you read on.

2

Theoretical perspectives informing our framework

Introduction

This chapter outlines our overarching framework for support and protection practice based on five interrelated themes. We begin with an overview of ecological perspective based on the work of Urie Bronfenbrenner and his colleagues, and follow with a commentary on lifecourse perspectives. While these are the two main theories that underpin the five-theme framework that follows, there are a number of other theories of relevance that we summarise in Figure 2.1 and address in detail throughout the book. These relate to power and power relations, protection and support, transitions, relational cultural theory, presence theory, ethics and empathy. In addition, there are theories we do not cover in this book that are important to 'recap' on, and we direct you towards these.

Figure 2.1: Overview of our framework

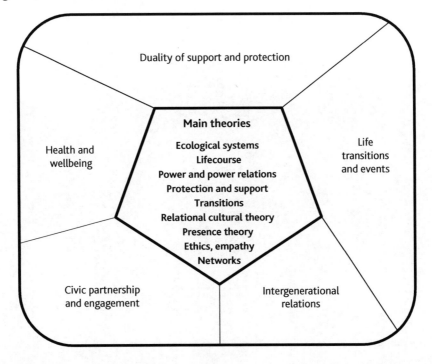

Following this, we summarise the five core themes of the framework:

- duality of protection and support;
- life transitions and life events;
- intergenerational relations;
- civic partnership and engagement;
- health and wellbeing.

Figure 2.1 encapsulates the five themes and the various theories that we relate to these.

Bronfenbrenner's ecological model

We developed our five-theme framework through the use of an ecological approach that recognises layers *of influence from micro to macro*, as developed in Bronfenbrenner's original work (1979). We use in particular his later development of the bio-ecological approach (Bronfenbrenner and Ceci, 1994; Bronfenbrenner and Morris, 1998, 2006; see also Bronfenbrenner, 1988, 1995). Figure 2.2 is a snapshot of the scope and focus of how we use this model in this book. This is developed further later in this chapter, to incorporate the five themes. These

Figure 2.2: Overview of the adapted bio-ecological model applied to our framework

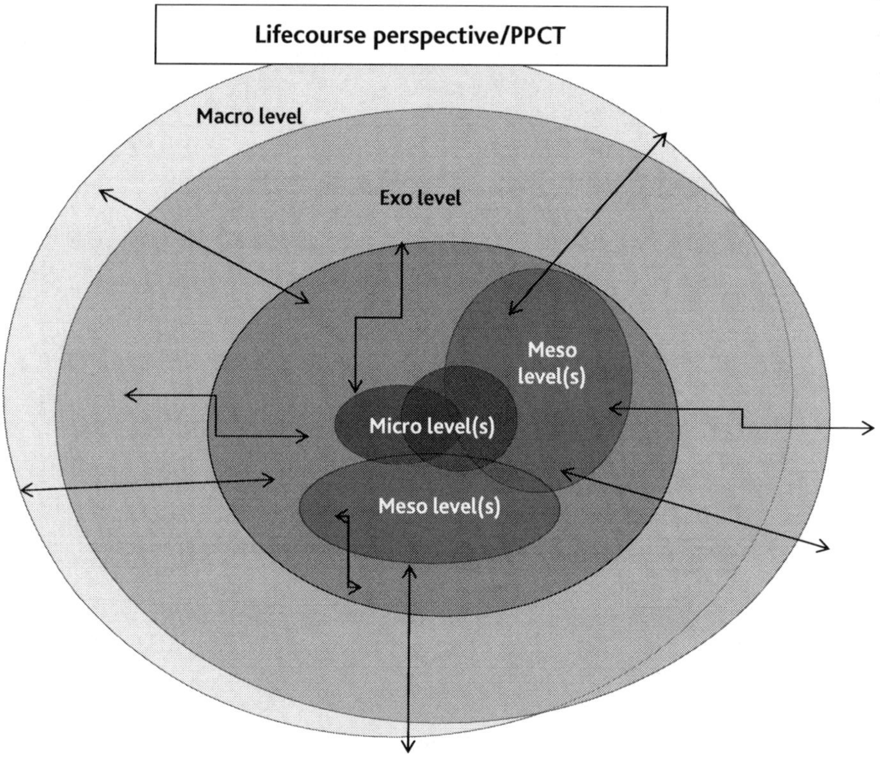

Source: Adapted from Bronfenbrenner (1979) and Bronfenbrenner and Morris (2006)

figures should be viewed as work in progress, which we refer back to and develop throughout the book.

Use of the ecological model provides a more differentiated picture of the 'person–in–environment' by breaking the 'environment' up into different layers. Many of you are likely to be very familiar with Bronfenbrenner's work as it is used so widely in social work and related areas. For those new to this work, however, core references are provided in the 'Recommended resources' at the end of this chapter. It is important to note that this work evolved over Bronfenbrenner's lifecourse. Here, we set out our interpretation and adaptation of the model, and throughout the book we explore how we can adapt from and build further a critical ecological framework.

The original ecological model offered by Bronfenbrenner (1979) gives a context to add depth to an analysis of interactions between the person (micro) and environment, where environment is broken into meso, exo and macro. This allows levels of concern such as family relations (micro–meso), community or school context (micro–exo) or wider policy context (micro–macro) to be specified and identified rather than just thinking about the 'environment'. It also focuses on interactions and relations between the different systems. The bio–ecological model (Bronfenbrenner and Morris, 2006) develops the context (micro–meso) in relation to processes, people and time (PPCT). This later model gives more emphasis to the person in the system (focused on biological, psychological and social context) and the dynamic interactions between the person's micro and wider context. For example, 'process' can refer to relationships, interventions and interactions. 'Person' refers to the individual (the worker, the service user or the young person, for example). Bronfenbrenner and Morris (2006: 811) refer to aspects of the person in relation to force (personal factors), resource (individual and wider resources) and demand (characteristics such as age and gender). 'Context' refers to the layers, from micro to macro. 'Time' includes micro (moments), meso (patterns) and macro (chrono) levels, relating to trends at a moment in time (for example, the current role of digital technology). This focus on time also resonates with a lifecourse perspective that emphasises history, culture and context. A focus on the PPCT aspect of the ecological model enhances a framework for practice for relational social work based on interactions and mediation between the person and the impact of wider environmental factors on individuals, families, groups and communities. It offers both a tool for mapping and planning work as well as targeting interventions and decision-making (McCormack et al, 2020). However, it also has limitations that should be highlighted from the outset.

Tudge et al (2016) have criticised the application of the ecological model, arguing that it is often misused. Another criticism is that it assumes order where the systems – like Russian dolls – each fit well into each other. While this may be the case for some people, for most who come into contact with social work, their systems and relations between their bio and micro levels and their meso (family, for example), exo (community, for example) and macro (legal status, for example) are likely to be more complex. There is also a need to develop the model to take account of diversity and possible multiple micro or meso levels for a person in regular transition, such as certain children in care (Devaney et al, 2019). Norris et al (2013) focused on use of the approach in nursing with older people and proposed a critical bio-ecological approach that takes account of the more dynamic and fluid dimensions. Winter and Burholt (2018), also writing in relation to work with older people, make the case that culture – usually identified at macro and/or chrono level – should, in fact, be viewed as crossing all dimensions, from micro to macro, given its centrality. McGregor and Devaney (2020b) suggest that the ecological model can best be activated through use of network theories and practice, and position the person at the forefront and the process as the interaction connecting these back to the micro–meso context. The ecological model needs to be developed further to take account of environmental and sustainability issues to emphasise a focus on the physical and environmental as well as social ecologies.

In the bio-ecological model, personal resources can also be identified as beneficial or harmful, but there seems to be a need to have a wider dynamic approach to categorising interactions and proximal processes according to their benefit or otherwise to the person in the micro system. For example, Bredewold et al (2020) highlight the importance of a critical consideration of all aspects of the ecosystem, not just at micro level, in their study on deinstitutionalisation for people with an intellectual and psychiatric disability. They found that a move to the community did not automatically lead to greater integration, and sometimes led to greater social difficulties for some individuals due to negative forms of interaction. The global movement to close large orphanages with an estimated population of at least eight million children is another example that highlights the complexities of engaging at exo and macro levels. This approach is shared as a policy direction through use of the ecological approach across the major non-governmental organisations (NGOs) including UNICEF, Lumos, Better Care Network and Hope and Homes for Children. Practices involve engaging with families and services to enable family reunification through enhanced informal family support, with community service provision including community social work. The Lumos approach, for example, reflects a chrono-level concern 'to create global, meaningful change in the way children are cared for, we partner with advocates and allies at every level: from international decision-makers to children and their families' (Lumos, 2019).

We mostly use the bio-ecological model in this book, with critical awareness of its strengths and limits. We argue that it is particularly helpful because it helps to break up the 'social' and the 'environment' into more detailed contextual interactions (micro–meso–exo–macro–chrono). In so doing, it gives depth and specificity to the analysis of social work as mediation between the person in their environment throughout the lifecourse.

The following points summarise how we have adapted its use within our framework:

• As a necessarily relationship-based discipline, practice begins at the micro–meso level through relationships and interactions between service users and social workers. For some, these interactions will be mostly at the micro–meso level (for example, interactions in relation to social support and therapeutic intervention). For others, they will be interactions focused on the micro to the exo (for example, mediating interactions between a service user and an organisation in relation to seeking adequate services) and/or the macro (for example, mediating interactions between a service user and the legal system to challenge and advocate for rights to services such as disability support).

- We focus on PPCT to make connections between the person and environment as a process of mediating interactions in the social. We refer to person–process or process–person to denote the relationship and interaction between workers and service users/groups/communities. We refer to the context as the layers of the ecological system that are the focus of concern and action. We refer to time as *both* the specific moment of interaction (relationship) *and* the current trends in society (for example, the impact of the personalisation agenda on access to disability services).
- We adapt the model to account for the critiques about 'consensus' and to enable consideration, using the layers of the model, for more complex micro–meso interactions, contradictions, dynamic and fluid relations that can take account of intersectionality and superdiversity and embed culture throughout the context.
- We connect the ecological chrono level to a lifecourse perspective that activates further the notion of time in particular.
- We propose that community and social development theory and network theory can be used to develop a more critical analysis of the ecological context.
- We recognise the need for ongoing development of the model, especially in relation to environmentalism and sustainability and social work.

Lifecourse theories and assumptions

The lifecourse reflects the intersection of social and historical factors with personal biography and development, within which the study of family life and social change can ensue (Elder et al, 2003). A lifecourse approach focuses on human growth and is based on the assumption that this will take different directions. The *Handbook of the Life Course* (Shanahan et al, 2016) provides a comprehensive overview of a range of lifecourse perspectives. Lifecourse implies that life is best judged as occurring through a series of journeys rather than as a single linear path. As Hutchison (2005) explains, it is about the interplay of human life that links past history and present circumstances. Reflecting on the relevance for social work in 2019, Hutchison reiterates her lifecourse perspective that focuses on five concepts: cohorts, transitions, trajectories, life events and turning points. These are discussed in relation to six interrelated themes of links between people's lives, links between past and present, individual choice, development and diversity (Hutchison, 2019).

A lifecourse perspective is also about developmental risk and protection, diversity in lifecourse trajectories and the role of human agency in making life choices (Shanahan et al, 2016). As a concept, lifecourse is an emerging interdisciplinary theory that seeks to understand the multiple factors that shape people's lives from birth to death. It situates individual and family development within historical and cultural contexts (Hutchison, 2005). As an emerging field of research and practice, it infers working towards a better understanding of the elements and dynamics of an individual's life journey, and how this is influenced by socioeconomic conditions, political context and culture. This journey can be viewed through normative development (growing up and growing old), life transitions (dependency to interdependency) and life events as they occur over time (planned and/or unexpected). Lifecourse also includes how unforeseen and unwanted circumstances can play a part that requires human responses and adjustments. These can sometimes be both drastic and immediate, for example responding to the sudden and untimely death of a parent or the urgent requirement for residential care for an older parent or grandparent.

Taking a lifecourse perspective should be viewed as both an ecological concept and part of wider work planning. It can contribute to better service design and practice delivery as well as improved policy. Time, concept and process are key. Ageing and developmental change, therefore, are continuous processes that are experienced throughout life. Throughout this book we advance our commentary about lifecourse and develop it with a particular emphasis on lifecourse, transitions and disruptions. Our five main themes, set within an ecological context, are, in our view, a way of advancing the practical application of lifecourse thinking to day-to-day practice.

One critical point to note is that while our understanding of working within a lifecourse context and perspective often includes focusing on broad issues such as poverty, disadvantage, social exclusion and adversity, with a particular interest in how these affect people's lives, two other key factors can be overlooked, namely, culture and life spaces. The role of culture within a lifecourse framework is one that goes beyond cultural competence (understanding) and needs more fulsome consideration. Despite the extent to which families are integrated within local communities, there are often mores, which may seem hidden but which impact on family functioning. For example, filial piety differs across populations where in some cultures elders are revered for their wisdom, resulting automatically in offspring, including children and grandchildren, having a strong sense of commitment to care for older family members; in other cultures this is less common, and can be seen very differently. From a practice perspective, despite intended and desired outcomes, the social worker needs first to understand the cultural norms within the lifecourse pattern of the family in order to then work within that context. For example, issues such as parental norms (good and safe responsible parenting) for admonishing a child's behaviour can differ, with corporal punishment deemed to be acceptable in certain cultures as opposed to others. Social workers have to delicately mediate between respecting and understanding cultural differences in childrearing (for example) while assertively applying children's rights and best interests. The second 'sometimes missing' factor in relation to working within a lifecourse context comes in the form of understanding 'family spaces and time'. Contact is not the same as closeness between family members, and professionals can mistakenly confuse it. Closeness between family members changes over the lifecourse. For example, adult children often return to greater levels of contact with their parents only on the arrival of the first grandchild. This is not just to enable childcare-sharing duties, but also relates to emotional attachment between generations. Just as the adolescent moves away from parents in order to become independent, once achieved this can be followed by 'returning to the nest to some extent' later on. Understanding where family members are in their life journey of connectivity is important. Rather than judge this as being aloof or distancing in families, it is important to be cognisant that just as relationships change over time, opportunities and the need to connect also change. So, lifecourse is entwined by the provision of social support, a need for belonging and the factor of time within families. A key function for the social worker is not just to understand space in the lifecourse as a 'moveable feast' in families, but to also have a good sense of when to encourage both greater connectivity or better distancing dependent on life circumstances and need. In our framework, we emphasise in particular the lifecourse themes of intergenerational relations, life events and transitions and health and wellbeing, which are discussed in 'Five key themes' later in this chapter.

Other theories that inform the framework

Table 2.1 provides a summary of other theories we cover within our framework. The core theories covered in this book are outlined in bold; these are directly connected to the framework and explained in the chapters that follow, as set out in the table. Other theories are referenced as 'recap theories' for you to draw from, especially in relation to learning about theories of human behaviour, human development and the social environment, which are covered substantially in other texts. With regard to 'recap' theories, many theories of human behaviour, growth and development in particular are referred to in this book but are not explored in depth. Instead, we revert to core texts and guides. We use texts such as Sudbery and Whittaker's *Human Growth and Development: An Introduction for Social Workers* (2019) and Walker and Horner's *Social Work and Human Development* (2020) to introduce the relation of the main theories to human growth, behaviour, development and the social environment. For student readers, each social work programme will have their own specific core texts for this essential subject relating to biological, psychological and cognitive theory that you can draw from. Whatever the text, some of the most relevant theories, as covered by Sudbery (2010), are:

- attachment;
- stages of development;
- grief and loss;
- learning and behavioural theories;
- ecological and systems theories.

Table 2.1: Overview of the main theories covered in the book

	1–2 General overview	3 Protection and risk	4 Family and social support	5 Resilience through social support	6 Transition	7 Disrupted development	8 Networks and social ecology
Chapters							
Common themes covered in all chapters			Duality of protection and support Life transitions and life events Intergenerational relations Civic partnership and engagement Health and well being				
Additional/related theories used relating to human development, human behaviour and the social environment	Ecological theory Lifecourse Lifespan	Safeguarding, risk management and protection Power and power relations Social construction of childhood and adulthood	Family support Social support Relationship and relational practice	Resilience Cultural relational theory Presence Empathy	Child and adult development Transition	More detailed focus on lifecourse, transition and disruption of development Grief and loss Attachment	Social ecology (including family support cupped model and a look back to protection theories) Community and social development Network Formal–informal Bio-ecological Technology

(continued)

Table 2.1: Overview of the main theories covered in the book (continued)

Chapters	1–2 General overview	3 Protection and risk	4 Family and social support	5 Resilience through social support	6 Transition	7 Disrupted development	8 Networks and social ecology
Sample of practice domains discussed in detail for illustration (including use of relevant research studies)	General discussion on social work	Adult safeguarding/ protection Child protection	Working with marginalised youth Youth justice Partnership with parents Children's participation	Family support Social support Mental health Families affected by poverty	Children leaving and after care Work with recent migrants Asylum-seekers and refugees Transition of people with intellectual disability from childhood to adult	Parental mental illness Move to alternative care for older people Child sexual abuse Severe child neglect	Child and adult protection and support Sociolegal practice in mental health, safeguarding and criminal justice practices Social policy, advocacy and networked practices
Note: additional examples are also provided in more summary form							

Theories about the impact of trauma are also influential, as shown by Lotty et al (2020) in relation to children and families, and Spira et al (2020) in relation to adult trauma. Critical considerations include taking account of trauma within an ecological context, such as historical trauma linked to colonial histories (Atwool, 2019), trauma experienced by refugees and asylum-seekers (Naseh et al, 2019; Ballard-Kang, 2020) and ethnic and racial differences in response to trauma (O'Hare et al, 2019).

Advancing your knowledge further, Parker and Ashencaen Crabtree (2020a, b) provide a comprehensive overview of a range of traditional and contemporary theories relating to children and adults. While not specifically set in a lifecourse frame, their perspective resonates with the position of our book that lifespan development is not a linear path but rather a complex process, different for everyone. Chapters in this book emphasise especially that ethnicity, race, gender, sexual orientation, age, class and so on influence this development. Parker and Ashencaen Crabtree (2020a, b) emphasise the importance of social workers engaging critically with traditional theories. This does not mean they should be debunked. Rather, they need to be placed within wider critical contexts to take account of environmental and ecological factors. Parker and Ashencaen Crabtree (2020a, b) encourage use of broad critical theories such as feminism, spirituality, anti-discriminatory and anti-oppressive practice (Thompson, 2020) and critical best practice (Ferguson, 2008a).

In terms of understanding the complex context of people in their environments, there is currently particular emphasis on Adverse Childhood Experiences (ACEs) and their impact on adult health and wellbeing outcomes (Felitti et al, 1998; Bellis et al, 2014). ACEs have featured strongly in discussions about connections and disruptors between childhood experiences and adulthood and warrant separate study in their own right (Spratt et al, 2019). Theories about ACEs show the importance of addressing issues of abuse, alcohol misuse, violence, criminality and mental health across the lifecourse to prevent adverse outcomes. Spratt (2012) discusses the notion of MACEs (Multiple ACEs) to capture this complexity. While advancing our awareness of these important factors, the risk of over-generalised use of ACEs is cautioned. The following all impact on how people respond to and overcome adversity: cultural and personal diversity; differences in how people cope; what family and social support they have; what resilience they have built up; and how formal services have engaged (Kelly-Irving and Delpierre, 2019; Siagian et al, 2019). A lifecourse perspective enables a critical and dynamic view on the complex relationship between experiences in childhood and their impact on adult life.

Five key themes

Duality of protection and support

Support and protection in social work is a simultaneous role that can be traced through history in relation to the duality of care and control and the sociolegal function of social work.

The emphasis of social work on support and protection changes depending on the wider social and governance context. For example, in the Scandinavian countries, there has traditionally been a greater emphasis on welfare and support, whereas in Anglo Saxon and US contexts, the child protection and legal aspect is more to the fore (see Merkel-Holguin et al, 2019). We argue for a 'dynamic duality', informed by the work of Devaney and McGregor (2017) and McGregor and Devaney (2020a, b), who frame child welfare work as 'protective support and supportive protection'. Even in fields that do not have an explicitly defined legal mandate for social work – such as aspects of clinical practice – the role of offering support and protection enabled and constrained by legal and policy contexts remains a constant feature. In delivering a dual mandate to care and control, social support and family support theory is central to the delivery of social work (Pinkerton et al, 2019).

To adequately problematise this complex duality of support and protection there remain 'unknowns' in the literature and practice guidance about how best to deliver this contradictory dual mandate. In our view, we can address these unknowns through in-depth reflection. Family support and child protection theories reflect the tension between partnership and solidarity with families, on the one hand, and 'the technocratic pursuit of classification and management of risk' (Pinkerton et al, 2019: 49), on the other. The same can be said for adult protection. Chapters 3 to 5 are devoted to building up our knowledge of some of the main theories about protection and support. In Chapter 3, we focus specifically on child protection, adult safeguarding and risk management across the lifecourse, with an emphasis on power and power relations. In Chapters 4 and 5, more detailed theories of family and social support are explored. Following from this, continued attention is paid to this fundamental duality applied to a range of practice contexts.

The remaining four themes are interrelated, each helping to advance critical ART about this dual feature of support and protection in social work.

Life transitions and life events

Under this heading, a broad range of theories of human behaviour, human development and the social environment are relevant. It is important to distinguish between lifespan and lifecourse theories. Lifespan theory is commonly used to map life transitions and events for children and adults, and draws from a body of knowledge based on biological, sociological and psychological theory (Walker and Horner, 2020). Erikson's lifespan frame goes from infancy to late adult development (Erikson, 1974, 1994). A lifespan approach is important for mapping the development of newborn babies and toddlers to help understand how a child is developing, and to determine any additional assistance they may need with aspects of this in relation to disabilities or developmental delays, for example. However, for understanding human development and behaviour more broadly, the lifespan approach is too deterministic and does not reflect most people's lifecourses. For example, the child scale from ages 0–18 may map well enough onto Western democracies, but is less relevant in contexts where children's development is more accelerated into work, marriage and/or participation in war long before the age of 18. The early adulthood stage that ranges from 20–39 spans many different developments and transitions in a person's life. Mid-adulthood spans a massive 40–59. Moreover, late adulthood is from age 60 onwards! Joan Erikson, Eric Erikson's wife, added a ninth stage relating to age 80 onwards (see Erikson and Erikson, 1998; Bugajska, 2017), but the linear nature of the lifespan, on its own, is still limited.

The main critique of the lifespan approach is its linear nature. Those who do not follow a linear path of lifespan may feel 'outside the norm' – for example, a person who stays single, a teen parent, a person with developmental 'delay', a person with a learning disability, and so on. Alternatively, the lifecourse perspective encourages a non-linear approach to understanding human development. While lifespan theory derives more from psychology, lifecourse theory derives more from sociology and cultural studies. It generally implies that we look at childhood, adulthood and older age as interconnected and interrelated.

A lifecourse approach also implies a biographical approach. This involves seeking to understand our own development in order to be able to work with others, using lifecourse mapping. We emphasise the importance of social work students and practitioners engaging in a lifecourse approach that recognises their own lifecourse. In the 'Tips for critical ART in practice' we suggest how drawing the lifecourse and using lifecourse mapping can aid assessments and interventions.

Intergenerational relations

'Intergenerational relations' connects to both lifecourse and ecological perspectives. This theme crosses many disciplines, including social work (see, for example, the *Journal of Intergenerational Relationships*). As shown in Part II, we need to think about intergenerational relations in many different ways. First, it is about the relationships between different generations, parents, children, grandparents or younger and older people. Awareness of the range of commonalities and differences across cultures in relation to intergenerational relations is essential. For example, Timonen (2019), who examines grandparenting around the world, illustrates how societal constructions of age, parenting and intergenerational relations affects day-to-day relations. Examples from Southeast Asia and Africa (Timonen, 2019) refer to multigenerational co-residence, where many generations reside in the same household. In later chapters we highlight further the impact on intergenerational relations where family members are separated due to economic or social needs for migration or emigration. Also on the theme of grandparenting, Capous-Desyllas et al (2020) consider the challenges for grandparents who become unexpected carers later in life due to difficulties experienced by their adult children in relation to parenting, thus changing the nature of these intergenerational relations.

Second, an intergenerational approach shows how childhood may be very present in an adult life, for example because of the impact of childhood abuse, and conversely, how 'children' can take on 'adult' roles of caring for parents or grandparents or working to earn for the family. We need to move away from being over-paternalistic, yet sufficiently protective, when it comes to working with young people. Satka et al (2007) explain this very clearly with regard to Finland, showing how policies relating to youth protection and youth 'delinquency' are linked to a larger-scale change in the generational relations and governance of young people. Using a perspective relating to social work in the social, they highlight a curious dichotomy whereby policies and practices concerned with promoting the development of children and young people treat children more as objects of concern rather than as co-subjects in this generational transformation. Their solution is to move away from 'narrow conceptions of citizenship that exclude non-citizens and citizens under a certain age' (Satka et al, 2007: 134). They optimistically and helpfully remind us of our capacity to take a more subject-oriented and citizenship-based approach to challenge adult-centred practices of 'normal', where they argue that: 'The fact that past generations of social workers have obviously had the means to construct innovative tools and appropriate theoretical knowledge to enable such development is a good indication that the current and future generations might well be able to carry on this tradition' (Satka et al, 2007: 134).

Third, we need to consider disability from an intergenerational perspective. Goodley (2010) captures the layers of oppression and discrimination relating to biological, social, cultural and political constructions of disability. These can lead to:

- denial of human rights (see, for example, Murphy and Bantry-White, 2020, in relation to Ireland);
- stigmatisation (see, for example, Kayama et al, 2019, in relation to India);
- ableism (see, for example, Shier et al, 2011, in relation to Canada);
- 'differentiating and disabling' social work practices (see, for example, Engwall et al, 2019, in relation to Sweden).

Much of this comes from adultism and disablist attitudes (Flynn, 2019a, b, c). One example of this relates to approaches to sexuality and relationships for people with learning disabilities. Feely (2016: 725) describes 'the subtle but effective' ways that the sexuality of disabled people is being controlled in policy and practice (discussed further in Chapter 6). Like Satka et al (2007), Feely (2016) highlights how practitioners and service users can effectively challenge and resist this. His research showed a range of effective practices of courage and resistance by staff and creativity resistance and resilience by disabled people in escaping social control in day centres. This emphasises the importance of constant critical awareness of practices that may seem benign and protective, within an intergenerational perspective.

Civic partnership and engagement

Partnership and participation are cornerstones of contemporary social work practice and a welcome shift away from more traditional paternalistic approaches. When reading about practices in the 1970s, for example, there is a significant difference to note in the tone, nature and focus of the work with 'clients', 'service users' or 'consumers'. Reading about relationships in the 1970s (Perlman, 1979) will have common features with contemporary accounts (Bryan et al, 2016; Ruch et al, 2017) with regard to its centrality in social work, but will differ greatly in terms of the way power relations between the 'client'/'service user', the worker and the system are articulated. Through activism among patients, service users, clients and families in relation to working collaboratively, social work now pays far more attention in its work to partnership, participation and power relationships (Beresford and Croft, 2001, 2019). Collaborative and partnership-based practice is complemented by advancements in the involvement of service users in direct social work education and assessment, including co-publication and co-leadership with service users (Duffy et al, 2017; Tanner et al, 2017).

Munford and O'Donoghue (2019) provide a range of chapters on new innovative theories for social work that emphasise approaches focused on the democratisation of knowledge and practice, decolonisation and attention to specific indigenous cultures within and between countries. As Ife (2019: 10–11) argues in introducing Munford and O'Donoghue (2019), social workers are well aware of the challenges and advocate for the importance of people 'actually having significant agency in determining the nature of the services they need, and being able to articulate their own hopes and aspirations rather than these being assumed by well-meaning bureaucrats and managers' (Ife, 2019: 11). Two examples to note from Munford and O'Donoghue are the use of mana-enhancing practice in Aotearoa, New Zealand and Pacific social work. Mana-enhancing practice operates from three recognition points of: significance of history, promoters of identity and Māori concepts of wellbeing (Ruwhiu, 2019). Pacific social work is based on principles of love, relationship and humility (Mafile'o, 2019). This points to complex processes that require detailed knowledge of culture and context. As Ruwhiu (2019: 208) advises, what is needed from the worker is 'authenticity and humility'. There also needs to be willingness and openness to recognising the power of learning from practices outside our own context, and the ability to learn from specific contexts to adapt to our own critical ART. The four main elements of practice identified by Munford and O'Donoghue (2019: 307–17) resonate with the approach we take in this book:

- relational practice;
- integrated evidence-informed practice working at multiple levels, working to principles of human rights and social justice, as defined by the IFSW;
- operating in context and promoting local and indigenous knowledge;
- reflection on practice.

Collaborative leadership through a network-based approach can also help subvert inequality, as shown in by Herrera-Pastor et al (2019) in relation to one area in Spain. We can also look to the fields of mental health (see Mossberg, 2019, in relation to strategic collaboration in mental health services in Sweden), disability (see Hutchinson and Sandvin, 2019, in relation to older people with an intellectual disability in Norway) and child protection (see Sulimani-Aidan and Paldi, 2020, in relation to youth perspectives on their parents' involvement in residential care in Israel) to learn how service user involvement has been embedded in service development and delivery. Generally, studies of service user views of social workers (see, for example, Kam, 2019, in Hong Kong) also highlight an expectation of partnership working and cooperation.

There is no one unified approach to 'service user involvement', and sometimes the challenge is to balance competing interests (Herrera-Pastor et al, 2019). Collaboration in child welfare practice can pose additional challenges of engaging both children and young people and their parents, especially in child protection situations that are contested or conflictual due to the tensions that can arise between parental rights and young people's need for protection (Wilson et al, 2020). The wider ecosystem concerns around politics, culture, history and social policy that shape the relations between society or state and the family are highlighted in the analysis of parental movements across Central and Eastern Europe and Russia by Fabian and Korolczuk (2017), who discuss 'rebellious parents' from a sociopolitical perspective (see also Kornbeck, 2019).

Here, we focus on how partnership and participation in social work can be progressed further through a focus on civic partnership and engagement, which is underpinned by a commitment to citizenship-based social work. Lister (1998) made a passionate appeal for greater attention to the development of citizenship theory in social work to develop it as both a practice and a status. Satka (2014: 201) describes a core goal of social work as the 'overall realisation of citizenship', and there are many developments of citizenship theory and practice to be found in the social work literature, such as welfare citizenship, immigrant and cultural citizenship, citizenship and mental health and age-related citizenship (mentioned earlier and discussed later).

One way for social work to advance a citizenship approach is through specific learning from practices of civic engagement, especially those developed in relation to marginalised young people (McGregor et al, 2020). From a civic engagement perspective, clients, service users, patients and consumers are framed as citizens and co-producers of solutions to individual and collective problems. From this perspective, the person, within their micro system, should always be at the centre. Engaging through practices of civic engagement, and with those we work with as fellow citizens, has potentially transformative potential with regard to developing shared approaches to addressing individual and social issues or problems. Having said this, we have to differentiate between the ideal (for example, full civic engagement and partnerships) and the reality (for example, an exo- and macro-organisational context that limits the scope to operate in an open and trusting way with staff and/or the public). We specifically draw from theories such as empathy, power, relational cultural theory and presence theory in this book to elaborate on this core theme.

Health and wellbeing

Health and wellbeing and social work is another key concept in our framework. A focus on health and health inequality requires critical interrogation. A wellbeing approach is strengths- and solution-based, and connects back to practices of civic engagement and partnership. There is a particular emphasis on wellbeing and health promotion in many areas of social work, such as mental health. This approach does not deny that problems occur – such as severe and enduring mental illness or child and adolescent psychiatric problems – but tries to address them through seeking co-produced solutions and looking for strengths. A number of relevant social work practice developments derive from a wellbeing stance, such as person–centred planning often used in disability services; capabilities models used in work with older people; motivational interviewing used in relation to addiction; the recovery model used in mental health; and Signs of Safety® used in child protection. Wellbeing concepts have been used to promote practices focused on partnership, power sharing and promotion of rights and interests of local indigenous populations. For example, in Aotearoa, New Zealand, holistic Māori concepts of wellbeing are applied, and include:

- *wairuatanga/wairua*, which relates to 'spirituality, ideology, paradigms, perspectives and beliefs' (Ruwhiu, 2019: 202–3);
- *whakapapa*, which is about ancestry and connectedness;
- *tikanga* and *kawa*, related to customs and protocols;
- *mana*, which encompasses 'power, prestige, authority and humility' (Ruwhiu, 2019: 203).

Long established as a key feature of social work and social welfare (Jordan, 2007, 2008), the notion of wellbeing is contested. For example, in the UK it is associated with debates about choice, self-determination and economics (see, for example, Ferguson, 2007; Houston, 2010a). As Simpson and Murr (2014) explain, wellbeing in social work has vacillated between a focus on the 'body personal' – linked to traditional, individual, value-based social work – and the body 'politic' – linked to more radical social work focused on social structures. Framed within the context of neoliberalism, many wellbeing approaches are argued to be caught up with cultural norms around economics and rationalisation.

In this book, we focus in particular on resilience as an example of wellbeing within a strengths-based approach. We argue that resilience is of particular relevance given that most social work is provided when there is a challenge of some form to wellbeing or health. It is difficult to have a sense of wellbeing when a person, family, group or community is experiencing a threat or a hazard. This may be violence in the home, being at risk in independent living or due to lack of family support. However, we know from resilience theory that people can and do 'bounce back' from such threats or hazards. Resilience, as defined by early pioneers, is about overcoming difficulty in the face of adversity through the use of internal and external resources (Rutter et al, 1998). Resilience theory in social work mirrors person–in–environment perspectives in that resilience can be found both within (for example, personality, traits, temperament and drive) and outside a person (for example, networks and quality of support). Essentially, a focus on resilience can enhance physical, mental and emotional wellbeing (discussed and critiqued further in Chapter 5).

Summary

Figure 2.3 gives a snapshot of the scope and scaffolding for the rest of the book. It attempts to show the way we can integrate our critical ART using the five themes within an ecological and lifecourse frame. The intention is to offer a

Figure 2.3: Snapshot overview of our framework mapped onto the bio-ecological PPCT model

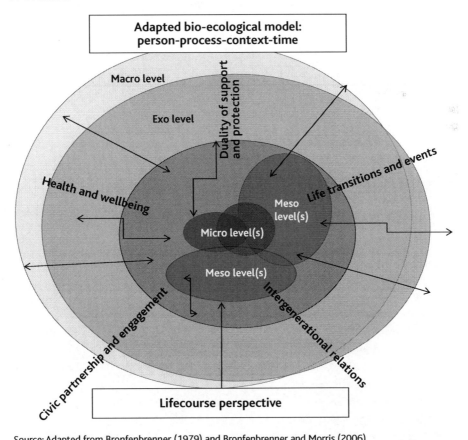

Source: Adapted from Bronfenbrenner (1979) and Bronfenbrenner and Morris (2006)

holistic and comprehensive critical frame for practice. We encourage you to complete the summary box in 'Tips for critical ART in practice' (see Table 2.3) to connect the main points about the five-theme framework with your own context and perspective.

Recommended resources

Social work and human development

Texts on human behaviour and the social environment provide a good grounding for some theories covered here. Our approach is to 'recap' on theories that have already been covered substantially elsewhere, and to focus specifically on selected theories here to illustrate our particular additional contribution to complement these resources. We recommend the following.

Two 2020 books from Policy Press are ideal companions to this book. Both are edited by Jonathan Parker and Sara Ashencaen Crabtree: *Human Growth and Development in Children and Young People* and *Human Growth and Development in Adults.*

John Sudbery and Andrew Whittaker's *Human Growth and Development: An Introduction for Social Workers* (2019) is a very good application of these theories to social work. The authors take readers through the different life stages, and cover a range of relevant theories to be applied, including attachment, ecological theories, psychoanalytical and humanist approaches and theories of ageing.

Janet Walker and Nigel Horner's *Social Work and Human Development* (2020) also introduces theories of human behaviour and social environment from a lifecourse perspective. See also Bruce Thyer et al's *Human Behaviour in the Social Environment: Theories for Social Work Practice* (2012).

Ecological model

A direct reading of Urie Bronfenbrenner and colleagues is highly recommended if you are not familiar with this work:

- Urie Bronfenbrenner (1979) *The Ecology of Human Development: Experiments by Nature and Design.*
- Urie Bronfenbrenner (2005) *Making Human Beings Human: Bio-Ecological Perspectives on Human Development.*
- Urie Bronfenbrenner and Stephen Ceci (1994) 'Nature–nurture reconceptualized in developmental perspective: A bioecological model'.
- Urie Bronfenbrenner and Pamela Morris (1998) 'The Ecology of Developmental Processes'.
- Urie Bronfenbrenner and Pamela Morris (2006) 'The Bioecological Model of Human Development'.

Lifecourse and life events

It is important to gain a general grounding in theories about the lifecourse if readers are unfamiliar with this. See, for example, Jason Powell's *Life Course and Society* (2018). For an excellent general overview of the main concepts and approaches involved in a lifecourse perspective, see Michael Shanahan et al's *Handbook of the Life Course, Vol II* (2016).

Tips for critical ART in practice

Lifecourse and life transitions – the use of mapping

Draw your own lifecourse map and mark out your significant life events, key moments and transitions. It might be linear, winding, disrupted or circular. Use flip charts and colours and see it as a work in progress. It will be different for you as different moments will be significant at different times and in different contexts.

After you are confident drawing your own lifecourse map, consider how you can use this with service users. Such mapping should be used as part of a planned intervention where the method is clearly defined. It is important that you carefully plan this work through supervision and support, and consider how best to use it depending on the specific approach you are taking. As Table 2.2 shows, there are many practice usages for lifecourse maps that can be developed as part of your assessment and intervention plans.

Here are some suggestions for your own and other maps:

- Encourage people to pick key 'moments' that are important at that particular time.
- A path may be linear, but don't impose lines.
- Connect personal development with environmental context.
- Be sensitive to the power of history:
  - only use it when appropriate;
  - it must be consented to;
  - it must have a reason;
  - never explore history without a purpose.

Table 2.2: Examples of where lifecourse mapping can be a useful practical tool

Examples of where lifecourse mapping can be used	Examples of areas of practice
Social histories	Medical/hospital/mental health services
Life story books	Children in care
Reminiscence work	Social support with older people
Memory work	Stroke victims, rehab
Solution focused approaches; 'projecting' the lifecourse and mapping the ideal future	Addiction/depression

With reference to an individual case or area of practice, consider how you can use the ecological systems approach to:

- *Map out* and *analyse* to what extent the issues you are addressing relate to intrinsic factors (individual behaviour, relationships, feelings, health) and to what extent they are related to extrinsic factors (housing, welfare issues, organisational access issues, discrimination, denial of rights).
- *Reflect on and identify your ethical and values position.*
- *Think* about the focus of your intervention and your chosen method as a result of this.

Use of the conceptual framework to plan your work

Consider how you might use our framework to inform your assessment work and decisions about what theories to use in practice (the framework will be developed throughout the book).

Table 2.3: Connecting our framework to your practice

Theme	Main points	Suggested practice examples	Your own examples from practice experience
Duality of support and protection	This denotes an adaptation of the care–control function of social work It can be seen in all aspects of work (explained further in Chapter 3)	Mediating the social in contexts of child protection Adult safeguarding Working with legislation relating to mental health, offending, health outcomes	
Life transitions and events	It is possible to locate each person you work with in the context of what the significant life events of that moment are, and the main life transitions that the person identifies as the most significant	Your own critical reflections on life transitions and the lifecourse help create empathy and understanding, especially at times of change or disruption; a focus on life transitions and events is helpful	
Intergenerational relations	Instead of separating out the 'child' and the 'adult' (using a lifecourse approach), we can focus on the importance of the dynamic of relations between generations past and present The 'intergenerational' lifecourse of the person is also important – eg their sense of being a child (eg past experiences still to the fore in adulthood), parent (to own child) and grandparent (to child's child)	A great deal of our work with children, older people, and people with a disability involves working intergenerationally with families and their wider networks Family work can focus on maximising the relations between generations – building support networks between younger and older people	

(continued)

Table 2.3: Connecting our framework to your practice (continued)

Theme	Main points	Suggested practice examples	Your own examples from practice experience
Civic engagement and partnership	A social worker can bring an approach to their work that is unpinned by a commitment to civic engagement and partnership A worker can also look for the social capital of the person(s) they are working with in relation to their own capacity for civic and political engagement	Partnership working is essential when working with people through social work services. A focus on civic engagement locates this partnership at both the individual and wider community and societal level. Service user or public engagement needs to be critically informed and challenge paternalistic approaches	
Health and wellbeing	Social work is focused on strengths and potential, thus a focus on health and wellbeing, rather than illness and harm, is important This does not deny the existence of illness but encourages, through resilience, a strengths and solutions approach Connecting health and social wellbeing is another important element here	In different clinical settings, including mental health and hospital social work Interdisciplinary working is core to social work and can be operated within the context of a commitment to health and wellbeing. Rather than having medical and social models compete, find ways to work with the patient at the centre, to maximise overall outcomes	

PART II

Applying our support and protection framework in practice

We know that no single book or approach can claim to cover all that must be known and understood for social work practice. Indeed, it is unlikely that any one social work course can even do this. We come from the perspective that learning from the specific to the general is the most applicable and effective way to combine theoretical learning with research evidence and practice and personal learning. With this in mind, the purpose of Part II is to combine theory, current research and practice wisdom with service user, carer and public knowledge in selected areas to bring forth learning in each of the theoretical domains identified in our framework. We provide specific in-depth analyses of aspects of a theme in order to enable general learning. Our intention is that this in-depth treatment of the subject can be transferred to other specific considerations using an enquiry-based approach. Throughout the chapters that follow, we maintain a focus on how the framework presented in Part I can act as a scaffold for critical analysis, reflection and thinking to inform decision-making about assessments and intervention. While the framework informs each chapter, there is more emphasis on some aspects than others depending on the chapter focus.

In Chapter 3, we focus on protection and safeguarding. We start from the knowledge that child protection, and, to a lesser extent, adult safeguarding, has a huge body of relevant theory, literature, practice developments and research you can draw on from other modules or learning sources. Here we want to add to this body of knowledge using our framework to emphasise the importance of thinking about protection and safeguarding from a lifecourse perspective in your practical day-to-day work. We view mediating in the social as a core sociolegal activity that leads us to think of power and think about framing policy law and practice within an ecological practice frame. We develop our discussion about care and control by relating this to child protection and safeguarding. Theories about childhood, adulthood, power and power relations will be covered with relevant research and practice links identified throughout. We demonstrate the importance of considering child and adult protection from a lifecourse perspective, and broaden this application to support and protection in adult safeguarding and social support.

This leads to further elaboration of family and social support in Chapter 4. Theories of family support and social support are core to our support and protection framework. These essential concepts are influential in many social care fields, but are not as fully integrated into social work theory and practice as you might expect, given that support is so critical to promoting people's welfare and rights.

To activate our support and protection framework, we dedicate Chapters 4 and 5 to applying these ideas to social work. Following a general overview in Chapter 4, Chapter 5 follows on from this to focus on theories of resilience and empathy in the context of social and family support. It also introduces presence theory and cultural relations theory.

Chapters 6, 7 and 8 advance the framework further by looking in depth at transitions and disruptions, and engaging in the wider exo and macro contexts. We argue that much of social work is about mediating between individuals and systems to facilitate transitions and to address disruptions in the lifecourse. This work involves the complex application of theories of human behaviour and the social environment and, as discussed in Part I, core texts of the subject are used in our teaching to provide this expertise. While we refer to some of these in the chapters that follow, we are primarily concerned to enhance these applications through the framework presented here, emphasising practice from a lifecourse and ecological perspective. Necessarily illustrative, we hope you will be fully engaged in critical ART and enquiry-based learning to adapt the content provided here to your own specific practice and context, drawing on your additional learning and expertise from related core texts and/or modules. For example, in Chapter 6, we focus on theories relating to the challenges faced through a lifecourse that happen at points of change and transition. We apply Bridges' theory of transition developed from the field of change management and adapted by Dima and Skehill (2011) in work relating to children in care. In Chapter 7, we focus on a selection of particular issues that arise in relation to disrupted development in the lifecourse. In Chapter 8, we focus on support and protection through networks and social ecologies. This chapter also focuses on social work as a networked profession (Frost, 2017), and reiterates the value of formal and informal supports in social work and social care.

Part III then brings together and integrates the framework to point towards future and ongoing learning.

3

Safeguarding, protection and support

Introduction

Irrespective of where you are working or whom you are working with, awareness regarding your duty and responsibility for the protection of children and adults at risk of abuse, neglect or harm must be to the forefront. Abuse, harm and neglect can take many forms, including physical and emotional abuse and neglect, child sexual exploitation, online abuse, child trafficking and gender-based violence. They occur across the lifecourse as major events, usually with a negative impact on health and wellbeing. Safeguarding and protection is a response to harm that has occurred, or that is at risk of occurring. It often involves complex intergenerational relations, and it can be challenging to find ways to work in partnership because of the complex, emotive nature of the work, influenced by different power relations and structures.

Globally, responsibility for child protection is one of the most common areas of practice for social work. Increasingly so, too, is adult safeguarding, although developments in this area have been more varied (Braye et al, 2012; Manthorpe, 2014; Butler and Manthorpe, 2016; Donnelly, 2019). Safeguarding and protection relate to actual or risk of abuse and/or neglect of people in the home, the community, within institutions or due to the structural conditions of people's lives (such as institutional abuse, neglect caused by socioeconomic conditions and/or discrimination against minority and marginalised groups).

While protection and safeguarding are some of the most common features of professional social work globally, most child and adult protection is not carried out by social workers or within designated child protection and safeguarding systems. Individuals, families and local communities do most of the protection and support work through informal systems of support. Where informal and natural support is insufficient or unavailable, it is the professionals working in frontline services, such as public health nurses, local community workers, youth workers, general health community practitioners and so on, who are often best placed to identify, respond and refer on concerns about protection and safeguarding. Working in partnership with formal and informal family and community supports, as well as formal child protection systems, is therefore crucial, as highlighted later in Chapter 8. Where this protection is not available, the role of frontline protection and safeguarding services is essential, and most often social workers are a primary profession employed within this context.

Practice in protection and safeguarding requires specific and complex mediation between the dualities of family and social support and sociolegal protection, as defined by the scope and limits of law and policy. McGregor and Devaney (2020a, b) refer to the mediation of child protection and family support as 'protective support and supportive protection'. This takes place across the continuum of need, from informal and universal support to sociolegal and criminal justice interventions. Donnelly (2019) offers a complementary framing for adult safeguarding as being about 'protection, empowerment and proportionality' (2019: 249). As mentioned, protection and safeguarding practice is necessarily connected with *lifecourse, life transitions* and *life events*, and most often involves *intergenerational relations*. Experience of abuse, harm, neglect or their threat usually negatively affects a person's *health (physical and mental) and wellbeing*. Responses that maximise *partnership and civic engagement* are optimum where possible.

With this opening commentary as our backdrop, the focus of this chapter is to:

- Expand a lifecourse perspective on risk, protection and support, highlighting commonalities and differences in adult and child safeguarding.
- Consider the social constructions of childhood and adulthood that influence lifecourses and ecologies and inform our critical thinking.
- Consider how theories of power and power relations in particular can inform protection and safeguarding practice and advance our theorisation of the duality of protection and support.
- Consider practice in the context of policy and procedure that represent the exo and macro levels of practice and inform, shape and constrain micro- to meso-level interactions.
- Discuss the importance and challenges of working in partnership from a perspective of civic engagement.

Since safeguarding, protection and risk management relate to an immense field of theory, research and practice, our contribution in this and further chapters aims to complement existing resources for this complex subject from relevant specialist modules (if you are a student) and prior knowledge and resources (if you are a practitioner). As Dingwall et al (1983) argue, the field of protection 'raises complex moral and political issues, which have no one right technical solution. Practitioners are asked to solve problems every day that philosophers have argued about for the last two thousand years and will probably debate for the next two thousand' (cited in Higgins, 2019: 349). While this is specifically about child protection, a similar point can be made about adult protection.

A lifecourse perspective on risk, protection and support

With regard to advancing our framework, a starting point is to consider protection and safeguarding for children and adults together, in recognition of the fluidity of the lifecourse. There are many parallels between child and adult abuse, such as victimisation of a weaker member in the family, concealment, issues of intrusion on family life and privacy and the need for multiagency working

(Filinson et al, 2008). Relations of abuse and neglect are often intergenerational (for example, adult-to-child, child-to-parent and cycles of abuse within families; see Coogan, 2017) and have an impact across family life (for example, domestic violence between partners and its impact on children) (Holt et al, 2017). They are also culturally specific. For example, Talpur et al (2018) highlight one barrier to addressing elder abuse as being the persistence of 'traditional rigid norms of the South Asian communities, as well as the changing cultural values of society' (2018: 203). Regarding child safeguarding in countries in the 'developing world' such as Africa, Sloth-Nielsen (2014) and Johnson and Sloth-Nielsen (2020) highlight the need to take into account country- and locality-specific cultural norms regarding gender, sexual violence, harmful sexual initiation rites and silence about addressing these issues.

While we address child and adult protection in parallel here, we are also aware that adult safeguarding systems are often too simplistically connected and compared with child protection (Montgomery et al, 2016; Donnelly, 2019). There are core differences to note with regard to rights to autonomy, dependency, self-determination and freedom (see, for example, Filinson et al, 2008). The histories of child and adult protection highlight the inherent diversity in understanding how different practices of protection of 'children' and 'adults' have emerged. With regard to child protection, historical and present discourses focus on:

- concerns about child rescue (for example, practices of philanthropy, often driven by the middle and upper classes, aimed at rescuing children from poverty, neglect or abuse);
- reform of parents (to become better parents as defined by a dominant discourse based on class, religion or state powers);
- control of families to meet state economic, social and cultural priorities, and the emergence of children's rights discourses.

Histories of mental health services, as one example of adult protection, expose complex discourses of:

- labelling;
- imposition of discourses of abnormality;
- containment and institutionalisation;
- stigma, discrimination and threats to human rights.

Mandatory reporting varies in child protection and adult safeguarding, with differences between countries and sometimes within countries on a regional basis. The difference in the role of 'mandated professionals' and members of the public is important to note when interpreting and applying a protection and/or safeguarding policy in your own jurisdiction. However, notwithstanding these crucial differences between adult and child safeguarding, a common purpose of protection practice is to promote support and protection, through preventive and participatory practices, and, where necessary, through the more formal court, criminal justice and legal system. Table 3.1 provides a snapshot overview of both common and distinctive features of child and adult protection and safeguarding.

'Childhood' and 'adulthood' are socially constructed. For example, in Ireland, with the change in child welfare law from the Children Act 1908 to the Child Care Act 1991, the age for 'childhood' was changed from 16 to 18, and practice had to adapt accordingly. Worldwide, we see varying interpretations of 'childhood' as defined by the law. A lifecourse approach implies that we operate beyond fixed legal definitions of childhood and recognise the broader context of 'age', such as the needs for young people leaving care into their 20s and the differentiation of

Table 3.1: Commonalities and differences between adult and child protection and safeguarding

	Adult	Child
Areas of practice	Disability, issues relating to older people, domestic and gender-based violence as well as general adult clinical practice, community-based, residential social work	Children in need of support, children who have been abused or neglected, children in foster and residential care, families in need of support, domestic violence, children with disability
Law and policy	Significant variation in law and policy regionally and internationally including laws (sometimes overlapping) relating to capacity (mental health legislation) disability, human rights, domestic and gender-based violence and criminal justice	Longer history of legal and policy development with more consistency in core features of law and policy regionally and internationally in civic and criminal law
International conventions	Mixed influence of international conventions including the UN Convention on the Rights of Persons with Disabilities (UNCRPD)	UN Convention on the Rights of the Child (UNCRC) more embedded in many child protection systems
Duality of support and protection	Recommended but not widely implemented – 'safeguarding' more closely aligned with a focus on protection	Protection and support services still most often discussed separately even though in relation to each other. However, considering the interconnections between support and protection, it is becoming increasingly commonplace in practice
Intergenerational relations	Focus in this area includes relationships between spouses or partners, grown children and parents and adult siblings	Focus in this area is mostly on adult-to-child relations but also includes peer-to-peer abuse, sibling abuse and child-to-parent violence

(continued)

Table 3.1: Commonalities and differences between adult and child protection and safeguarding (continued)

	Adult	Child
Civic engagement and partnership	User involvement is well advanced in many fields, but there is often a disconnect between the principles of partnership in policy and how this is experienced in practice	Partnership practice is commonplace in many contexts although complex with regard to balancing different perspectives. Young people are generally more positive than parents or guardians about their experiences of involvement with services. However, in order to be able to participate more fully, children and young people need more clear and comprehensive information about processes and more opportunities for engagement. Youth civic engagement tends to be led by not-for-profit voluntary and third sector organisations
Life transitions and events	In adult and child abuse, the impact can be a major life transition and event. This may include removal to alternative care, a support hostel, to live with other family members or relatives	
Health and wellbeing	Abuse, neglect and harm can have a massive detrimental impact on the health and wellbeing of individuals and their families	
Social work theories and methods used	Most social work theories and methods apply to practice across the lifecourse with some approaches being more commonplace than others in certain contexts	
Summary of common features	Prevention, early intervention, partnership, context-specific practice, empowerment, person-centred, rights-based, importance of the relationship	
	Similar theories to inform practice (anti-oppressive, anti-discriminatory, human rights, managerial, critical social, behavioural, psychodynamic, humanistic, and systemic, psychosocial, psychodynamic, attachment, cognitive behavioural, systemic, social democratic and social pedagogy)	
Summary of main differences	Adult abuse has more limited public awareness, understanding and sympathy than child abuse	
	Adult services are less well resourced in many contexts than children's services	
	Definitions of adult abuse are more fluid and varied than child abuse	
	A range of specific theories informs practice in different domains	
	Less integration of adult abuse issues that transcend services for older people, disability, domestic and gender-based violence compared to child welfare systems that are increasingly taking a more integrative support and protection approach under a common legal and service delivery framework	

needs for mental health support for young people transitioning from children's to adult services. As expressed in sociological analyses of the development of the 'family' in Western society (for example), childhood and adulthood are framed within discourses of dependency at both ends of the lifecourse. Modernisation is seen to have led to the intensification of a gender distinction between motherhood and fatherhood, due to a combination of economic theory (the expansion of industrialisation). The construction of childhood and adulthood is also deeply influenced by intersectional themes including race, ethnicity, gender, religion, class, nationalism, disability, older age and mental ill health.

The literature on the social construction of discourses relating to child and adult 'protection' is immense. Michel Foucault and authors who engage with his work consider the development of psychiatric services (see, for example, Foucault, 1973), the prison system (see, for example, Foucault, 1977) and child protection and welfare (Donzelot, 1979; Parton, 1991, 2014a, b; Hendrick, 2003). From such studies we can track how the regulation and/or protection of individuals was constructed around discourses of 'normalisation' (thus leading to an imposition of 'norms' and definitions of 'abnormal') and moralisation (focused on how individuals or families should behave based on imposed, dominant, societal, moralistic, patriarchal and/or religious principles). It is argued that the purpose of professions such as social work is to operate within discourses of normalisation and moralisation as far as possible (in Philp's terms, this would relate to potential subjectivity) and, where needed, to extend interventions towards a 'tutelary' discourse (Donzelot, 1979) based on legal constructions of 'morality' and 'normality'.

'Social constructions' are fluid. Gender constructions, for example, have been transformed over time due to the various feminist and anti–discriminatory practice movements (see, for example, Smart, 1989; Weedon, 1996) that challenge patriarchal assumptions about mothering and parenting. Yet, gender-based violence and gender inequality are a persistent global challenge. While there are some shifts in the construction of disability in society, it remains the case that in most contexts, society places greater emphasis on support and maintenance at individual levels rather than looking at wider social change. Informed by critical disability studies, there is a need to construct societies that are inclusive of people of all abilities rather than along the dominant 'normalisation' discourses that continue to prevail (Goodley, 2010).

Take the protection of children with a disability as one example. As Engwall et al (2019) argue in relation to children and disability in Sweden, children with a disability are 'profoundly victimised by power structures that favour the adult perspective in social services' (2019: 1025). With reference to Nilsson and Westlund (2007), they summarise three themes that explain violence against children with disabilities:

- Invisibility: linked to difficulties of communication and the fact that violence in relation to disability is not often treated as criminal violence.

- Vulnerability: 'exacerbated by disability because it is difficult for the person to defend themselves against assault or to understand their rights' (Engwall et al, 2019: 1026).
- Dependency: that implies a high level of reliance on other people to manage daily life activities.

There is widespread evidence to support the claim that within many systems children with disabilities experience exceptional injustices when it comes to child protection (see Flynn, 2019a, b, c). These issues transcend micro- to meso-level interactions and wider exo (for example, the services involved), macro (for example, policies that limit the scope for practice) and chrono levels (for example, social constructions of disability). Another chrono-level challenge, expressed by Flynn (2019a), is the need for a shift in the way we *think* about and theorise disability through a disablement lens in the first place in order to achieve a more rights-oriented approach (see also Flynn and McGregor, 2017; Flynn, 2019b). Flynn (2019a) argues for the use of critical disability studies (see Goodley, 2010) to inform this critical thinking (see also Kelly and Byrne, 2015).

It is unlikely that you will be citing social construction theory or histories of the present explicitly in your everyday contemporary practice. However, critical *analysis* is important to develop our *critical thinking* about the social forces that shape personal lives, with *critical reflection* on how we understand childhood and adulthood from our own perspectives, and how these implicit, historically situated processes impact on our day-to-day practices in protection and safeguarding work. We would argue that much of our discrimination and prejudice comes from social constructionism and the 'othering' this brings about. Some other themes to consider include:

- The status of children and young people (for example, liminal citizenship) and older people (dependency, autonomy).
- Attitudes to mental health and how psychiatric systems and theories have developed historically.
- Gender and the family (for example, assumptions about male and female roles).
- The role of culture, race, religion and ethnicity in defining expected norms, practices and intergenerational relations.
- Assumptions about the family (for example, the dominance of one family form over others, attitudes to gay and lesbian-led family, lone parenting, the role of grandparents, recognition of diverse cultural and family practices, the role of religion in defining family assumptions and expectations).
- Views on sexuality (for example, cultural or religious influences), sexual orientation and relationships (family privacy, authority, secrecy, role of authority).
- Dominant social values (for example, dominant norms and morals and public perceptions).
- Ways the current government supports and constrains family life in the construction of policies, laws, services and practices deriving from this.

Understanding protection and safeguarding in the context of power

Theories of power and power relations are central to social work, and even when not explicitly discussed, issues relating to power influence interactions throughout the ecological system and through a person's lifecourse. McGregor et al (2019), for example, show how, in a study about the permanence and stability of children in care, the theme of power emerged in the narratives of the children, young people, foster carers and parents of origin. Critical understandings of power are particularly significant to understanding abuse and neglect requiring protection, safeguarding practices, policies and legal intervention (see, for example, Houston, 2010b). System and individual responses to child abuse have often been criticised for not using enough powers to intervene. For example, the case of Jasmine Beckford in England (Blom-Cooper, 1985) brought criticism of not using enough legal power to protect a child, applying instead the 'rule of optimism' that the family would change (Stevenson, 1986; Kettle and Jackson, 2017). In many cases in the UK since, the question of whether more powers to intervene could have prevented a child's death has arisen (for example, 'Baby P'), and influenced how systems have sought to develop and improve child protection responses (Munro, 2011). A similar issue arose in an Irish child abuse inquiry, referred to as the *Roscommon Child Care Case* (Gibbons, 2010) (discussed again in Chapter 7), where decisions to continue to offer support were criticised for giving too much emphasis on offering support and not focusing enough on the legal protection of the children from neglect and abuse. In Philp's (1979) terms, this would be an example of a belief in the capacity to change overriding a response to the actual objective reality of the experience of abuse and neglect.

Notwithstanding the almost universal adaption of the UNCRC globally, in some countries the legal instruments for protection remain inadequate in protecting children. Johnson and Sloth-Nielsen (2020) highlight institutional and governmental constraints in developing an adequate child safeguarding system in line with the UNCRC and African Charter on the Rights and Welfare of the Child. In the adult service systems, for safeguarding of older people (for example), issues also arise about not having enough powers to intervene. Stevens et al (2020) highlight the limits of legal powers of entry for social workers in cases of concern for older and disabled people in England, and the challenge that 'balancing conflicting goals of support and more assertive implementation of policy and law to defend human rights is a typical social work dilemma' (2020: 18). They make the case for social workers gaining greater powers to be made explicit in their 'assumptions about vulnerability including the subjective experience of adults at risk, and its impact on autonomy' (Stevens et al, 2020: 18).

Conversely, there are also instances where too much power has been exercised. In England, the Cleveland Child Abuse Inquiry (Butler-Sloss, 1988) is a notable case where medical and social work practitioners were criticised for being over-zealous in relation to investigations of suspected child abuse (Ferguson, 2004). There is a concern across many jurisdictions about the over-use of legal powers to remove children from their parents, especially in cases where the factors affecting parenting were widely associated with poor socioeconomic circumstances or focusing on particular indigenous minorities (O'Donnell et al, 2019). Those who work in the child protection system often experience the feeling (especially when reinforced in the media) of being ever caught in a juxtaposition of being accused of using too much power and not using enough power to protect – 'damned if you do and damned if you don't'. This perspective belies the complex myriad of micro–meso and exo–macro–level factors that come into play highlighting the critical challenges for practitioners on the field (see Rogowski, 2015).

In adult safeguarding, use of legal powers (for example, safeguarding laws and the mental health capacity law) to protect individuals or others who are adults is highly contested and controversial. Any attempt to exercise legal powers against another adult's will raises questions of human rights and freedoms. Criticisms centre on potential intrusion into adults' lives without consent, thus threatening autonomy (see Preston-Shoot and Cornish, 2014; Donnelly, 2019). Filinson et al (2008) argue that there is generally greater public awareness and public sympathy when it comes to child abuse in comparison with adult abuse. They also highlight the fundamentally greater ethical dilemma posed around balancing adult protection with autonomy and avoiding the infantilisation of adult service users through a focus on empowerment approaches.

Power needs to be understood in the context of a 'family of theory' (Haugaard and Clegg, 2013) that helps us to think about the existence and relations of power in a number of different ways. Using enquiry-based learning, there are a number of theories of power to consider focused on the relationship between structure and agency, power and liberalism, politics and democracy, power and discourse, power and inequality, power and gender, culture and power, and power and exclusion, to name just a few. As Haugaard and Clegg outline in their introduction to *The SAGE Handbook of Power*, 'the concept of power is absolutely central to any understanding of society' (2013: 1). Power has been theorised by many key thinkers such as Thomas Hobbes, Friedrich Nietzsche, Talcott Parsons, Hannah Arendt, Steven Lukes, Jürgen Habermas and Michel Foucault. In our work, we draw especially from Foucault's work in relation to power, discourse, structures and the duality of care and control that connect with theorisations around social work in the social. Winter and Cree (2016) apply Foucault's theory to home visiting, to explore themes of power, knowledge and truth, and Chambon et al (1999) provide a comprehensive overview of Foucault's application for social work. Theorists such as Dorothy Smith help to expand understandings of power with more emphasis on subjectivity and materiality (see Satka and Skehill, 2012). Tew (2006) and Smith (2008) specifically interrogate power and power relations in social work, drawing on a range of perspectives.

McGregor (2016) sought to summarise theories of power for local practitioners to use in supervision drawing from some of the theorists mentioned above. Starting with the position that 'power is everywhere', as so commonly cited from Foucault's work, it is emphasised that it exists and operates in diverse ways that can be multidirectional and non-linear (McGregor, 2016). Thinking specifically of protection, risk management and safeguarding, we can think of power at many levels (see McGregor, 2016), such as the:

- power of the law;
- power of the abuser;
- power to resist and challenge abusive or neglectful behaviour;
- power to empower;
- power of the practitioner;
- power of the service user.

We can think about power in terms of:

- 'power over' a victim or survivor;
- 'power to' entrap, abuse, neglect or harm;
- 'power of' the law to protect;
- 'power with' colleagues and peers to collectively challenge and bring to account those who abuse and/or neglect (McGregor, 2016).

We can think about use of power in terms of:

- What power do you, as the social worker, have (legal, knowledge, positional)?
- What power does your service user have (power to resist, community support)?
- What power can come from internal sources (potential positive power of your own knowledge, confidence)?
- What power can come from external sources (networks, statistics and evidence, collaboration with other organisations)?

Smith (2008) uses the 'four P's' to consider power in social work as:

- 'Potential': for example, how can a worker use their legal powers positively to promote rights and justice?
- 'Possession': for example, who is deemed to have power and how much power is possessed?
- 'Process': for example, how is power used to promote rights, and how is power misused?
- 'Product': for example, what is the outcome of power processes? Has the use of power led to empowerment or disempowerment?

Tew (2006) discusses how power can be 'productive or cooperative, while limiting modes of power can be oppressive or collusive' (cited in McGregor, 2016: 13). As McGregor (2016), drawing from Foucault's work, sets out, 'Power is not in itself either good or bad – power exists and can be used to either effect' and 'where power exists, resistance will also be found – le resistance' (McGregor, 2016: 13).

For protection and safeguarding, the power of the law is significant as it defines, limits and enables the scope for interventions (see Mooney and McGregor, 2021). An ability to understand and embrace the power vested in social workers through the law is a fundamental requirement for sociolegal practice. In child protection (McGregor and Devaney, 2020a, b) and adult safeguarding (Keeling, 2017; Mackay and Notman, 2017) there has always been a strong interconnection between law and social work. Yet, in many jurisdictions, including Ireland, it remains a challenge to ensure social workers are competent and confident in their sociolegal practice (Coulter, 2015, 2018; Halton et al, 2018). Law, used in safeguarding and protection, requires a particular capacity from the social worker to be proficient at being able to:

- be assertive;
- read and interpret legal documentation;
- communicate legal responsibilities to the public;
- write clear and concise court reports;
- give evidence;
- make decisions and judgements about thresholds of harm, abuse and neglect;
- act decisively and in collaboration when thresholds of harm have been met in relation to both those who perpetrate harm and those who experience harm (see also Mooney and McGregor, 2021).

As discussed in more detail later, risk management and decision-making within a sociolegal context brings with it a range of further complex challenges in child protection and adult safeguarding that can be considered in the context of power and power relations, such as:

- balancing between individual and organisational factors in an ecological context that impacts on decision-making (McCormack et al, 2020);
- responding to the impact of algorithms and their power over decision-making as electronic systems become more widely used (Gillingham, 2019; Keddell, 2019);
- addressing the challenges of ethical decision-making relating to rights to autonomy of adults, who, for example, self-neglect (Braye et al, 2017).

Safeguarding and protection policies

Protection policies and laws represent the exo and macro levels of practice in the ecological system that inform, shape and constrain micro–meso-level interactions. These are not benign instruments. They reflect social constructions of childhood and adulthood and attitudes to the balance between freedoms and regulation. Social workers must be critically aware of the exo, chrono and macro forces that influence their practice and the lives of their service users. Underpinned by relevant law, each child welfare and safeguarding policy in a specific jurisdiction is influenced to greater or lesser degrees by international and regional law and policies. These instruments are implicitly shaped by theories (beliefs) about the:

- role and position of the family in society;
- nature of intergenerational and intergendered relations;
- role of the state;
- way risk is constructed in their own society;
- freedom and its limits that can be afforded to families;
- views about the nature of childhood, adulthood and ageing (for example, dependency vs independence and stereotyping).

Regarding safeguarding, for example, Donnelly argues, 'reporting systems reflect the context, ideologies and intent that underpin the development of adult safeguarding in different countries and states' (2019: 244; see also Montgomery and McKee, 2017). It is important to view these exo, macro and chrono lifecourse forces as fluid and temporal. For example, Talpur et al (2018: 193), with reference to cultural assumptions about families in South Asia, argue that: 'while older people have traditionally been venerated and respected in the culture and religion of South Asians ... changes in family structure, familial roles and expectations caused by recent occupational mobility and a stressful demanding lifestyle ... has made such cultural and religious assumptions questionable.' They also highlight the lack of safeguarding policy and law in South Asia and for South Asians overseas, and argue that this needs to be addressed in both policy and practice.

A thorough critical analysis of child protection and safeguarding policy and guidance is critical for practitioners to be able to see the implicit assumptions that shape, enable and constrain the protection and safeguarding of citizens. The skills and values of the social worker will significantly impact on how relevant policy is implemented in direct practice, recognising that the very nature of reporting and intervention is contested and often hotly debated. Protection takes place in the context of risk management and professional judgement. As discussed, it is commonly recognised that a focus on risk and a risk society is a feature of many present-day policies (Beck, 1992). This means that policy can be too orientated towards risk assessment, which can make practice risk-averse and overly risk-focused (Killick and Taylor, 2020; Lonne et al, 2020; McCafferty and Taylor, 2020). At times, and in certain contexts, there is stronger emphasis on 'risk assessment tools', but at other times, the emphasis is on the importance of professional judgement. It should not be a matter of 'either–or', but rather 'both–and', as Taylor (2017) argues with regard to using heuristic decision-making. A competent professional social worker should use bureaucratic or algorithmic tools alongside their own professional expertise and that of their peers. Risk assessment models and systems that derive from protection policies are there to support, not supplant, professional practice, and it is our ethics of professional life associated with practice that will guide our commitment to working in partnership. The implementation of safeguarding and protection law, policy and practice takes place within the context of ethical professional practice that combines logic and analysis informed by such codes, and guides with passion, empathy, emotions and imagination (see Banks, 2010: 129).

As discussed in Chapter 1, Banks (2010) identifies key ethical components in professional life, namely, commitment, character and context. This emphasis on the development of the professional self is crucial in protection and safeguarding. While there is much that is outside the social worker's control and that needs to be addressed at wider organisational and structural levels, an individual practitioner has the greatest power over their practice, leading to a professional life as an ethical and legally obliged practitioner.

Commitment includes:

- Recognising that protection from harm and safety is a right of both children and adults, noting that children have additional protection rights due to their development stage and their diminished access to civic and political engagement in processes directly affecting their lives.
- Noting differences of how to realise these rights is based on capacity, age and maturity across the lifecourse.
- Critical consideration of how we impose the discourse of dependency and vulnerability for children and adults in some of our 'care' practices.
- Seeing service users as fellow citizens and engaging as collaboratively as possible to protect and support through open and honest relationships.
- Seeing safeguarding and protection as a moral and civic responsibility that is everyone's business.

Character includes:

- Being critically aware of stigma, negative attitudes and judgementalism about people's lives, including our own attitudes and values about those who are harmed and those who harm.
- Proactive engagement with anti-discriminatory and anti-oppressive practice to tackle evidenced inequity in protection and safeguarding practices on the basis of age, class, socioeconomic status, ability, gender, race, identity, ethnicity, sexuality, religion or politics.
- Proactive engagement with colleagues in our own and related organisations to build networks and work in partnership to address issues of protection and safeguarding.
- A sense of responsibility and proportionality in the use of the law.
- An ability to recognise, critique and address issues of inequality, social injustice, poverty, lack of public will and marginalisation of some citizens and to challenge the inappropriate individualisation of social problems, for example, in incidences of alleged neglect caused by poor socioeconomic circumstances rather than individual intent.

Context includes:

- Critical engagement with the dilemma of requirements to report (for example, mandatory reporting) and protecting confidentiality, client relationships of trust and rights to self-determination.
- Responsibility in being able to differentiate between abuse, harm and neglect that is caused by social injustice, poverty, poor social services and so on, with that caused by individual and relational factors.
- Responsibility for direct action at the causes of harm, abuse and neglect, ensuring, for example, the avoidance of individual blaming for conditions caused or exacerbated by social circumstances and injustices.
- Responsibility for understanding the nature and causes of abuse from the perspectives of victims and survivors and their families and close networks and also the perpetrators' perspectives.

Protection and safeguarding through power sharing and partnership practices

Partnership working in protection and safeguarding takes place in the complex interplay of risk, rights, inclusion, social justice, human rights and relationship-based practice. In relationships affected by neglect and abuse, there is very often attachment, trust, love, reliance and intense connections between people spatially, psychologically, emotionally and socially. Partnership has to be worked out in relation to power relations between social workers and service users as well as power dynamics between people who have experienced harm and those who perpetrate the harm. Multiple resources are available to guide user involvement and adult safeguarding (SCIE, 2011; Butler and Manthorpe, 2016; Montgomery et al, 2017; Carr et al, 2019; Southall et al, 2019) and parent and child involvement and child protection practice (see, for example, Corby et al, 1996; Slettebø, 2013; Buckley et al, 2019; Kornbeck, 2019; Sulimani-Aidan and Paldi, 2020; Wilson et al, 2020). However, there are many specific challenges when it comes to partnership working in safeguarding and protection, including:

- Significant evidence of a lack of trust based on experiences of the child welfare system, wider organisational systems and social systems. For example, Tembo et al (2020) explored immigrant parents' perceptions of the Norwegian welfare system. They found a dominant view about over-surveillance and lack of trust. Fabian and Korolczuk (2017) provide many examples from 'rebellious' parents' engagement with child welfare systems in Eastern Europe and Russia. Haight et al (2017) discuss 'moral injury' by parents involved in child protection in the US, and Buckley et al (2011) used the term 'walking on eggshells' to depict the experience of child protection service users in Ireland.
- It is not always possible to achieve joint decision-making or full participation. Sometimes sharing information and consultation (Bell, 1999) are all that can be

achieved. For example, Wilson et al (2020) provide a comprehensive summary of young people's perspectives on their experiences of child protection, highlighting a deficit in the first basic principle of participation – having enough information in the first place to be able to meaningfully engage.

- There are many structural barriers to promoting partnership practices from the perspective of civic engagement and citizenship. For example, Murphy and Bantry-White (2020) found that, in Ireland, people with an intellectual disability were not regarded as citizens capable of full inclusion in society. They raise a number of critical issues regarding capacity, maturity, dependency, human rights and lack of opportunities for meaningful participation.
- Many gaps between service user and professional expectations exist. For example, Mossberg (2019) found that professionals tended to categorise service users more from an individual perspective, whereas service user representatives constructed their needs more within a structural and collective perspective, with an emphasis on wider citizenship.
- Often 'service user involvement' does not include all aspects of the relevant micro–meso system relationships. For example, Sulimani-Aidan and Paldi (2020) report on the views of young people in care in Israel to highlight gaps in the involvement of biological parents in the children's lives. A study in Ireland (Moran et al, 2017) showed a similar exclusion of parents in particular, when children were in long-term foster care.

How can we respond to these challenges? This is something for us to address more fully as the book progresses. For now, however:

- Partnership approaches should lead to empowerment, as Montgomery and McKee assert in relation to adult safeguarding, describing it as a 'rights-based, empowering and person-centred approach, encouraging consent-driven practice and promoting partnership with the wider public' (2017: 203).
- Sometimes the commitment to shared power and participation can seem at odds with the assertion of a person's legal power to protect at the same time. Critical engagement with theories about power and power relations is needed to inform critical analysis, reflection and thinking about this core duality of balancing care and control, regulation and support. Managing dualities of support and protection requires excellent skills to use powers positively, authoritatively, sensitively, openly and honestly with service users, carers and the public.
- Partnership working requires a sharing of power, and this often means having to relinquish certain powers while exercising other powers under legal or profession remits.
- Being open and honest about what power and responsibility we have, what we can share and what we cannot share is crucial to enable effective partnership working through mediation support and protection.
- Models of practice such as family group conferencing, used in child protection, youth and adult criminal justice and working with adult abuse, are specific

examples of where these power relations can be explicitly and openly negotiated and worked out.

- Partnership working takes place at a number of levels, from engagement with informal family systems, universal services, targeted support and protection services and legal and criminal justice systems.
- Irrespective of the levels (or thresholds) of intervention, social work mediation should happen through relational practice. The centrality of trusting relationships that enable service users to feel safe and in a position to engage is evident in both child welfare (see, for example, Munro, 2011; Ruch et al, 2017; Ferguson et al, 2020) and adult safeguarding (see, for example, Hopkinson et al, 2015). Greater attention to civic engagement and citizenship-based practice can inform and advance our mediation practices.

Summary

Social workers have a particular responsibility for protection and safeguarding given their position as mediators in the social. It is arguably one of the most sensitive and challenging areas of practice that requires a complex web of knowledge, values and skills. It requires social workers to work across their ecological system directly with individuals and families, their organisations, related organisations, and formal and informal networks. We have focused here on safeguarding and protection as mediation across the lifecourse, and remind readers again of the importance of consulting the wealth of literature on the many specific considerations in relation to child protection and adult safeguarding. Later in this book, and within the framework, we focus on further themes, including:

- The importance of engaging in work that differentiates individual and wider societal or structural causes of some forms of abuse and neglect, especially physical neglect due to poverty and socioeconomic disadvantage.
- Critical consideration of the impact of abuse and harm on individuals, families, groups and communities.
- A focus on specific challenges in relation to child sexual abuse and exploitation.
- Examining transitions to alternative care for children, young people and adults.
- More focus on sociolegal practice specifically within the legal and criminal justice system.
- Consideration of the disruption caused to individuals' and families' lifecourses by different kinds of abuse and neglect.
- The importance of empathy and understanding of the perspectives of all parties involved.
- The centrality of interdisciplinary and interagency practices and networking.

Prior to this more detailed analysis, Chapters 4 and 5 go on to focus on social and family support theory and practical applications that crucially inform support and protection practice.

Recommended resources

Power

In a brief paper written specifically for local practice, Caroline McGregor's 'Balancing regulation and support in child protection: Using theories of power to develop reflective tools for practice' (2016) provides a number of tables for use and adaptation in relation to exploring power and power relations in social work practice and supervision (see www.lenus.ie/bitstream/handle/10147/617865/SupportChildProtect.pdf?sequence=1).

Protective support and supportive protection

For a comprehensive overview of the duality of support and protection framed as 'protective support and supportive protection', we recommend Caroline McGregor and Carmel Devaney's 'A framework to inform protective support and supportive protection in child protection and welfare practice and supervision' (2020b). This article takes an ecological approach and proposes networking as a means of activating the mediation of support and protection across the levels of the ecosystem. While related to child welfare and family support, the framework can be applied to other fields of practice, as we discuss further during this book.

In relation to adult protection and safeguarding, we recommend the dedicated *Journal of Adult Protection* that provides comprehensive and specific papers covering the themes of protection and support across all areas of adult practice (see www.emerald.com/insight/publication/issn/1466-8203).

Tips for critical ART in practice

Applying the framework to protection and safeguarding practice

Consider how you might use our framework to inform your protection and safeguarding practice, and adapt Table 3.2 to your own specific practice context.

Sample application of 'children and disability' to the bio-ecological model

Taking some of the themes from the discussion on social construction, these can be mapped as follows onto this tool for practice development, with some examples provided for illustration. We encourage you to adapt and complete this for your own context using an enquiry-based approach (remember from Chapter 1 this means that everyone brings some expertise to the table and no knowledge is without further questions and investigation).

Table 3.2: Summary of the main themes

Theme	Main points	Practice examples	Your specific practice examples
Duality of support and protection	This is central to all safeguarding and protection work	Elder abuse, domestic violence, child abuse and neglect, adult abuse	
Life transitions and events	An experience of abuse, neglect or harm is most often a major life event for the persons involved	Impact of retrospective abuse Links between trauma and abuse	
Intergenerational relations	While children and adults can be harmed outside their own close network, much safeguarding and protection work is focused on close intergenerational relations	Adults abusing their own children or those of relatives Peer abuse such as older children abusing younger children Child-to-parent violence Abuse between partners	
Civic engagement and partnership	While participatory processes are now well advanced in the field, more work is needed in relation to engaging with service users through concepts of citizenship, social capital and civic engagement with policies not just affecting themselves, but society more widely	Use of family group conferences Youth civic engagement practices used within child protection contexts Work with disability movements to promote and support greater partnership work with children and adults with a disability Engagement with formal and informal networks to build safety and protection for individuals and families	
Health and wellbeing	Abuse, harm and neglect can have lifelong damaging effects on the individuals who experience them	Counselling services Connecting protection with wider service provision (eg disability, mental health)	

Table 3.3: Sample discussion tool for practice development: mapping practice with the bio-ecological framework

Bio-ecological level		Issues for specific practice	Issues for own professional development	Examples of skills or values comment
Person		Construction of violence towards children with a disability in relation to dependency, vulnerability and invisibility	Have you the knowledge and skills to address these challenges? What are your own assumptions? How does this impact on your practice?	Active empathy – what has been the experience of abuse or neglect? What impact is it having? Use a critical ART approach to prepare for practice
Process		Valuing children with a disability Critical disability studies Protective support and supportive protection	Have the protection issues been prioritised and acted on? Are you familiar with the current arguments from a critical disability studies perspective? How do you share power? How do you balance protection and support?	Interagency working (child protection and disability services) Direct open and honest communication Advocacy
Context	Micro	This links back to 'person' above Communication barriers Lack of power	Can you identify the specific rights and justice issues arising in particular individual cases? What is the impact of this on the individual or family? What are the concerns about health and wellbeing? What are the key intergenerational relations?	Information sharing skills (about rights and entitlements)

(continued)

Table 3.3: Sample discussion tool for practice development: mapping practice with the bio-ecological framework (continued)

Bio-ecological level		Issues for specific practice	Issues for own professional development	Examples of skills or values comment
Context (contd.)	Meso	Supporting families and communities to maximise support	How are the interactions with the social worker (you?) or team helping or hindering? How are the legal requirements being explained and implemented? To what extent is there a partnership approach?	Skills of partnership working Sociolegal skills Connect back to the notion of 'ethics of professional life' and apply it to this scenario
	Exo	Service and organisational constraints Difference in how child welfare and disability services operate (short-term vs lifetime focus)	How do you ensure effective joint working between disability and child protection services? How do you interact with the relevant exo system? Have you networks? Do you build relationships? Have you advocated?	Sociolegal skills Networking skills Confidence to work collaboratively including challenging practices where needed Advocacy skills
	Macro	Power structures Injustice Inequality	Have you taken time to critically understand these issues? Work in partnership with service users to specify how they directly affect people you are working with Prioritise the issues that must and can be addressed	Influence up through management and relevant organisations to report and highlight specific issues Advocacy Ability to clarify roles of different actors
Time	Chrono	Social construction of disability	Reflect on your own attitudes and perspectives regarding disability. What do you observe in your own local and wider societal context?	Analytical skills to connect present assumptions with a critique of social constructions
	Moments	How does the person experience your intervention at this moment?	Awareness that your moments of interaction can have great power	Ability to see and analyse power relations, including your own use of power

Source: Adapted from McGregor and Devaney (2020b, Appendix A), reproduced under Open Access Creative Commons CC-BY 4.0 license)

4

Enlisting family and social support

Introduction

The relationship between family support and child protection has been long established in child welfare (Parton, 1997), although right up to today there remains a perceived 'tension' in this relationship (see Devaney and McGregor, 2017) and a disconnection in the aims of protection and support. However, family and social support have always had, by nature, an emphasis on protection built in. As Dolan and Frost (2017: 383) conclude, practices that are 'good' for child protection are likewise 'good for family support'. We assert the same can be said for adult protection. These practices include working in partnership, a strengths-based approach, offering services based on need, including basic poverty, using the community for support, relationship-based and reflective practice and upholding social justice and rights. Referring back to McGregor and Devaney (2020a, b), we emphasise the importance of an approach of 'supportive protection and protective support'. While we focus here on elucidating in particular the theories and practices emerging from family support and social support discourses, the assumption of duality of support and protection underpins this commentary.

This chapter draws mostly from the proven track record and pioneering work of Pat Dolan and colleagues (see, for example, Canavan et al, 2016) and related publications about family and social support theories. It connects parenting and family support to underpinning social support theory, and demonstrates the relevance of family support as a broad overarching practice of support and protection with children, families and vulnerable adults. This includes a focus on *lifecourse and life events, intergenerational relationships, civic engagement and participation* and *health and wellbeing* as underpinning frameworks for social work. Towards the end of the chapter the practice focus and illustrative research themes covered include working with marginalised youth, youth justice, partnership with parents and children's participation.

Understanding family support

From a social work perspective, family support is a key and primary function. Supporting parenthood in all its forms is one particular focus within family support and not separate to it. Typically, both parenting and family support are often merged and perceived within a deficit model as a response to the very wide-ranging problems in families, most typically poverty, or child underdevelopment or maltreatment. However, this is not a fair orientation of the far more positive purpose and benefit of family support. For example, well-established programmes such as Strengthening Families, developed by Molgaard and Spoth (2001), focus on building support for families. Similarly, policies that provide families with clear tangible support as basic as children's allowance weekly payments, for example, assume the innate positive functions of local parent and community support. For over 20 years, there has been a focus on the importance of early childhood development and education as a universal form of family support (Belsky, 2009). The importance of reducing issues such as adolescent risk of self-harm or being marginalised has also come to the fore and is now included as part of the 'staple diet' on a social worker's menu of interventions.

In a commissioned report for UNICEF, Daly et al (2015) provided a robust policy definition for family support, and within this framework more specifically for parenting support. This builds on the earlier definitional and conceptual work on family support by Dolan et al (2006). The UNICEF report states that: 'Family support is a set of (service and policies) activities oriented to improving family functioning and grounding child-rearing and other familial activities in a system of supportive relationships and resources (both formal and informal)' (Daly et al, 2015: 12). It further adds that parenting support is a set of service activities oriented to improving how parents approach and execute their role as parents, and to increasing parents' childrearing resources (including information, knowledge, skills and social support) and competencies.

Within the functions of family support itself, there is rightfully now a much greater focus on parenting competence rather than professionals judging parents. This represents a paradigm shift towards enlisting joint working with parents on how best to care and positively enable good child development. Importantly for social workers, this does not and certainly should not lessen the need for direct casework with families. This includes helping where at all possible to enable 'self-help', family functioning and amelioration of poverty through locally sourced and other basic means.

While Daly et al (2015) focused family support on information and education provision, training and skill development as key goals, Dolan and Pinkerton (2007) have highlighted that in many ways the basics of pure 'coping' should not be forgotten or underestimated. In their international study of 'expert pioneers and veterans of family support', Devaney and Dolan (2014) found the quality of the relationship between the social worker and individual or family as the key factor and 'secret sauce' in family support. This implies that 'relationships outweigh interventions', or, in other words, that the likelihood of the intervention by the social worker being successful is partly dependent on the quality of their relationship with the parent or family. This factor was also found to be the case in a national study on what works in family support by Brady et al (2004), and links back to earlier discussions about the importance of relationship-based practice.

Family support and social work practice

Just as social work has a long established history (Skehill, 1999, 2003, 2004), similarly, according to Frost and colleagues, within the UK the provision of formal family support through person-to-person services has a long tradition dating back to the early 19th century (Frost et al, 2015). For over 20 years, Pat Dolan and colleagues (Canavan et al, 2000, 2016; Dolan et al, 2006; Pinkerton et al, 2019) have traced the evolution of family support. They have conceptualised and summarised its core dimensions as follows:

- range and flexibility;
- characteristics for service development;
- style of practice and a domain for social research;
- its capacity to work with and not just for families in need.

Pinkerton et al (2019) have recently argued for a renewed connectivity between family support and social work practice. However, they have also highlighted the clear limitations of family support, including its sometimes-perceived confusion with the concepts of prevention and early intervention. There can also be an 'over-collective grouping' of what are distinctly differing aspects within the field, namely, the remedial, protective and developmental functions of family support (Canavan et al, 2016: 8). More positively, their work has collectively contributed to the enablement and recognition of family support as a key orientation within social work policy and practice. Family support is now part of the common language of social work, ranging from a fundamental consideration in seeking alternatives to state care placements for children in adversity, to having a clear functional role in prevention of and intervention for child and older person protection and abuse. Gilligan (2000) situates social work practice in family support as:

- *developmental*: for example, supporting a lone parent who is a first-time parent;
- *compensatory*: for example, working with a young person leaving care to cope with the care experience and enhance independent living; or
- *protective*: for example, ensuring Signs of Safety® are ever-present for a young person or parent experiencing domestic violence.

We suggest that outcomes, which essentially means a desired agreed positive result for a family and social worker and, in fact, for all civic society, function at differing levels. This starts with the basic result that a family functions better due to the family support on offer to them and enlisted by them. In certain contexts, helping others cope at the micro level is an important basic social work practice function. This often occurs with an associated set of activities (including programmes) that families engage in with the support of professionals, leading to a set of clear outputs. Examples could include a teenager's acceptance of and attendance at a local community youth work group invitation, or a parent engaging with and attending an addiction support service. This leads to a set of outputs that are clear and measurable. The intention (hope and desire) is that through better coping and stated outputs, better outcomes will accrue for a family, such as better functioning, improved standards of living, greater closeness and improved relationships, or a reduction in harm.

However, it can also be that success comes from unplanned sources that have little or nothing to do with professional intervention. This can be due to renewed and better natural support from extended family or pure efficacy on the part of a parent him or herself, regardless of the family support on offer. Importantly, a critical reflective social worker remains optimistic and open to all sources for improvement, and discerns between coping, outputs and outcomes. This includes being able to gauge the difference between implementation – how much they have been able to do – and impact – what difference their work has made. This judgement is key as it keeps the focus rightfully on the family and away from perceived service success, including service-designed key performance indicators. This may seem a little basic, but it is essential. This differentiation between coping outputs and outcomes is presented graphically in Figure 4.1.

Finally, it is important to restate that despite the best intention of any one professional or their social work team and allied professionals, there are limits to success. As Daly et al (2015: 31) have suggested, understanding outputs and outcomes is a dual process:

> One way of achieving both is to conceive of outcomes in terms of particular categories encompassing the situation of the child and adolescent, parents, families and the community (understood in an immediate sense of the actors involved locally but also in a more general sense of the resources and capacities of the local area as well as the nation as a whole).

One of those limits must be recognised when the problems for families are due to wider exo- and macro-level factors, thus requiring a differentiated response targeted at the environment, as we discuss later with reference to the range of

Figure 4.1: Differentiating between the implementation and impact of family support interventions

Outcomes as a practice focus

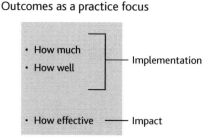

paradigms of social work, from reform to transformation and from individual to collective approaches (McGregor, 2019).

Family support principles at differing career points

Based on a review of evidence from research and literature, Dolan and colleagues (2006) developed a set of 10 family support principles, originally designed for policy and multidisciplinary practice in the field of child welfare. These principles were adopted from the Irish context with application to the UK (see Davis and Smith, 2012; Churchill and Sen, 2016; Pinkerton et al, 2019). In essence, they encompass the key range of policy and practice elements required to support families and individuals effectively. To support your understanding, at the end of this chapter we present an exercise for you to complete that will help you identify and match your social work practice with each of the family support principles. As a guide to applying these principles for practice, a range of direct actions for a student of social work, a newly qualified social worker in the field or a veteran senior social work practitioner are outlined with these typical practice responses matched against each of the principles. In Chapter 5, we revisit these principles in more detail for social work. For the remainder of this chapter, we broaden our focus to social support within a social work–specific context and from a lifecourse perspective.

Social support across the lifecourse

From their research, McCubbin and McCubbin (1992) have shown that social support implies active assistance between people that enables coping and personal sustenance. They also frame social support as occurring within systems that tend to function in two fundamental ways. First, they protect the individual or family from the negative influence of the stressor. In this way, support systems act as a 'buffer to stress', working between the stressor and the stress. In the main, individuals and families who have support systems will experience less stress or cope better with stress if it occurs than poorly or unsupported individuals who are subject to the same stressor. Good support systems also enable individuals and families to recover more quickly from stressful events, which build their resilience and adaptability. Thus, families who have active support systems will self-repair more quickly from a crisis than those who remain unsupported while experiencing the same crisis.

Social support and family support are not just connected but also interlinked, and for most of us with (thankfully) plentiful support in our lives, the two act like a 'hand in glove' function and motion. However, while social support theory has been used within many professional disciplines and research and education contexts, such as community development, social psychology, anthropology, geography and the broader humanities and social sciences, this has, to some extent perhaps, weakened its impact, in that it has no one particular home (Cutrona, 2000).

That said, this can also be seen as its strength in that this multidisciplinary usage and ownership has the potential advantage of connectivity across professions in relation to something that is essentially organic and innate in all of our lives. One could argue, in fact, that social support is so embedded and automatic in our lives that it is only when we don't have support and really need it that we fully value it. Despite its multidisciplinary features, we focus here on social support as theory for applied sociology and through the lens of social work practice in particular. In Chapter 5, our focus is on mapping the 'fundamentals' of social support including definition, description, types and qualities; here, the emphasis is on its usage in social work practice. Based on the evidence, we now consider 10 key aspects of and challenges for social support enlistment through effective social work.

1. Perceived vs received support

Having social support available is core to our daily existence in terms of our relationships with family, community and society. It is integrally connected with the social ecological model. In many ways, its lack of supply or the personal cost in accessing support is a key issue that social workers deal with on a daily basis. In terms of emancipatory practice, social workers should remain cognisant of the fact that the support a person believes to be available can be equally as important as the amount of support actually accessed (Cutrona, 2000). This is for two core reasons. First, if the person does not perceive the availability of social support from others, they will probably never access that support. Second, even if the available support supply is actually not as good as the person thinks, this may not matter as their self-efficacy is the key factor and they may never actually need to access the support anyway. Good social work practice does not, of course, include encouraging anyone to be unrealistic about available support; however, the guiding rule here in relation to support availability is 'what you believe can sometimes be as good as what you receive'.

2. Power of hidden support

Within social support, the power of hidden or anonymous help should similarly be considered in social work practice. Research by Bolger and Amarel (2007) found that where support is provided and the donor of the support is unknown, the impact of the support is stronger than if the recipient knows the person providing the support. This may seem obvious in that if the donor is anonymous, the person in receipt of the help does not feel beholden to anyone or required to 'thank' the person or 'pay back'. However, it may also mean that the recipient could feel that if they overcome the negative life events experienced, and do well in life, they can remain somewhat anonymous. For social work, the implication here is to be cognisant of not matching the need of a person for support to their being labelled as 'needy' in the present and into the future.

3. Size and range of issues in a social network

Our third social support and social work consideration relates to understanding the issue of size and range of sources. One common false assumption that professionals make is to assume that the more sources of support a person has, the greater the amount of support they receive. This is, in fact, not necessarily true at all – very often we can access plentiful support from a small range of people – as low as two to four that may typically, but not always, include family members (Dolan and McGregor, 2019). It is common for a social worker to do a social network assessment with a family and discover multiple nominees for help, but when this is explored somewhat deeper, to discover that some of those selected are more toxic than helpful and/or actually don't supply much support at all. Similarly, whereas support from multiple family members can be helpful, having sources that are outside the family network, typically friendships, are sometimes deemed to be better. This is simply because sometimes, if a person falls out with a family member, they may fall out with all the family as a consequence, leading to a total isolationist status in terms of support. Thus, when mapping social supports with individuals or families, using your ecological model, it is important to not only identify the key people in the micro and meso system, but also to determine the quality and nature of those relationships.

4. Allowing for the burden of support

One of the most under-estimated threats to social support provision is the burden of caring, which, over time, can lead to burnout on the part of the support donor. It is key that the social worker is aware of self-burden in offering support, but also in encouraging other supporters to be aware that helping can take its toll. For example, where the number of people in families providing the support is just one person or a few, support can deflate and the capacity to provide help wears out. Or, in the context of providing daily and personal care for older people, including people with dementia, the burden of caring is particularly difficult (Gillespie et al, 2015). Here, apart from seeking regular respite breaks for the carer and the ongoing provision of esteem support and emotional encouragement, the social worker also needs to watch out for the risk of carer breakdown, or simply not assuming the automatic availability of social support every day and all of the time.

5. Transferability of emotional support in social work

One of the unique features of social support theory lies in the power of emotional support and its transferability function. Unlike practical support or advice, which, if offered in the wrong context does not suffice or can even be perceived as negative and/or unhelpful, emotional support that is genuine is always valued and valuable. For example, if a child is struggling with learning in school, ongoing emotional support is not just a comfort but can also be the lynchpin that enables the child to overcome problems. Of course, the receipt of emotional support is not just connected to a better sense of one's belonging to and with others, but also acts as a buffer to stress. This is particularly unique to and connected with empathy. Empathy can be considered the bread and butter of the core skills and values of the social work profession; without emotional connectivity by and from the social worker, there is no real relationship with the family as a whole or specific individual members, and thus no foundation for mutually desired outcomes.

6. Convoying social support

In working with families who face multiple adversities at the same time with poor levels of social support, an assumption can occur that because one person in a family has a problem, all, including the extended family, are problematic. However, Mary Levitt describes convoyed support, where one positive and responsive network member can be identified from among more toxic supporters, leading to the transformative provision of social support (Levitt, 2005). Essentially, through 'convoyed support', the network of the one positive member can be accessed as new sources of help to enable the central family member with whom the social worker is engaged overcome issues through the buoyancy of new sources. However, it is important that the social worker, in encouraging this unique usage of the network of others, is not overused or taken for granted.

7. Immediate help vs later support

Our supply chain of social support is not static for any of us; like the moon, it waxes and wanes at differing times. One of the key functions in enabling others to cope with or overcome a specific adversity is to consider the timing of any help offered. This supports what Sheppard (2009) calls clear social integration for service users during and after a crisis. For example, following a family bereavement, mourners typically receive almost too much support from well–intended sympathisers during the period of the funeral, and it may only be six weeks later, when the support is waning, with no one calling, that the shock subsides for the person and core feelings of loss really occur.

8. Maintaining the value of support while addressing safeguarding

One of the common mistakes in social work in working in child or older person protection is that on discovery of harm to a person, the importance of social support becomes lessened or even forgotten. Unintentionally, the combination of shock, anger and upset of the discovery of abuse in a family (particularly sexual abuse) of one or more of its members leads to a lessening of the focus on the need for social support (Dolan and McGregor, 2019). This can occur for non–abused family members and for social workers engaged directly with the family. For the former, the key issue can be pure coping with shock, and for the latter, the social worker may be so engrossed in detection, assessment and ensuring due procedures are followed that the familial need for social support is lost.

9. Risk of overruling natural support

For those of us who experience adversity, we continue to receive social support from informal contacts (family, friends and neighbours) and formal services (professionals, including social workers) as well as semi-formal sources (paid volunteers). A key function for social work is not to undermine the natural helping systems that families have or that are potentially available to them (Dolan and Brady, 2012). For example, in a case where a social worker with the best intent is offering emotional support to a lone parent on a regular weekly basis, similar support might also be available to the parent from an estranged sister who lives nearby. Enabling this more natural source of support is a better course of action as, if successful, it is more likely to be available in the long term as well as being a more naturally occurring support and cost–effective use of resources.

10. Social support across the lifecourse

Finally, part of the focus of this book relates to understanding the functions and influence of the lifecourse as part of the pathway in coping and thriving. Social support provision and receipt acts as a thread throughout the lifecourse in that we start off in life as dependent children, and if we live long enough, we will very likely end up (to some extent) as dependent older adults. We start off indebted to others, including our parents, for our support needs, and may end up similarly socially in debt to others, most typically our children or other family members. During the in-between periods, as we move to independent living, adulthood and, in many cases, parenthood, we grow to become the main providers of social support, although this pathway will be diverse and varied rather than linear and progressive. One of the functions of robust social work is to understand these differing 'flows' of social support as they occur, and to help ensure a solid supply of help is available when needed from a lifecourse perspective.

Having mapped out the key factors of social support, it is also important when working with individuals and families that the principle of optimal matching is upheld. This relates to the rule that the specific type of support sought and/or needed by an individual or family equates to the social support provided (Cutrona, 2000). Conversely, a mismatch of support not only leads to poorer outcomes, but also weakens the partnership and trust with professionals working with and for the family. The optimal matching rule is now considered through the lens of the key framework for this book, namely, lifecourse and life events, intergenerational relationships, and civic engagement and participation.

Connecting lifecourse, life transitions and life events

Whereas lifecourse involves the reasonably predictable journey via transitioning through childhood, adolescence, early and older adulthood entwined by differing social dependencies at different stages, it should not be assumed that these transitions occur at the same rate or in the same context for everyone (as discussed in more detail later, in Chapter 6). Much has been written on lifecourse and transitions from a developmental psychology perspective, most notably Erikson's renowned concept of life stages (Erikson, 1950). However, the less-well-thought-of sociological construct of lifecourse trajectory (which has strong applicability for social work) has relied on debates through wider descriptions, for example, life transitioning in the context of social human and economic capital (Portes, 1998). In this context, lifecourse has also been described as getting by (surviving) and getting ahead (thriving) through bonding and bridging capital. This is attained over time as part of the lifecourse flow from childhood dependency on family and community to independent adulthood and returning to older life dependency.

There is a very distinct difference between life transitions and life events. Lifecourse, to some extent, has predictability, which implies a capacity to plan ahead and cope. Conversely, whereas some life events occur more naturally as part of life transitions, for example getting a job or getting married, in the main it is sudden unpredictable negative life events that most likely lead to families needing a social work service. For example, this could be the sudden death of parents through a car accident, leading to admission to the care system of their young children, or the sudden onset of schizophrenia in a young adult, leading to hospital admittance, or vascular dementia, leading to placement in a nursing home for an older person. Compas et al (1986) distinguish between serious life events and daily hassles as major and minor life events, but note that families under stress often become excessively distressed about minor hassles while not giving due attention to major life events. In relation to both lifecourse and negative life events for social work, social support is key.

Intergenerational family support

In relation to both life transitions and life events, intergenerational transference of social support between families is key. This is frequently looked at through reciprocal support between generations – parent to child, child to grandparent, grandparent to child, and parent to grandparent. However, that overview can be misleading as well as an over-simplification, as intergenerational connections are dependent on other issues such as place. Place includes factors such as proximity. For example, grandparents can really only provide childcare if they live close to their children and grandchildren, but can offer emotional support over video calls, for example, when living far away from their children.

Financial support between generations is often overlooked but can be key, not least where older generations find themselves in need of basic support, and through 'filial piety' their adult children provide ongoing monetary assistance (Ní Léime and Street, 2016). However, although in the minority, from a social work practice point of view it is unfortunately often the case that whereas there can be robust support between generations, there can also be strained and even toxic relationships with a long history of animosity. Often such relationships between family members across generations cannot be rectified. Here, the social work function may, in fact, be to keep generations apart and seek new relationships, or to engage with untapped existing sources of support.

A key function of intergenerational support relates to both care and protection in unison and not as separate. While rightfully the protection of minors and vulnerable older adults is the responsibility of all civic society, as mentioned in Chapter 3, in the main, family protect family from harm regardless of age or stage in life. For most of us, the capacity to care for family is innate and ingrained from an early stage, and providing protection and safeguarding is foundational and a core part of caring. In fact, it is from familial care and protection that community caring for others is modelled. The effect and legacy of positive intergenerational relationships and support provision culminates in stronger and safer communities and societies. This is pivotal to health and wellbeing and leads to positive living conditions. Within the ethics of the very foundation of social work as a profession, as outlined by the Abbot sisters in the 1930s (see Leighninger, 1986), this is a legacy goal for any social worker.

Civic engagement and participation

As discussed, civic engagement is an underrated aspect of social work. For example, the potential benefits that accrue from the positive engagement of family members who are recipients of social services being involved as volunteers and providers of help in their community are manifold. First, by engaging in civic activities, ranging from volunteering in a local day centre for the elderly to being a sports coach on a local football team or helping in a church group, a person gains respite from their problems, and their difficulty is not their sole focus. Second, civic engagement also leads to the development of positive casual and even close friendships over time with others who are outside the family and unaware of the difficulties the person faces. Third, in terms of self-efficacy, where a person can successfully engage in participation in the community, this can enable and support a 'self-belief' in a personal capacity to overcome problems and issues. Despite these very real benefits, however, this potential may be overlooked or deemed as less important in the context of what are deemed more serious family concerns or issues. Finally, it is important to note that civic engagement can come in differing forms apart from *social* civic engagement described above (Dolan and Brennan, 2016). Other variations of civic engagement can be *economic*, for example helping on a farm or family business; *political*, including lobbying for better local amenities for others; or *moral*, which involves advocating for social justice. Finally, ahead of focusing on specific populations and the connection between social support and enabling better individual and family functioning, we present an interwoven model of the types of social support (described in more detail in Chapter 5) and their interface with our core framework components as described above, including the encirclement of support and protection. This is illustrated in Figure 4.2, and connects (clockwise) as follows:

- emotional support, such as providing comfort to a family in light of a sudden life event or major transition;
- advice support, offering guidance between generations in a family, most typically older to younger in light of having to make a major life-changing decision;
- through successful civic engagement and community participation, the growth of esteem support from professionals to service-using family members;
- the enhancement of better health and wellbeing through the provision of practical help to a person in need of direct and immediate sustenance.

Figure 4.2: An interwoven model of types of social support

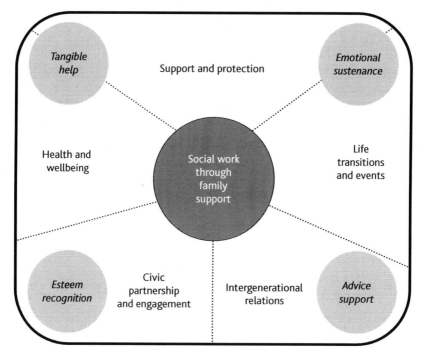

Practice and research examples

Working with marginalised youth and youth justice

One of the main functions of social work in supporting both marginalised youth and those who are engaged with the youth justice system lies in the development of the young person's resilience (to bounce back and overcome the odds) and self-efficacy (their own belief in self), discussed in Chapter 5. Here, we focus on the importance of social and familial support in relation to youth who are marginalised and who often 'act in' in terms of mental health issues and/or 'act out' through destructive or violent behaviours. This can lead to involvement in youth justice systems where work involves supporting young people while also addressing criminal behaviours. Richard Learner's theory of positive youth development (PYD) takes a strengths-based support approach. It contains 'five Cs', which act as a good orientation and framework for social work practices, particularly in terms of direct social support to youth in support, protection or justice services. They are:

• Competence;
• Confidence;
• Connection;
• Character;
• Caring (Lerner, 2005).

Based on effective working with the young person and relationship building for them, the objective is to support personal competencies through the provision of tangible support. Confidence and connection building relate in many ways to both esteem and advice support, while character and caring are oriented through the provision of emotional sustenance. That said, the personal skills of the social worker or related professional are often most tested in working with marginalised youth, and often require strong 'stickability' on their part. There is strong emerging positive evidence that youth leadership development, including active civic engagement (Redmond and Dolan, 2016) and empathy education (Silke et al, 2019), can lead to better outcomes for marginalised youth underpinned by both a PYD approach and robust supportive and genuine relationships. The potential for extending this to a focus on civic and political engagement, with an emphasis on citizenship practice, is also significant (Chaskin et al, 2018).

Partnership with parents

To illustrate partnership working with parents, we use an example from Northern Ireland. Over the last five years, family support hubs have been developed and operate as interagency and intersectoral mechanisms to enable the matching of family support provision to need. They operate as a community of professionals and citizens with a shared interest in supporting parents and families. They facilitate professional and parent self-referral to a wide range of services, providing both practical and more intensive types of support. They operate in local environs, both urban and rural, including the voluntary and community sector, and centre on the delivery of support services that are easily accessible and timely in nature. Most importantly, they are flexible and non-stigmatising for parents and family groups. The trust of engaging in the hubs is a key factor, encouraging parents to seek help when issues emerge safe in the knowledge that services can only occur through the hub with full informed consent and participation based on the parents' volition.

This model reflects a fit-for-purpose form of assistance to parents through a pragmatic model of social support, and is echoed in similar models elsewhere in the UK (Davis and Smith, 2012). Using a similar cooperative parenting support model in Ireland entitled 'Meitheal', key simple positive messages are modelled for parents (Rodriguez et al, 2018). These include the following core guide statements in relation to positive parenting, which:

- is strong, but caring (authoritative), and is not bossy (authoritarian);
- is supportive, warm and responsive;
- is understanding of children and their daily lives;
- expects children to follow age-appropriate rules, gives explanations and is not controlling;
- involves children in decision-making and encourages two-way communication and discussion;
- is non-violent;
- promotes dignity, recognising children as individuals in their own right;
- assumes full responsibility for the quality of the relationship with the child (see Rodriguez et al, 2018).

These positive approaches to parenting also apply to those who are parenting under stress. They mirror the findings from earlier research by Gardner (2003) regarding parent support from social workers and professionals in the UK – the issue was not about quality but quantity, with parents and families more likely to be dissatisfied with the social work support on offer (not enough) than dissatisfied with it (not helpful).

Supporting children's participation

The human right to participate in the family, school, community and within civic society is one of the general principles of the UNCRC. Article 12 protects the rights of the child to express their views freely in all matters affecting them, and requires the state to give 'due weight' to their views in accordance with the age and maturity of the child. According to the UN Convention on the Rights of the Child, participation embodied in Article 12 highlights the role of the child as an active participant in the promotion, protection and monitoring of their rights (see Lundy, 2007). In the first instance, at an international policy level, it can be easily argued that the child's right to participation in itself is a form of support to them, leading to the child's views being expressed.

Hart's ladder of participation is a renowned model for conceptualising, monitoring and measuring children's participation (Hart, 1992). It promotes the utilisation of leadership in young people, which, he notes, can range from tokenistic encouragement (bottom rung) to full support across family, school and community and, for those who need additional help, professional services (top rung). There is also the Lundy model of child participation (2007), which is widely used to inform the development of participation strategies with children and young people within child welfare systems (Tierney et al, 2018; Kennan et al, 2019). Whereas since 2010 many fora have been developed to encourage children's civic participation from political (national) to community (local) level, the participation of children in need or experiencing some form of adversity has been less evident. A key function of the duality of family support and child protection in relation to the promotion of these children's participation lies in ensuring that through robust familial, in school, community and services participation, their voices are heard and listened to, and acted on in terms of reasoned actions. This is a very measurable form of tangible social support.

Summary

This chapter has focused on family support and its strong and innate connection with social support theory and its centrality to social work. It is a primary protective measure to ensure early intervention, prevention, support and protection. Taking these concepts, the implications for robust social work practices have been considered and interwoven throughout. In particular, we have considered both family and social support in social work and its potential across the lifecourse, intergenerational working, civic engagement and participation, using the contexts of working with marginalised youth, parents and children's participation as specific exemplary contexts. The themes raised here are revisited in Chapter 5, which focuses on the implications for requirements of social work, empathy and resilience.

Recommended resources

For a foundational overview of social support principles, see Carolyn Cutrona's 'Social Support Principles for Strengthening Families' (2000).

For an updated overview of family support, building on their body of work developed over the past 20 years in the field, see John Canavan et al's *Understanding Family Support* (2016).

For reading on youth mentoring and supporting young people in care, see Pat Dolan and Bernadine Brady's *A Guide to Youth Mentoring: Providing Effective Social Support* (2012) and also Bernadine Brady et al's *Mentoring for Young People in Care and Leaving Care* (2020).

Tips for critical ART in practice

Matching social work practice to family support principles

Situating yourself as either a student of social work, as an early career practitioner or in a senior management position, building on the suggested prompts below (see Table 4.1), fill in the blanks with short, sharp practice responses to each of the principles of family support. While we have focused mostly on family and parenting support, children and families, these principles should be applied to practice across the lifecourse. It may be useful for practice teachers to use this table in supervision with students or as a tool for self-reflection and personal development.

Self rating with key factors in social support provision

This table lists the 10 principles of family support that were published in the *Agenda for Children's Services* (Office of the Minister for Children, 2007). For each principle, we have developed this table to identify areas for reflection for the student social worker, the early career worker and the senior practitioner, and encourage you to use this as a template to develop your own reflections. It may be useful for practice teachers to use in supervision with students or as a tool for self-reflection and personal development.

Table 4.1: Family support principles for social work across career contexts

Principles of family support	Student social worker	Early career social worker	Senior social worker/manager
1) Working in partnership with children, families, professionals or communities	Learn how all views are heard in assessment and used in the intervention		
2) Family support interventions are needs-led and strive for minimum intervention required		Don't lose sight of the core need to be addressed, and don't be a 'professional helicopter'	
3) Requires a clear focus on wishes, feelings, safety and the wellbeing of children (vulnerable adults)			Provide oversight to ensure that the welfare of the individual and family remain foremost at all times
4) Family support reflects a strengths-based perspective that is mindful of resilience as a characteristic of many children's and families' lives	Seek ways to help the person bounce back using their inner and outer strengths		
5) Effective interventions are those that strengthen informal support networks		Use social network assessment to mobilise existing family/friend supporters or discover new natural sources of help	
6) Family support is accessible and flexible in respect of timing, setting and changing needs, and can incorporate both child (older adult) protection and out-of-home care			Seek domiciliary care for children or older people and review and change the plan regularly if it's not working

(continued)

Table 4.1: Family support principles for social work across career contexts (continued)

Principles of family support	Student social worker	Early career social worker	Senior social worker/manager
7) Facilitates self-referral and multi-access referral paths	Let families use their voice to access services – avoid 'red tape' autocratic actions		
8) Involves service users and frontline providers in planning, delivering and evaluation on an ongoing basis		'Co-produce' the family support plan with the family and regularly test the genuineness of their involvement	
9) Promotes social inclusion, addressing issues of ethnicity, disability and rural and urban communities			Test out that you and all staff are demonstrating cultural competence and taking a rights-based inclusive perspective
10) Measures of success are routinely included to facilitate evaluation based on attention to outcomes for service users, and thereby facilitate quality services based on best practice	From the outset, discover the difference between outputs (doing what you promised to do) and outcomes (making a difference), and seek ways to do it better		

Table 4.2: Rating key factors in social support provision

Aspects of social support	Rank order your prior knowledge as 'weak', 'reasonable' or 'strong'	Further exploration required 1 = None 2 = A little 3 = Substantial
1 Received vs perceived support		
2 Power of hidden support		
3 Size and range of issues in a social network		
4 Allowing for the burden of support		
5 Transferability of emotional support in social work		
6 Convoying social support		
7 Immediate helping vs later support		
8 Lessening the value of social support while focusing on safeguarding		
9 Risk of overruling natural support		
10 Social support across the lifecourse		

Notes and observations:

5

Empathy, resilience and social support

Introduction

This chapter explores the importance of empathy and resilience as key underpinning functions for effective social work based on family and social support principles and practices. We explore how social support as a core practice emerges from empathetic responses from the social worker, manifested through a presence approach and real connectedness. This positive engagement, in turn, enables individuals, families and communities to achieve resilience, and is demonstrable as by their continued capacity to cope. As highlighted elsewhere in this book, the importance of contextual relationships of support and protection across the lifecourse, within the ecological model, is highlighted. Social support enlistment that builds resilience for individuals and families can then form a lynchpin for active empathy by social workers. We explore these approaches in practice contexts. Finally in this chapter, we look at a set of three social work practice tasks as illustrative, namely, working with people living with mental health issues, families in poverty and family support partnership and prevention approaches.

Activating social empathy as common practice

We should not presume that although integral to social work practice, empathy is always present and being demonstrated by the practitioner. As has been well documented, there are many situations where social workers are suffering personal trauma themselves; sometimes, although not always, it is work-related, which hampers their capacity to remain empathetic to those they work with and for. In such instances, while it may be that the social worker is more unable (for whatever reason) than unwilling, the impact is, of course, detrimental for the service user (Segal, 2011). Empathy is the capacity to understand and identify with what another person is feeling and/or experiencing. Broadly, it is categorised as cognitive – understanding the person's plight – and affective – emotionally connecting with the person at some level. From a social work practice perspective, it is professionally and ethically incumbent to seek to work from the latter perspective. This can best be manifested in practice by seeing empathy as static and/or active, with the latter evidenced in providing demonstrable actions with the intent of making situations and outcomes better for service users.

Empathy in social work is connected with wider values such as the desire for human rights, social justice, the global need for the public to embrace cultural respect and the critical need to understand poverty and discrimination. Its essential connection to direct practice may be somewhat overwritten, with a modern focus on programmatic interventions and project-based working. Similarly, the historical connection of some social work with religiosity and faith-based NGOs, and conversely, the focus of social work as a robotic statutory function in child protection may, to some extent, have muted the empathy component to good practice.

In effect, empathy in social work is underpinning and foundational, not least for the energy being empathetic brings to the social worker on a daily basis, as found by Ferguson (2018) in his UK study on the everyday work of social workers. It may be that social workers feel empathy but do not always show it. The literature on social work and reflective practice clearly indicates that the capacity for a social worker to think in action on their actions (essential reflexivity) may well be a core lynchpin for them to demonstrate empathy and, ultimately, compassion.

Self-empathy or self-compassion is an important consideration here. Self-compassion includes the capacity to understand that you are limited despite perceived skills, and that doing your best is all that you can do and there are many situations that are out of your 'gift' to resolve. It is interesting that this promotion of self-care has been less prevalent in social work than it should be, perhaps, in part, because of the continuous stream of child protection failures and scandals including child death. We would argue that for almost 50 years, since the death in the UK of Maria Colwell in 1973, the social work profession has rightfully or wrongfully received constant criticism for what it is doing wrong much more than for what it is doing right.

Underpinning empathy through the presence approach

We believe that Andries Baart's theory of the presence approach is key to underpinning empathy development and maintenance in social work practice (Baart, 2002). The social worker who can show full presence demonstrates active compassion in a tangible way, and this is discernible in that it includes 'being there for' in addition to 'being there with' the person (Kuis et al, 2015). Baart initially developed a set of eight associated principles as key to describing and understanding the presence approach. This, in turn, was further developed by Kuis et al (2015) to inform the design of a self-evaluation tool for practitioners in nursing, but with what we believe has strong applicability for social work. We see these as empathy enablers for social work. These eight principles, amended for our book, are:

1. *To be free for:* rather than being tied up in administrative and regulatory requirements and other time constraints, social work practitioners guarantee to provide free space for what service users bring up.
2. *Open for:* 'presence' social workers set aside preordained or determined decisions and remain open to what the person brings up as their solution(s).

3. *Attentive relation:* at a basic level, social workers pay attention to what the person may need from them, and seek to respond without prejudice.
4. *Connecting to what exists:* presence social workers accept and connect simply to the other's life and circumstances.
5. *Changing perspective:* this applies when practitioners accept that the conditions for those they work with is not static but that circumstances change, and an associated change in the perspectives of all is required.
6. *Being available:* social workers who demonstrate engagement and their presence ensure they are there in terms of skills and abilities.
7. *Patience and time:* despite the tumultuous nature of the pressures social workers endure, sometimes, and to an exhaustive extent, ensuring ample time and space for those they work with is key.
8. *Loyal dedication:* presence social workers are loyal and never refuse to help, even where they may occasionally or even often have this loyalty tested.

Whereas we see the presence approach as a basic practice orientation for social work that can ultimately help enable resilience stemming from activated social support (Dolan, 2012), it is closely aligned with the innovative foundations contained within relational–cultural theory (RCT). Pioneered by the late Jean Baker Miller and colleagues in the 1970s, RCT has a clear focus on the importance of growth-fostering relationships of worth, which is core to successful support and interventions with individuals, families and communities. Although originally developed as a feminist construct and for marginalised groups, it now has a wider individual, family and community focus. The core message within RCT is that the conditions under which relationships thrive are based on relationships that are built and connected person(s) to person(s) rather than through separation and individuation. It is also based on the premise of what we know about people who live in isolation, disconnected from family and community, and often coping with chronic loss. Importantly for social work, it challenges perspectives and assumptions around power privilege and marginalisation that occur in differing cultural and social contexts and settings. In many ways, it is a strong underpinning framework for understanding and enabling cultural competence practices in social work (to which we return to in later chapters).

Understanding relevant resilience for social work

Adapted by Gilligan (2001, 2009) and others, the concept and prospect of resilience as a social work practice method has gained much attention and prominence. The concept of resilience is not in any way a new phenomenon, and can be found in many human medical and life sciences contexts (Rutter, 2012). The term 'resilience' itself has become very much part of common language in civic society, now being used in fields as diverse as explaining the progression of the animal kingdom to solutions to responses by banks in economic crises to reference to structural fault solutions in engineering. Concisely defined with a social context by Masten (2001), resilience is the capacity to thrive in the face of severe adversity. It enables the 'bounce-back' factor in life, whereby a person, family or even a community not alone cope with stressors but go on to become stronger. Because of its appeal, it has, perhaps, become somewhat over-used as a term in the context of basic coping with minor life hassles or daily stressors rather than that for which it was originally conceived.

In the context of social work support, two conditions need to prevail for resilience to be enabled. First, the underlying situation needs to be an extreme adversity, and second, the person's capacity to overcome his/her adverse difficulties needs to be positive and substantial, with their doing better than expected with long-term sustainable outcomes.

As indicated earlier, the source of a person's resilience may come from 'inside' and is self-derived, such as personal temperament, drive and self-efficacy or ego strength – or, to put it more bluntly, from a person's 'self-determination'. Resilience can also be derived from 'outside' the person, through a range of family, community, professional and societal sources. This indicates that rather than seeing the occurrence of resilience as the sole responsibility of the individual, professionals, and social workers in particular, have a dual role. First, notwithstanding the importance of direct work with the service user in terms of a one-to-one casework approach, the social worker can also enable resilience-building by mobilising family, community and other professional support for the service user. For example, Gilligan's *Promoting Resilience: A Resource Guide on Working with Children in the Care System* is an excellent direct work guide and toolkit for social workers seeking to support children and youth living in care through the pursuit of leisure activities as respite from negative life stresses and as a self-efficacy builder (Gilligan, 2001). Conversely, the emergence of numerous programmes, for example family group conferencing, seek to work with the external set of supporters to the person of concern and through the actions of others, to create the conditions for the central client or family to demonstrate resilience (Connolly and Masson, 2014). This latter approach is strongly connected with the social ecological or person-in-environment theory.

It is fair to say that there has been some debate about the role of social work with a tension between doing less direct face-to-face work with families in lieu of wider, almost external, case management. There is a concern that the former is diminishing to the cost of the 'traditional purpose and mission' of social work itself in light of neoliberal and managerial social work contexts in particular. We argue here that it is not a choice of one way of working over another, but (as will be discussed further in this book) that effective social work requires both direct relationship-based, one-to-one, face-to-face working and using case management processes as well as indirectly working through a mediation of systems, processes and networks. Being resilient is not an end in itself but rather a process demonstrated through effective coping. What is key is that the social worker understands the personal strengths, timing and context to help the service user understand their personal 'ebb and flow' of sense of being resilient.

Just as debates on the internal and external sources of resilience need to be tied to the functions of good and robust social work practice, so is clarity also required on viewing resilience pathways as either resulting from specific turning points or mundane events in a person's life. While resilience has a strong individual behaviour emphasis, it is also deemed to stem and grow from key moments in the course of a person coping with difficulty, frequently referred to as 'turning points' (Masten, 2001). These stem from the belief that in the course of a person's journey from an inability to function and cope (which, in part, led to their needing a social work or professional intervention) there comes the lowest point in the journey where determination to overcome the adversity 'kicks in', usually identified by the person as a kernel moment. This is then followed by a personal resolve, with professional support leading to the problem or adversity abating over time or demonstrable resilience.

There is a view that resilience can only occur as a 'personal epiphany' and can only happen when the person is at their lowest point. The alternative model to this view of resilience suggests that it is the mundane, regular and consistent supply of support from others that matters most. Referred to as 'ordinary magic' by Masten (2001), resilience occurs because of persistent and unconditional help and guidance from others, perhaps one person in particular. It is not spectacular and can be automatic assistance as well as esteem support from others that, over time, helps a person to thrive. In terms of grounding the concept of the 'mundane' within resilience enablement, the use of the 'five R's' developed by Gilligan (2009) is helpful. These include ongoing and regular maintenance of:

- ensuring the existence of solid and key Relationships of worth;
- the provision of continuous Reciprocity of support;
- ensuring that personal, family and community Rituals occur despite trauma or fractured relationships;
- sticking to a sense of daily and weekly normative life Routines;
- upholding Respect for self and others despite interpersonal tensions and challenges.

We advocate for a view of resilience as being somewhat heterogeneous, that is, occurring both within the person and in the wider social ecology, which varies between sudden turning points or longer term life experiences. Ungar (2012a, b) has described this as being a 'pathways approach' to resilience. This implies and affords a more flexible option for the social worker as they seek to work with the service user on designing best fit-for-purpose approaches to being resilient. In addition, there are limits to when one should focus on resilience. It is especially useful at micro–meso-level interactions. If the presenting issues are clearly due to, or compounded by, issues of structural inequality of socioeconomic disadvantage, a focus on the wider exo and macro levels will be required rather than focusing on a person's resilience to withstand conditions they should not be experiencing in the first place.

Social support as enablement practice in social work

Whereas in Chapter 4 we focused on social support and its connectivity with family support, here, we return to matching the fundamentals of social support with social work as practice enablement. The 10 practice considerations outlined remain relevant for the discussion that follows. As discussed in Chapter 4, social support, pioneered in the 1970s (see Cassel, 1976), has become well established as active theory in varying fields, from social psychology, education, community development and within social care and social work. Social support is defined very simply as direct assistance that occurs between human beings (Tracy and Whittaker, 1990). We have discussed how most typically these acts relate in particular to specific types of help on offer, notably the provision of tangible or concrete supports, emotional sustenance including comforting, advice in terms of decision-making or working and esteem support from others to a person or people in need (Dolan and Brady, 2012). Further important factors of quality of support include closeness between donor and recipient, durability or strength of relationships, a capacity for allowable and acceptable positive criticism of the central recipient and reciprocity or balanced exchange of support (Cutrona, 2000). Both type and quality of support need to be attended to.

When considering social support practice, the importance of relationships deserves further mention – with the role of the social worker–client relationship as core and central. However, in order to value the power of a positive professional, the social worker should and must engage relationally (Daniel and Wassell, 2002). Research has shown, for example, that in palliative care contexts, the relationship between the social worker and hospital patients was the key ingredient to perceived successful interventions. Finally, closeness in social work relationships should not be viewed as 'all or nothing' or a 'friend or foe' option; it has degrees of connectivity, just like all relationships.

'Positive admonishment' or the 'capacity to provide constructive and useful criticism' often feature as a social work task and is a core function of good social support provision. This is where the provision of carefully and sensitively delivered criticism(s), with suggested solutions gently provided by the social worker to the service user, can lead to better outcomes. It should go the other way, too, where service users can also constructively deliver criticism to a social worker. Positive and constructive admonishment is totally contingent on the quality of the relationship between the parties and the basic difference is that what is being focused on is neither the behaviour (blame) nor the person (profiling), but rather it is the issue at hand that needs change or resolution.

In the context of the emerging interest and attention on 'co-production' as a social work practice method, it is the underlay of reciprocal social support. This implies that by exchanging support between parties, problems are discussed and solutions are discovered with mutual respect. Given that the service user from a family is part of the 'solution discoverer' and not alone, not only are they more likely to engage, they are also more likely to maintain any success in the longer term. Ironically it may well be that of all the social support qualities linked to social work practice, the one that should be the most simple to provide – namely, 'durability' – may be the hardest to achieve. We return to this point later in the context of expanding our reflections on practices of civic engagement and partnership.

Working on the assumption that the presence approach by the social worker is in place, delivered with a steady supply of empathy with a view to resilience building, the next question is, how do social support practices play out in real-world contexts? In order to answer this, we briefly explore possibilities for social support practice across three typical social work practice situations, namely, in relation to mental health, working with families in poverty and family support.

Mental health

Given the need for and importance of reassurance and genuine caring between the social worker and a service user living with a mental health issue, a mixture of ensuring a presence approach and empathetic responses is key. Often the social work function is perceived as limited to sociolegal functions and/or enabling coping alone, as if that will suffice. While this is important, it can underestimate the possibilities of what more can be done. For example, a strengths-based practice approach (looking to build on the positives, no matter how small or slight) has been found to be a key function in working with people with mental health issues to ensure support and protection simultaneously. Furthermore, ensuring emotional support (personally connecting) and esteem support (belief in the other's capacity to thrive) marks the difference in the social worker caring for as opposed to just caring about the person, and these are key ways of offering sustenance. Furthermore, good social work interventions seek the right time to intervene, with the correct amount of support at a given time. Additional important assessment and practice factors include seeking answers to the following set of simple questions:

- Is the person at home, safe and physically okay? (Safety check-in.)
- Has the person's perceived condition worsened or stayed at a low point recently, and if so, what actually prompted this change? (Condition assessment.)
- How can the person's own network of family, friends and community be enlisted to help? (Social support audit.)
- What helped or worked previously for the person, and can this be reactivated? (Personal resilience enablement.)
- ꞏIs the person's engagement with you as a social worker real or just tokenistic? If the latter, what can you do to change this? (Desirability gauge.)
- What are the immediate and reasonable next steps for you to enable working with the person over the coming weeks? What interim goals can you set? (Goal planning.)

Given the response to these key questions, the social worker can better derive methods for interventions. This follows a clear pattern, beginning with a crude check-in and condition assessment; social support, with a view to resilience enablement; factoring in desirability to engage; leading to goal planning and a set of steps and barriers with mitigation.

Working with people living in poverty

Working with people living in poverty is a very common and, at the same time, a very complex set of conditions for social work practice. You could argue that a traditional view of social work is that it is about working with the 'have–nots' (not just in monetary terms) and enabling them to 'have'. One example is the move in UNICEF to advance cash transfers to those in need as opposed to more costly professional interventions, albeit somewhat crudely applied (Daly et al, 2015). While necessary, this does not address the underlying conditions and intergenerational aspects of how poverty occurs for families. Indeed, it is as if the social ecological model is working in reverse, whereby it is totally focused on the microsystems, with a person's social capital in negative equity. In relation to responding to the existence and effects of poverty, the social worker should be a key critical agent operating across the ecological system. With the precondition of genuine empathy and being present in place, the task is to work directly with the person, family and community and, at an advocacy level, to achieve *both* immediate support *and* long-term positive possibilities, including education and employability, as well as housing and social integration and inclusion prospects.

Importantly, ahead of intervention and outside any programme (of which there are many), it is key that the social worker understands at the most basic level what the term 'poverty' means (Silke et al, 2018). Empathy grows from knowledge and understanding. Having the capacity to use a presence approach here requires solid knowledge and understanding of poverty. This includes the social worker knowing about minimum income standards, the concept of intergenerational poverty, relative and absolute poverty, material deprivation and destitution. In involves awareness of ever-emerging new forms of poverty from increased homelessness and new populations of people living in Direct Provision as well as 'in-work' poverty, where families have work and some money, but not enough. It requires a theoretical and conceptual analysis of poverty and its effects, and the capacity to apply this to the practice context. This includes critical analysis of the connection between poverty in families and the maltreatment of children, older people and people living with a disability, also recognising that this should not just be assumed. In fact, we need stronger acknowledgement of how remarkable many individuals and families are in their capacity and ability to survive and thrive, despite the impacts of poverty. This is done alongside, and not instead of, critical analysis, framing and actions regarding the factors leading to poverty at the exo to macro levels. Finally, and importantly, from the point of view of affective empathy in practice, the social worker needs to emotionally identify with the plight of a person who literally cannot afford basic food supplies. In other words, while addressing poverty at wider systemic levels is essential, we also need to ensure that in day-to-day practice, we empathise with the immediate and direct effects of poverty, and are willing to do something practical and material to address this through our own practice or through networking with others to harness resources. When we discuss the complex and contradictory nature of social work, the issue of how we tackle the impact of poverty on people's lives is one of the major challenges in terms of balancing individual and environmentally focused responses to this. As discussed later, in Part III, the way we construct theories and methods does not always help us in this regard, for example when individual practice and collective action are presented as two separate 'paradigms' of practice. As detailed below, our argument here is for a *both/and* approach.

In sum, the task for the social worker in relation to tackling poverty for and on behalf of others requires direct and indirect interventions. Having established a good understanding and engagement with the nature and plight of poverty for the person or family, the primary key function for the social worker is to focus on the immediate reliefs necessary, including basic tangible support, to ensure basic needs are met. This may be in the form of comfort provision, such as food and accommodation, and addressing urgent health issues for the person, which cannot be assumed to be readily available or accessible. Beyond this immediacy, the key function is to work at personal betterment over time towards self-sufficiency through a programmatic or planned approach. This can be in the form of either a formal poverty support programme or adaptation of one, or by creating an 'on-the-spot, fit-for-purpose' version. It requires engagement and partnership as an entry requirement on the part of the social worker. One very simple method, or 'working compass tool', for social work staff for use in collaboration with others, not least family members, is to use the well-known 'SMART' principles in goal setting to abate and end poverty. Adapted here, these include the following target steps:

- Specific: with targets that are helpful and address ameliorating poverty directly and indirectly.
- Measurable: any goal set has meaning and is clear to all, especially the person or family.
- Achievable: it has to be in the collective gift of the family and social worker, and it can be achieved – failure will lead to deeper poverty.
- Relevant: addresses clearly the issue with a matched resolution regarding what is not out of reach for the family.
- Time: timelines for the intervention in terms of readiness for the intervention so that resilience can occur using a 'success building on success' method.

It is important that in using this SMART approach, the wider ecological contexts of the occurrence of the poverty are not lost or replaced by narrow solutions being offered by the social work team. Critical awareness of the impact of poverty and deprivation on social problems that are too often individualised – such as child neglect – is crucial (see Bywaters et al, 2018; Featherstone et al, 2018).

Anti-poverty practice requires an approach that addresses *both* the individual impact of poverty on families and communities at the micro–meso level as well as the wider exo–macro-level factors across the ecological system. The *Anti-Poverty Practice Framework for Social Work in Northern Ireland* (Morrison et al, 2018) provides an excellent guide for practitioners regarding how to understand the impact of poverty on different groups and individuals. This is connected with anti-oppressive practice (using Neil Thompson's 2020 personal, cultural, structural [PCS] model) to implement anti-poverty practice in day-to-day interactions as well as at wider management, organisational and community-engaged level. Our focus on civic engagement and partnership implies the starting point as co-production, reminding workers that it is not their perceived narrative of poverty that should be the lead issue, but rather, the perspective and experience of the people affected. The guidance includes achievable and practical advice, similar to that for social support, on how to support people in poverty to access their benefits and entitlements. It also provides practical ways to support people to improve their material circumstances alongside advocacy and social justice practice. The framework encourages leadership by social workers at all stages of their practice, to talk about poverty, identify it and address it, research it and educate others about anti-poverty practices. We return to how we can develop these practices in Chapter 8, with an emphasis on maximising critical use of the ecological model and development and enhancement of networking skills and approaches within the context of civic engagement and partnerships.

Returning to family support principles

As discussed in Chapter 4, while family support has at last rightfully gained prominence in social work practice in recent years (Dolan et al, 2020; McGregor and Devaney, 2020a, b), it has long been embedded as a key function for the profession. Through the 1980s and 1990s Jack has advocated for family support as a practice orientation (Jack, 1997). Furthermore, Gilligan (2000) neatly categorised it as being primarily developmental, compensatory or protective. Dolan and Frost (2017) have also described it as being a primary (prevention), secondary or tertiary form of intervention (in cases of extreme adversity). We would strongly challenge the myth that social work and family support have separate functions. As has been argued by Bilson et al (2017), both need to be brought together now more than ever. Furthermore, family support and social support are intrinsically linked, and here we focus on its connection to empathy and resilience. To do so we suggest using the 10 family support principles established earlier as a reflective practice tool for social work. Here, we insert brief social work 'practice actions' for each principle, in order to ground this further:

1. Working in partnership is an integral part of family support. Partnership includes children, families, professionals and communities. *The social worker checks regularly that this is genuinely in place.*

2. Family support interventions are needs-led and strive for the minimum intervention required. *All proposals from the social worker are tested for need and over-intrusiveness.*

3. Family support requires a clear focus on the wishes, feelings, safety and wellbeing of children. *The social worker demonstrates active empathy to ensure this is in place.*

4. Family support services reflect a strengths-based perspective that is mindful of resilience as a characteristic of many children's and families' lives. *The deficit approach is abandoned in favour of a solutions-only focus.*

5. Family support promotes the view that effective interventions are those that strengthen informal support networks. *The social worker ensures that network members are enlisted based on natural sources and willingness to help.*

6. Family support is accessible and flexible in respect of location, timing, setting and changing needs, and can incorporate both child protection and out-of-home care. *Any intervention used is a moveable feast where the social worker allows for attrition or temporary fall-off.*

7. Families are encouraged to self-refer, and multi-access referral paths will be facilitated. *The social worker ensures information on access is easily understood and available.*

8. Involvement of service users and providers in the planning, delivery and evaluation of family support services is promoted on an ongoing basis. *The social worker fully engages with a model of co-production as a core practice method.*

9. Services aim to promote social inclusion, addressing issues around ethnicity, disability and rural/urban communities. *The social worker uses anti-discriminatory and anti-oppressive practices and self-tests regularly for cultural competence.*

10. Measures of success are routinely built into provision to facilitate evaluation based on attention to the outcomes for service users, and thereby facilitate ongoing support for quality services based on best practice. *An open and honest communication exists between the social worker and the person or family that celebrates what works but contritely acknowledges shortcomings.*

Summary

When you unpack what is core to successful social work in various and often challenging contexts, some clear messages emerge. The possibilities for successful outcomes stem from:

- the success of a social work intervention;
- a person's innate capacity to not just cope with but to overcome ongoing problems, and an ability to deal with sudden or new ones;
- living within harmonious relationships of worth;
- the availability of informal family support.

It also includes a common wish for a reasonable lifestyle free from worry, all this culminating in the person or family's right and ability to live freely and independently. As Pinkerton et al (2019: 60) argue, social work and family support 'provide and promote support through a managed and negotiated partnership process' and 'undergirding that is a shared commitment to respectful, empathic, human solidarity'.

As part of scripting this recipe, we have explored how resilience, empathy and social support theories can be actualised as useful to social work interventions. In particular, we have focused on social work itself, matching potential practices to what is known. Overall, we have suggested that empathy is essential to relationship working, the key and primary tool in the armour of social work. If this is in place, it can help ignite activated social support provision to enable a person or family's journey on the road to resilience.

As with Chapter 3, we recognise that there is more to consider in relation to family and social support (explored later in this book). In particular, we need to expand further on the notion of family and social support within the context of social capital and integrated social ecology (see Pinkerton et al, 2019). We need to continue to integrate support and protection as a duality in further chapters. We also need to explore more fully and critically the relationship between family and social support and social justice on the basis that 'innovative collaborative working necessitates a greater understanding of how hierarchy, power and politics work in organisations and the systems around the child, parent, professional and community' (Davis and Smith, 2020: 147). While referring specifically to child welfare, we contend that this argument by Davis and Smith resonates through family and social support across the lifecourse. We emphasise the importance of critically considering concepts of need and wellbeing to ensure an 'inclusive, anti-discriminatory, rights and social justice' approach (Davis and Smith, 2020: 147). As Davis and Smith (2020) argue, family (and social) support works best when it:

- 'enables service users to stop negative chain reactions, self-empower, become more analytical about why issues arise in their lives' (Davis and Smith, 2020: 146);
- is based on notions of minimal intervention, partnership, community-based support and a strengths perspective;
- recognises the capabilities of the people involved;
- engages with principles of diversity, social inclusion and anti-discriminatory practice.

Recommended resources

To support this chapter, we recommend the following as key reading, specifically in relation to resilience and empathy:

Robbie Gilligan (2009) *Promoting Resilience: Supporting Children and Young People Who Are in Care, Adopted or in Need.*

Elizabeth Segal (2011) 'Social empathy: A model built on empathy, contextual understanding, and social responsibility that promotes social justice.'

Charlotte Silke et al (2018) 'Factors influencing the development of empathy and pro-social behaviour among adolescents: A systematic review.'

Michael Ungar (2005) *Handbook for Working with Children and Youth: Pathways to Resilience Across Cultures and Contexts.*

Tips for critical ART in practice

Working on building resilience with individuals and families

One of the key challenges for social workers is to translate messages in resilience building as usable aspects of practice. For example, Gilligan's work on resilience building in children and youth (2009) is a useful example, as is Grotberg's model for developing better resilience in early childhood (Grotberg, 1995). Martin and Marsh (2006) have developed five factors that predict academic resilience. These factors are: enhancing self-efficacy, enhancing planning, greater persistence, addressing uncertain control and working on reducing anxiety (Martin and Marsh, 2006). Developing this table further in line with our framework, we propose a framework for putting resilience 'in action and in place', as outlined in Table 5.1. The factors we suggest should be focused on are: developing self-belief, better personal goal setting, not giving up on goals, living with uncertainty and sticking with what is positive.

Using Table 5.1 in direct work with a young or older person or family group, mind map, create and co-produce one 'doable' action per factor. Then, in a month's time, using the views of all parties (completed independently and then together), review, rate and discuss levels of success. In reviewing, explore what worked and what didn't, and what are the barriers to overcome etc.

Table 5.1: Putting resilience 'in action and in place'

Factor focus	Action	Current status: 1 Not at all 2 Sometimes 3 In place
Developing self-belief		
Better personal goal setting		
Not giving up on the goals		
Living with uncertainty		
Sticking with what is positive		

Source: Authors' own, part informed by Martin and Marsh (2006)

Practising a presence approach as an empathy-building tool using the Kolb model: a focus on reflection

1. Using the Kolb experiential model (see Kolb, 1984), which contains core elements of reflective practice, on completion of a session, consider an engagement with a service user (for example, a home visit) that went well with them.

2. Starting at the point of reflection (at the upper point, concrete experience), consider the extent of your presence throughout the session, at five-minute intervals. Do this by developing a word cloud of what you believe you did well, for example, good eye contact; attentive listening; asking the right questions; timely responses; nodding appropriately. List in another cloud things you could have done better (if any), for example, taking a phone call; not listening at a critical moment; being too quick to recommend an action to the person.

3. Over time build up a series of presence response word clouds, both positive and negative, and review for the direction of travel (with a view to positive word clouds increasing) through self-reflection by returning to the cycle of learning model shown within the Kolb cycle.

6

Transitions across the lifecourse

Introduction

Many of the challenges faced throughout a lifecourse happen at points of transition, such as from child to adulthood, into or out of care, adaptation following a loss, a break in attachment relationships, a move from home to elder care and loss of a partner. As Storø (2017) articulates, the concept of transition, as used in professional language, has become central in fields of research, such as studies of young people leaving care, but remains undeveloped theoretically. Storø (2017) provides an in-depth consideration of the meaning of transition, arguing that both diversity and common patterns are important. Even though it is focused on transition from care, Storø's paper has much wider applicability (as noted in 'Recommended resources' at the end of this chapter). Meleis et al (2000), writing for the field of nursing, provide another useful and relevant theory of transition. Considered by Joly (2016: 1254), it is outlined that 'properties of transitions include awareness, engagement, change and difference, time span and critical events'. Using this theory, Joly highlights how multiple transitions can occur at once, and that 'the goal of transitions is to achieve a state of well-being, reformulated identity and mastery while avoiding vulnerability' (Meleis et al, 2000, cited in Joly, 2016: 1254). Joly (2016) proposes a combination of transition theory and the bio-ecological model to inform transitions in nursing care.

For this chapter, we focus on support and protection in relation to transition across the lifecourse. The transition theory we apply is from Bridges (2002), which was developed within the field of change management. We advance our support and protection framework further, with a focus on social work as a process of enabling, supporting, protecting and managing change and transition as a core function and purpose.

Transition involves a process of changing from one condition or situation to another. Transition, for the most part, is a natural and necessary part of life. We transition through our individual development, from infants through to adulthood. Transitions can relate to house moves, career moves, new relationships, separation and divorce. Transition also occurs at wider organisational and societal levels.

While transition for individuals will usually bring a certain amount of challenges as well as opportunities, we tend to manage these through our own personal resources, coping mechanisms and/or the support of our close networks of family, friends and local community. However, in some instances, transition can be particularly difficult, and there is a need for additional support and protection, be it formal or informal. This is the focus of our chapter, when transition requires social work and related supports and protections. For illustration, we have selected three areas of transition to focus on:

- young people leaving residential or foster care;
- migration, especially for those who are refugees or seeking asylum;
- transition from childhood to adulthood for people with learning disabilities.

We then summarise a range of other examples where transitions theory can be used effectively, discuss core practice values and skills, and make connections with ongoing themes we can develop as the book progresses.

Bridges' theory of transition

William Bridges, a change consultant, developed a transition model in 1991, which highlighted that transition involved three stages:

- ending, losing and letting go;
- neutral zone;
- new beginning.

Bridges' book, *Managing Transitions: Making the Most of Change* (2002), provides guidance on how to manage transitions. Anghel and Beckett (2007) applied this theory of transitions to relevant social work contexts in Romania in relation to the transformation from communism to post-communism. It has also been applied and adapted in relation to understanding and responding to young people leaving care in Romania (Dima and Skehill, 2011; see also Dima and Bucata, 2015; Dima and Pinkerton, 2016).

As Dima and Skehill (2011: 2534) explain, Bridges distinguishes between 'change' and 'transition', whereby 'change is situational, external and focused on the new context (eg the new site, the new roles), while transition is internal and related to the psychological process people go through to come to terms with the new situation'. The neutral zone is described as 'the no-man's-land between the old reality and the new one, between the old sense of identity and the new', characterised by 'a time when the old is gone and the new doesn't feel comfortable, a time of chaos, confusion, anxiety, ambiguity, uncertainty, and search' (Dima and Skehill, 2011: 2534).

While Bridges calls the middle section of transition 'neutral', Dima and Skehill (2011) suggest that it is better described as the 'in-between phase', which can entail a complex process of attempting to let go and moving on. They suggest that care leavers (for example) can sometimes be caught in this phase for years as they grapple with the challenges of moving from a care-experienced childhood to independent living (see Figure 6.1). This transition is both social and psychological and does not happen in tandem. For example, a person can be transitioned 'socially' to new accommodation, employment or education but psychologically remain more focused on the ending and/or the in-between phase. In their research, Dima and Skehill found that 'professionals tended to be a step forward, while care leavers tended to be a step behind. Yet, for a successful transition … rhythms have to be correlated and the complexities understood' (Dima and Skehill, 2011: 2537).

Figure 6.1: Phases of transition

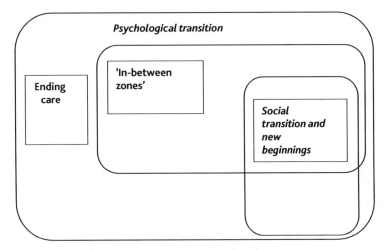

Source: Adapted from Bridges (2002: 70) by Dima and Skehill (2011). Reproduced by permission Elsevier

In this chapter, we consider how social workers can gain greater empathy with individuals with regard to major transitions and changes in their lives, including an understanding of both the psychological and social implications. We develop the 'social' aspect of transition by placing it within the bio-ecological frame to differentiate between the dimensions of that social context at the different ecological levels. We emphasise the importance of a focus on interactions between micro (depicted here as the emotional and psychological dimensions for the person[s] in transition) and the wider meso–macro levels (depicted as relating mostly to the broader social dimensions). As Bridges' theory has been most widely used in relation to understanding transitions from foster and/or residential care (see, for example, van Ryzin et al, 2011; Fenton, 2015; Dima and Bucata, 2015; Dima and Pinkerton, 2016), we start with this theme as our first illustration.

Transitions from care

Transitioning from care for young people involves various forms of residential and family-based care, and requires a return to developmental theories relating to adolescence. Arnett (2001) refers to this as 'emerging adulthood', and emphasises the particular features of this transitionary period for young people. The 'focal model of adolescence', developed by Coleman (1974), attempts to bridge psychological and sociological accounts of adolescence and to capture the complexity and diversity of this phase in the lifecourse. It recognises that there are many dimensions of transition for adolescents, and they tend to deal with this by tackling an issue at a time, spread over a number of years, and usually with the support of family and other adults (Coleman and Hendry, 1999). The issue for young people leaving care is that they are faced with what we could call the 'normative' processes of adolescence (what all young people experience, to a greater or lesser extent) and 'non-normative' processes specifically relating to transitioning from care. As Hollington and Jackson (2016) suggest, young people leaving care can find it more difficult to pace their transitions as per focal theory, because of additional disruptions, challenges and uncertainty.

International literature on transitioning from care (see, for example, Mendes and Snow, 2016; Atkinson and Hyde, 2019) identifies many important themes to consider, including identity theory, attachment, loss and separation and resilience (Stein, 2005a, b, 2006, 2008; Dixon and Stein, 2006; Munro and Stein, 2008; Stein et al, 2009, 2011; Pinkerton, 2008, 2011, 2021; Pinkerton and Rooney, 2014; Ward et al, 2009). Literature on youth civic engagement and citizenship emphasises working in partnership with young people in a youth-friendly manner, as citizens in the here-and-now (Chaskin et al, 2018; McGregor et al, 2020), with a vested interest in their own and their peer's futures (Kelly et al, 2020). Many organisations exist to maximise individual and collective participation from young people in care, and include EPIC (Empowering People in Care) in Ireland (www.epiconline.ie), VOYPIC (Voice of Young People in Care) in Northern Ireland (www.voypic.org) and INTRAC (International Research Network on Transitions to Adulthood from Care) (https://globalintrac.com). Global dialogue and 'mutually respectful discourse' about factors that impact on leaving care – for example, between the Global North and Global South (Africa, in this instance) – are emphasised by van Breda and Pinkerton (2020; see also, Pinkerton, 2011). It is important to be mindful of specific challenges for certain cohorts of care leavers, including those with additional needs due to disability or mental health difficulties (Kelly et al, 2014).

For young people leaving care, we can use Bridges' model to create a greater understanding of the process of transition from alternative/out-of-home care to adulthood by focusing on the three-stage model of 'endings', 'in-between' and 'new beginnings'. Learning from the study reported in Dima and Skehill (2011) about transitioning out of care in Romania, the importance of an understanding of the complex interplay between psychological and social transition was emphasised. The study highlighted the importance of social transition (for example, physically moving, getting accommodation, getting a job or going to college) and psychological transition (for example, grappling with moving on from a 'care identity', mixed experiences of loss and separation, the challenge of moving from enforced dependency to enforced independence) on health and wellbeing. This led to recommendations from the study about ensuring both social and psychological support and protection for young people, including recognition that the pace of transition is likely to be different. A person may complete their 'social' transition but still be very much struggling with the psychological transition.

Van Ryzin et al (2011) use Bridges' transitional model to develop programmes for support for young people and their carers to enable and support transition through care and after care. They designed a youth experience of transitions (YET) measurement, and found that: 'youth who became more comfortable and more open and reflective regarding change and transition were better equipped to handle the change they experienced, resulting in lower levels of internalizing symptoms such as anxiety and depression' (van Ryzin et al, 2011: 2271). In particular, they found that 'bolstering the awareness of transitions as an internal process and creating increased openness to change seemed to improve youths' ability to cope with the changes they were facing' (van Ryzin et al, 2011: 2271).

Referring back to Dima and Skehill (2011), another notable finding was that although differences in policy, context, time and space exist, there were many common issues identified irrespective of context – such as the experience of stigma. In later work by Dima and Pinkerton (2016), the importance of taking advantage of both informal and formal supports is emphasised, although they argue that it must be recognised that over-reliance on informal approaches (for example, for economic reasons of cost saving) also needs to be critiqued.

By placing Bridges' model within the bio-ecological framework, we can further differentiate between the complexity of the wider range of social factors that impact on a young person transitioning from care. This is especially important when considering how young people transition from children's to adults' services in differing country contexts (Tysnes and Kiik, 2019). It is also important to recognise that for some young people in care, they are possibly interacting between two or more micro–meso systems, denoting their care home and their home of origin, for example (Moran et al, 2017; Devaney et al, 2019) (see Figure 6.2). Eco-mapping can also be used to highlight supports and intergenerational relations that may be beneficial or harmful. Overall, a broad ecological approach, with an emphasis on social and psychological transition, can help to identify how best a young person can not only survive, but also thrive, in their lifecourse journey, through psychological wellbeing as well as social and civic engagement with society (for example, feeling part of society and connected).

When it comes to considering our next theme, transitions in the context of migration, the ecological map remains useful to capture the complex dynamics of interactions across and between system levels.

Figure 6.2: Relationship, communication, service support and continuity within a socio-ecological framework

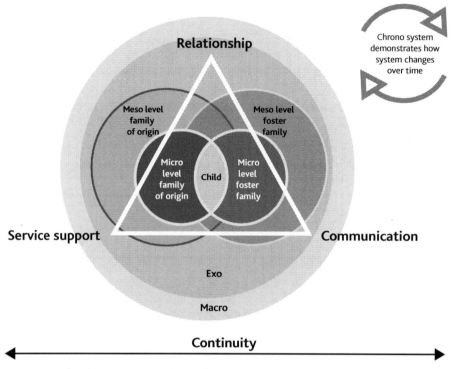

Source: Moran et al (2017, Figure 26: 68). Reproduced by permission The UNESCO Child and Family Research Centre, NUI Galway

Transition through migration

Migration involves moving from one place to another and entails not just change, but also significant transition at many levels. Migration is usually a major life event and life transition. In a global world, migration is a natural process that happens for many social, economic, political, cultural and personal reasons. Mobility of work practices across borders is common, and has positive and negative impacts on familial relationships and individual wellbeing (Götzö and McGregor, 2016). One form of migration is especially pertinent for social work, and relates to what we call 'forced' migration or migration under threat of war, hunger or abuse. The concerns of undocumented migrants raise specific challenges (Jolly, 2018). Here, we focus specifically on social work with refugees and asylum-seekers.

The UNHCR (UN High Commissioner for Refugees) highlights that 'every two seconds, somewhere on the planet, someone is forced to flee. Yet too often the world views their plight with indifference, even hostility' (see https://donate.unhcr.org/development/p2p1/~my-donation). And even though there has been a UN Refugee Convention since 1951, the needs, interests and rights of refugees and asylum-seekers remain a major global concern with regards to social justice and human rights. In whatever jurisdiction you are reading this book, there is likely to be a cohort of social work service users who are either themselves (or their families) having to flee or who are in your country having come to seek asylum or refugee status. This includes children, adults, families, and those travelling alone or in groups, including unaccompanied minors.

Supporting and protecting refugees and asylum-seekers is a global macro issue that requires an international, as well as a specific regional, response. One of the most important starting points should be to promote empathy and understanding of the issues. In the media, the movement and arrival of refugees is often objectified to numbers and generalisations, yet it is only through subjective engagement with people who have experienced migration as a refugee or asylum-seeker that both the psychological and social impacts of this transition can be fully understood. The impacts of the process of transition in relation to health and wellbeing are immense.

One group of migrants who require particular attention are unaccompanied minors, sometimes referred to as 'separated children', who represent a diverse group in terms of culture, ethnicity, religion and personal experiences. The in-between phase for young people is most likely to have been a traumatic, complex and challenging one, moving from their country of origin to their final destination. The psychological impact of their experiences before, during and after arrival, and their social contexts, can leave them open to exploitation, risk of abuse, lack of family and/or social support, isolation and retraumatisation. While these vulnerabilities are important, however, Horgan and Ní Raghallaigh (2019), writing in relation to the Irish context, are rightly critical of the tendency to construct young people arriving on their own solely as victims and open to vulnerabilities, as opposed to recognising their agency, capacity and resilience (see also Ní Raghallaigh, 2013).

Additional transitional challenges for unaccompanied minors relate to their moving from childhood to adulthood. As Ní Raghallaigh and Thornton (2017) highlight, while unaccompanied minors in Ireland are in the statutory care system until they are 18, they are denied the usual supports other children in care receive, and must instead use the punitive and highly criticised 'Direct Provision' residential centres. These centres are where all asylum-seekers in Ireland are forced to reside, with limited control over their lives and environment, until their case is heard (Arnold, 2013: IRC, 2013). As Ní Raghallaigh and Thornton (2017) argue, this environment has a detrimental impact on individual wellbeing, family life, child development, child protection and human rights. They describe this as a situation where 'the placement of aged-out separated children in direct provision, to our mind, can be viewed as a form of punishment for (continued) exercising of a legal right to claim protection' (Ní Raghallaigh and Thornton, 2017: 399).

The experience of transition from the ending of life in one country to the commencement of life in another (possibly even a different continent) as an asylum-seeker or refugee (either as a minor, family unit or adult) has to be recognised as a major concern for social work in relation to support and protection. We provide one case study of Amira and her son Jamal who migrated from Syria to Ireland as asylum-seekers in the 'Tips for critical ART in practice' at the end of this chapter by way of illustration. Reflecting on this case, we argue that the starting point for your practice should be empathy with and interest in how the transition was experienced, and where the person is (using Bridges' model) in their new situation. People may, for example, be socially in their destination country, technically safe, but psychologically still experiencing loss and trauma linked to the life that was left behind. Moreover, what was in-between is most unlikely to have been 'neutral' and much more likely to have been fraught, traumatic and complicated.

As a recent study in Germany argued in relation to best practice with refugees, 'Social workers emphasize the importance of learning to see people "eye-to-eye", cultivating empathy, cross-cultural competence, overcoming personal biases, and self-reflection' (Hagues et al, 2019: 1). This micro-level attendance to interactions as a starting point opens up the possibility for building relationships based on partnership, supporting the civic development of the person as a world citizen rather than as someone caught waiting to 'become a citizen'. This connection builds capacity to work, in partnership with others, to address the wider exo–macro-level concerns. Social workers need to make particular efforts to acquire specialist knowledge and ability to support individuals and families about entitlements relating to immigrants, refugees and asylum-seekers. In discussing the role of social work with undocumented migrants, Jolly (2018) calls for an 'anti-defeatist stance' to overcome the potentially overwhelming position social workers find themselves in with regard to helping a person negotiate a complex and specific welfare and regulation process.

We propose the critical use of the bio-ecological model as one constructive way to guide practice focused on supporting transition. As shown in Amira and Jamal's case later, the ecosystem of an asylum-seeker is complex, requiring at least two discreet or overlapping bio-ecological maps to denote the context that has been 'ended' and the new context that is being adapted to.

At a micro level, issues to consider for ecological contexts of 'endings' and what was left behind and 'new beginnings' of what is present and in the future include attention to identity (cultural and personal), psychological wellbeing (and possible trauma from past and/or present context), noting individual strengths, resilience and capacities. At the meso level, it is likely that the interactions and proximal processes are dramatically changed from the ending to the new beginning with regard to family and social networks, connections to peers and social activities. At the exo level, likewise, in a new country there is a completely new system to negotiate, with regard to, for example, school, sport and community outlets. In addition, at the macro level, processes such as asylum application management, laws (international and national) and policies and processes (such as very long delays, in the example of Ireland) massively impact on the person claiming asylum. At the chrono level, differences in trends, cultural practices and societal relations need to be considered in the context of how the person interacts with these complex layers surrounding this 'new beginning'. One of the benefits of the bio-ecological model is the focus on the interaction from the micro level (the person) to the wider meso–macro levels. However, there is still a tendency in much policy and practice to focus on the vulnerabilities and the way the system impacts 'down to' the individual. Using concepts of civic partnership and engagement, a more participative and power-sharing approach to practice can emerge where social workers can act as intercultural mediators to enable individuals to critically engage with systems rather than merely 'experience their effects'.

Throughout this consideration, there is a need to pay specific attention to aspects of culture, race and ethnicity throughout each level of the ecological context mapping, and at each point of the process of transition. Williams (2020) summarises social work research in relation to the focus on race, noting that while we have advanced our abilities to look at complex interactions and intersections between aspects of race, ethnicity, migration, cultural diversity and superdiversity, there has been a disappointing lack of progress in advancing practice that lives up to the principles of co-design and challenging normative assumptions. As we discussed earlier in relation to critical bio-ecological theory, culture is so imbued in a person's life and ecology, it needs to be considered at every level of context, from micro to macro, in all aspects of our practice. This focus must be absolutely to the fore in working to support asylum-seekers and migrants in transition.

Transition from childhood, through adolescence and adulthood, for people with a learning disability

For all individuals, life has many transitions to face, including the development from childhood through to adolescence and into adulthood. Here, we look specifically at the transition from childhood to adulthood for a person with a learning disability. The area of disability is one that starkly highlights the problems with a 'normative' approach to lifespan development, which automatically presents disability as, in some way, problematic, delayed or behind expected developmental patterns. As discussed earlier, a lifecourse perspective on disability allows a much more fluid consideration of development that can be attuned to the individual's own trajectory rather than against some generalised assumptions about what should be expected and when.

Webb et al (2020) reviewed service user decision-making in relation to both disability and mental health, taking a peer researcher approach, and found three aspects people wanted in relation to decision-making: 'practical support including more accessible information, emotional support … and sometimes the options to choose from' (2020: 1282). Specific emotional support included 'peer support, encouraging service users to be independent, providing reassurance on decisions, and having a wide support network' (Webb et al, 2020: 1288). In this approach, the importance of engaging with well-established disability rights activism groups is key to ensure that the responses we develop are not those imposed but are fully informed in participation with citizens most affected by the issues – in this case, people with intellectual disabilities. This includes direct inclusion of adults with intellectual disabilities in co-teaching, as developed by Feely and colleagues in Ireland (see the 'Supporting Adults with Intellectual Disabilities to become Co-lecturers in the School of Social Work and Social Policy: An Experimental Participatory Action Research Project', www.tcd.ie/research/profiles/?profile=mfeely).

From the literature on the developmental challenges for young people transitioning from childhood through adolescence and adulthood, the term 'bridging' comes up frequently in most jurisdictions, where it seems many education, health and social services are organised separately for children and young people and adults. Often the structures for delivering these services differ, and there are many examples of where there are barriers and challenges specifically for people with disabilities that belie what we know and understand about the complexities of the lifecourse to transition in this sphere. While it may not be possible to change services towards lifecourse provision, great attention to support and protection at points of major transition between services is needed.

Transitions for people with learning disabilities to adulthood impact on intergenerational relations. While it is generally assumed that a child moves from dependence to independence from their teens through to their 20s, often the 'child' status of a young person with a disability can be prolonged and protracted by over-protection, paternalism and insufficient support for parents and carers to help manage that transition to independence. Referring back to Bridges' theory, individuals who are developing into adulthood can be caught in the 'in-between' phase, where childhood has ended, but the opportunity for new independence is protracted or suspended, sometimes indefinitely. Kelly et al (2019), from a review of support to families in Ireland, highlight a number of challenges and additional strains for families supporting relatives with an intellectual disability (citing Barroso et al, 2018; Patton et al, 2018), especially in light of the evidence that most families, if possible, prefer to care for their relatives at home rather than through out-of-home placements. Kayama et al (2019), with reference to experiences of disability in India, provide a stark example of the relationship between family experiences of disability and sociocultural issues relating to gender, caste, socioeconomic issues and stigmatisation. They make the case for an intersectional approach to disability that can capture these complex, interconnecting themes. Furthermore, they emphasise that these themes are experienced differently by individuals, and 'it is necessary to examine their everyday experiences in their relationships with others, including at home, at school, and in the community, as well as beliefs, practices, and policies pertaining to disability embedded within Indian sociocultural contexts' (Kayama et al, 2019: 2–3).

One of the critical aspects of this challenge is the transition for people with learning disabilities in relation to developing adult intimate relationships. While this transition to sexual relations and development of one's own sexuality is a feature of lifecourse development, especially from adolescence onwards, for people with a disability, this basic developmental right can often be constrained. This is highlighted in Feely's work (2016) through his research with service users and service providers from a specific agency in Ireland. Using the theoretical work of Foucault and Deluze, and relying primarily on the narratives of the research participants, Feely presents an in-depth and critical insight into the extent to which 'sexual surveillance' was evident in the practices and experiences of those interviewed. In the quote below, he captures the interplay between wider structural and organisational discourses and individual practices, showing both surveillance, regulation and resistance in relation to the rights of adults with intellectual disability to what tends to be assumed as a 'normal' lifecourse transition in other contexts:

> It is not that people necessarily are sexuality conservative; it is that they must be seen to be sexuality conservative. Nonetheless, and despite the considerable risks involved, staff members often demonstrate considerable courage in resisting practices they believe to be unfair. Meanwhile, service users also remain extremely resilient and resistant, finding creative ways to escape sexual control within day-centres. Institutional architecture, for example, doesn't simply facilitate surveillance; service users also creatively re-appropriate architectural spaces (eg relaxation rooms) as sexual spaces to escape surveillance. Similarly, information technologies don't just aid surveillance; they also allow for new forms of resistance (eg accessing sexual information or online dating sites). (Feely, 2016: 746)

Supporting and protecting through transitions

As Storø (2017: 777) argues, 'Different actors involved in ... transitions, such as young people themselves, caregivers and other professionals, may understand both the process and outcomes quite differently.' It is important that this starting point informs our approach by recognising that what a social worker may consider a key challenge of transition may not have the same significance for their service user. In addition, as emphasised in this chapter, when working with transition, both the *process* of transition as well as the *outcomes* of transition are essential to attend to. In this chapter, we have selected just a few examples of transitions and note a number of other examples we could have used, such as transitions relating to:

- separation and divorce;
- managing cyclical transitions for individuals and their families in relation to enduring mental illness;

- social workers themselves transitioning between different countries to work;
- changes, often rapid, that have to be made due to social unrest, a pandemic (for example, COVID-19), political violence or other significant societal change at local and/or global levels;
- moving into or out of institutional or foster/adoptive care;
- many other examples from your own perspective (see 'Tips for critical ART in practice' at the end of this chapter).

Although implicit within many social work approaches, it is interesting to note that transition theories do not dominate as much as you would expect, given that so much of social work support and protection takes place within the context of working with people in transition. So what might be the additional values, practice and skills considerations? As discussed in particular in relation to migration, it seems most useful to consider transition theory – such as Bridges' – within a wider ecological context, so that the layers of social and psychological effects can be mapped more precisely.

From the discussion so far, the following summary points can be emphasised for practice:

- While 'change' is situational, external and focused on the new context, transition is internal and related to the psychological process people go through in moving from one context or situation to another.
- Transition in any context can be multifaceted and diverse for each individual involved.
- Transitions occur in many different ways, each posing specific challenges and opportunities.
- Superdiversity is a useful organising concept to ensure we maintain awareness at all times of the multifaceted core issues around identity linked to culture and ethnicity.
- While transition is multifaceted and diverse, there are some common features captured in Bridges' (adapted) model relating to a process of 'ending', being 'in-between' and 'new beginnings' that can be further developed using an ecological and lifecourse frame.
- Whatever the transition, it is crucial that attention is paid to *both* process *and* outcomes of transition, with attention to the maintenance of health and wellbeing through a critical understanding of the disruption some transitions cause for individuals and families.
- Greater awareness of the psychological impact of transition will lead to greater empathy towards those experiencing change at particular periods or moments in their lives.
- Critical awareness of the different interpretations of the meaning of transition is crucial: a worker may see 'new beginnings' such as securing a job and accommodation as most significant, whereas the person they are working with

may be still in the 'endings' stage, experiencing loss, confusion and separation. As Dima and Skehill argued above, 'rhythms have to be correlated and the complexities understood' (2011: 2537).

- Related theories or concepts to consider the psychological aspects of transition in particular include identity theory, attachment, loss and separation and resilience.
- Related theories or concepts to consider the wider social aspects of transition include critical bio-ecological theory, cultural awareness, cultural competence, superdiversity and intersectionality.

Summary

Transitions are a natural part of a person's lifecourse. For social workers themselves, this could include transition to studying social work, becoming a social worker, and changing location and role. Just as citizens who migrate or seek asylum bring a diverse culture and experience with them, so, too, do social workers, who traverse borders to practise in different international contexts. Reflection on the very experience of transition can aid the development of greater empathy for its impact. Reflecting back on lifecourse mapping, turning points are often used to pinpoint key moments. The use of Bridges' model, to acknowledge the psychological and the social – often moving at different speeds – can give a scaffold to aid conversation and understanding. Use of the bio-ecological model helps us to consider the challenges at different levels, and the need to continue more critical applications of the model (for example, in relation to culture) has been highlighted. Critique of the theory we have used (as always) is also important. For example, in the detailed case study provided in 'Tips for critical ART in practice' at the end of this chapter, questions are raised, using the five-theme framework, about whether the notion of 'ending' and 'beginning' always works for the transition context.

In Chapter 7, we focus on a selection of particular issues that arise in relation to transition that results in 'disrupted development' as further illustration of how the framework can enhance better understanding and application.

Recommended resources

For insights into transitions from care across the globe, see Philip Mendes and Pamela Snow's *Young People Transitioning from Out-of-Home Care: International Research, Policy and Practice* (2016).

Jan Storø's article, 'Which transition concept is useful for describing the process of young people leaving state care? A reflection on research and language' (2017), provides a detailed account of the meaning of the concept of transition. It is applied to young people leaving care, but has wider relevance for understanding the diversity and complexity of the concept of transition as it has been adapted into the professional world of social work.

The 'Stories of social inclusion' in Ireland for people with a disability include recommendations for practice that are relevant for transitions, such as an emphasis on choice and control and the importance of self and peer advocacy: https://inclusionireland.ie/19-stories-of-social-inclusion

Tips for critical ART in practice

Personal reflection using Bridges' model of transition

Reflect on a period of transition in your own lifecourse. Draw a map using Bridges' model, outlining the significant 'ending', 'in-between' and 'new beginnings' phases.

- What were the main psychological factors?
- What were the social factors?
- Did you find that these happened at a different pace?
- What can you take from this to apply to your own practice context?
- Could you use this map to talk about transition with service users?

Consider how transition theory, with an ecological model, can be used to inform practice in relation to forced migration

Refer back to the figures in Chapter 2. Use them to guide a drawing with the person you are working with to identify their ecological system (for example, to establish any psychological and social need for support). A sample is provided in Figure 6.3, which can also be used to reflect on the illustrative case study. This shows overlapping micro and meso interactions, mostly separate exo and macro systems denoting different country structures, policies and laws. There is likely to be some overlap at chrono level that can be used to denote common themes, such as the displacement of people globally, racism, ethnicity and issues relating to cultural competence. Different chrono influences are also relevant, such as differences in culture and religion. The expectation is not that you attend to all levels at one time; instead, the model should be used specifically to map out the *relevant systems and interactions*, from your conversations with the individual, family or group you are working with, that can aid assessment, understanding and planning for intervention and support. In reflecting on the use of the map, keep the five themes in mind for understanding and responding to the needs for support.

This is a practical tool to use within the context of an agreed planned method or approach you are using. It is useful to enable a conversation about experience of transition that is often overlooked. While there may be a specific presenting issue you are focusing on – such as a child welfare and family support concern, as in the case example we provide here – it is crucial from the point of view of empathy and relational practice that you recognise that a person's recent experience

Figure 6.3: Two ecological systems to consider in the context of forced migration

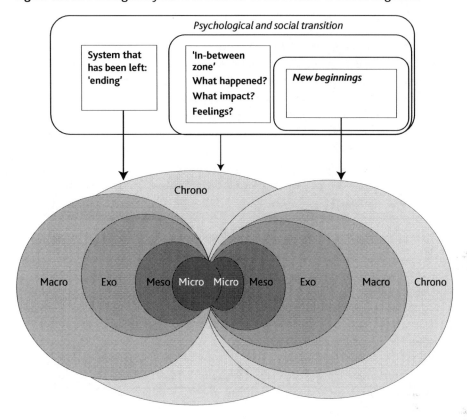

of transition due to forced migration is most likely to have been traumatic and impactful on the person, whatever the specific present issue is. It is about asking not 'what is wrong?' but 'what happened?'.

Case example

Amira, a 30-year-old mother, and her son Jamal, aged 10, are referred to the Irish Child and Family Agency. The family are originally from Syria. They left in 2016 due to conflict in their region, and after spending time in a refugee camp in Lebanon and then in Greece, they arrived in Ireland three months ago. They are referred to the child and welfare agency for a child protection concern due to the perceived neglect of Jamal with regard to malnutrition, poor hygiene, signs of some developmental delay and disruptive behaviour in the Direct Provision centre (the holding centre for asylum-seekers in Ireland). The director of the centre made the referral. Following assessment, however, it is decided that the conditions of neglect are mostly associated with Amira's social circumstances: her recent arrival in Ireland as an asylum-seeker due to being part of a resettlement programme led by the Irish Embassy, disruption of their lives in the past few years as asylum-seekers and socioeconomic issues due to poverty, not being able to work and living in Direct Provision conditions known and recognised to be limited and unsuitable for family life.

The personal factors are associated with Amira's own ability to cope due to these circumstances and the toll this has taken on herself and on Jamal. It is therefore deemed to be a case for family support rather than child protection investigation. The social worker is asked to work with Amira and Jamal to make a family support plan, but also needs to keep the importance of protecting Jamal on the agenda. The recommended practice approach of the agency is a strengths- and relationship-based approach, as used in child protection (for example, Signs of Safety®) and family support. The first task for the social worker is to build a relationship with Amira and Jamal, to do a further and more detailed assessment of needs for support and to make a recommendation for the best intervention plan (agreed with Amira) to the supervisor.

Source: Informed by Bronfenbrenner and Morris (2006) and Dima and Skehill (2011)

As part of the tools to support this work, Table 6.1 summarises ways the ecological model, using transition theory, could be used. These are just for illustration, and are focused on Amira as an example. Readers can develop this exercise or use one from their own contexts:

- Preparation: use an enquiry–based approach to collect basic information about the Syrian conflict, the resettlement programme referred to, the local Direct Provision centre, and other relevant information.
- Focus on Amira and Jamal, the *people* affected.
- Recognise your role (*process*) as offering support and protection.
- Reflect on the *context* to determine the most significant interactions or needs for support to address.
- Focus on *time* to appreciate the key moments in the family's life that may have been significant (for example, time spent in a previous refugee centre).

Table 6.1: Draft practitioner tool for critical ART

Understanding and discussing transitions	Micro	Meso	Exo	Macro	Chrono	Critical ART
'Endings' (possible areas that might be discussed with the five-theme framework in mind)	Important intergenerational relations? Impact of recent partner and family loss?	What were your important networks and relationships in Syria?	Involvement in school, welfare, child welfare services in Syria as sources of support for health and wellbeing?	Government and national policy? Impact of the conflict? Feelings towards what has happened in relation to the country?	While living in Syria is ended for now (social transition), the psychological connections with culture, society and life may still be very strong	For example, think about the psychological impact of the experience on micro-level relationships or macro-level feelings of being let down or not protected by one's own country
'In-between' (possible areas that might be discussed with the five-theme framework in mind)	Ask about the transition. The other refugee camps? How did you cope? What happened to you? What happened to Jamal?	Who supported you? What relationships were important? Who looked after your wellbeing as a mother?	Ask about key services for support and protection (education, basic welfare, family support)	Analyse relevant statistics about displacement globally, know about the asylum process in Ireland	Experience of being an asylum-seeker in different countries. Knowledge about racism and discrimination and its impact	The need to reflect on what you are told or how you can show empathy. Think about what social workers can or should do to support transition at different levels of the ecosystem

(continued)

Table 6.1: Draft practitioner tool for critical ART (continued)

Understanding and discussing transitions	Micro	Meso	Exo	Macro	Chrono	Critical ART
'New beginnings' (possible areas that might be discussed with the five-theme framework in mind)	What does Jamal need most for support and protection?	What can we (services) do? What kind of support would be best to promote family health and wellbeing?	Focus on how you can mediate with relevant support organisations	Check out legal and procedural status. Role for advocacy or support in engaging with resettlement programme (eg to speed up process of moving on?)	Experience of being an asylum-seeker in Ireland. What is the dream now? What can Ireland offer?	Remember learning from theory – social and psychological transition happen at different paces

Also reflect critically on Bridges' model:

Is the 'ending' and 'new beginning' too stark? Many people who leave their countries want to return some day.

Does it allow for a full understanding of people's strong connection with identity (eg Syrian identity)?

Does it help to focus on the gap that can exist between where people are socially and where they are psychologically? (Reminding yourself of the psychosocial nature of work?)

What other learning or knowledge is needed (eg on identity, disrupted development, as discussed later, in Chapter 7)?

How can the five-theme framework be activated to maximise support and protection for the family?

7

Managing and challenging 'disrupted development'

Introduction

A lifecourse perspective that encourages us to view life as a series of journeys and transitions helps our critical understanding of the multiple factors that affect people's lives from birth to death. It is a multidisciplinary concept, and historical and cultural factors are essential to bear in mind. Social work by its nature is a lifecourse discipline, and whatever area we work in, such as medical social work, family practice or probation, interventions take place with attention to the whole lifecourse of the person as well as their intergenerational relations. Disruption to or within a person's lifecourse is one of the most common reasons people seek and use social work services so this theme already has relevance when considering protection, safeguarding, family support, social support and transitions.

In this chapter, we advance the discussion further, focusing more closely on disruption. Disruption in a person's lifecourse may be ongoing and reoccurring, such as persistent neglect of a child within a family, enduring mental ill health or a need for lifelong disability support. Disruption can also occur at specific moments, such as the impact of loss through death or separation. Sometimes it is a whole systems change that causes disruption, such as, for example, the transition from communism and the re-establishment of social work in Eastern Europe in the late 20th century (Schilde and Schulte, 2005; Hering and Waaldijk, 2006), or the disruption caused by sectarian conflict, as in Northern Ireland (Duffy et al, 2020). Much of social work is focused on mediating at times when there is a disruption to people's development and lives. Theories of human behaviour, development and growth, such as attachment and loss, contribute greatly to our understanding of and response to disruptions. A range of methods (or processes) may be used in relation to disruption, such as crisis intervention, person–centred planning, strengths–based practice and psychosocial interventions. Care must also be taken in using these theories that we do not over-focus on micro–meso levels to the detriment of seeing the person within their wider lifecourse and ecological context.

We have chosen four examples that we use in teaching by way of illustration. These relate to examples of disruption due to:

• parental mental ill health;
• a move to alternative care for adults;

- severe child neglect and abuse;
- child sexual abuse.

In each instance, we consider how our framework can offer a useful critical scaffolding to inform practice. The importance of enquiry-based learning really comes to the fore at this stage of the book, as there are numerous other examples from your own experience and context that relate to the issues discussed here. In our examples, we refer back to the figures in Chapter 2 to further elaborate the use of the ecological model, and build on our discussion in chapters to date about its various uses and application. To keep developing our critical frame, we focus in particular on how certain bodies of knowledge can inform our further development of the ecological model to scaffold practice. For example, some theories, such as attachment and loss, focus mostly on the person, process and micro–meso-level interactions. Other research and theory focuses on the wider macro and legal factors. When summarising the literature in this chapter, we illustrate how we can break down the complex range of issues to take on board when critically understanding disruption, its impact and how best to respond by using an ecological framework. We also highlight the ongoing importance of looking to both the intrinsic and micro–meso level as well as wider extrinsic exo–macro-level factors. We use the 'Tips for critical ART in practice' at the end of this chapter to provide some case studies to further illustrate the discussion in this chapter, which can be adapted for your own practice and supervision contexts.

In each example, elements of the framework are central. We contend that *support and protection* underpin practice in decision-making to determine the balance between independence and risk to self or others when managing disruption. Each example demonstrates the importance of social work intervention at key points in *lifecourse trajectories and transitions* that can lead to physical, psychological, emotional and social disruption for the people involved. The range of interactions, within the ecosystem, that impact on this transition can be specifically identified using an eco-mapping approach. The impact on *intergenerational relations* is expressed in particular, in terms of how the caring roles between and within families can change due to many reasons, such as:

- a child supporting a parent with a severe mental illness;
- a parent failing to take on associated responsibilities to the point of leaving children neglected and at risk;
- an adult with dementia who was once the 'leader' of the family gradually becoming the 'dependant' (for example, an adult child abruptly becoming their parent's carer).

Disruptions like these impact on both wellbeing and relationships. Wider issues, such as the social construction of family life and cultural differences in family practices, are also important considerations. In some settings for social work, such as those that are clinical and health-related, the explicit emphasis is on promoting *health and wellbeing*, and in other settings, such as child welfare, it is framed with a focus on prevention and a strengths-based approach. In many instances, the health and wellbeing of a person with a mental illness, the need for support for older people or the need for protection for a child are a direct result of rights violations through inadequate support services, injustices in relation to failure to address inequalities caused by poverty, marginalisation or discrimination, and failure to implement legal entitlements and protection. We discuss in more detail in Chapter 8 how the ecological model can be advanced further as a critical framework for addressing oppression and discrimination, and for promoting rights and justice.

An approach to partnership in practice framed in the context of *civic engagement* is significant because one of the effects of disruption of a lifecourse can be a resulting disconnection or distortion of links with individual and family relations as well as the wider community and social context. Many people who experience grief, for example, describe the feeling of existing in a world that seems to be going on without them in it. For families where there is a member with a severe illness, isolation and disconnection are common themes, reinforced by stigma in relation to mental health and a lack of public and community understanding about the conditions and its impact. Moves to institutional care can result in a severing of ties from community and local connections and routines such as daily visits to a local village and connections with peers in the community. This can leave a person thoroughly disconnected from their ecological system. Experiencing neglect and abuse at home can leave a child disconnected from engagement in regular youth activities beyond statutory requirements such as schooling. Thinking from the perspective of civic engagement, the scope for partnership working is expanded beyond 'just coping' with health, education and welfare, for example, to focus on maximising a person's capacity to be an active part of society through activities, engagement with mentoring and volunteering, and critically understanding their own context and interactions within the wider systems that influence this. Overall, thinking from the perspective of citizenship underpinned by a civic engagement approach ensures that attention is paid to the whole ecological system, with a focus on interrelationships and interactions to inform activation of practices. The following four sections on our selected illustrative themes develop this discussion further.

Disruption due to parental mental ill health

For some people who experience severe and enduring mental illness or ill health (such as schizophrenia, severe manic depression or psychosis), their lives can be a series of circuitous transitions between community and institutional-based care. This can be disruptive for everyone involved, even when people are resilient and resourceful. As Hurley and Kirwan (2020: 340) argue, in relation to the Irish and Canadian context of mental health social work, 'prolonged adversity takes a toll on the resilience of the service user while social work practice, aimed at counteracting such structural adversity, takes a toll on the resilience of the practitioner'. They echo the warnings about resilience discussed earlier in terms of ensuring that wider structural and organisational factors that affect disruption are not overlooked when emphasising the resilience of either the service user or the social worker. Often in mental health practice the focus is on the individual, but increasingly, the importance of family-focused practice is being recognised, especially when it comes to working with parents who have mental ill health (see Foster et al, 2012; Reupert et al, 2015). These practices are ecological by nature in their focus on the person in their environment and interactions between both micro–meso as well as exo–macro levels. Yates and Gatsou (2020) review family-focused programmes and summarise both the opportunities and challenges in relation to family-focused practice, specifically in relation to parental mental illness. The range of challenges they identify are as follows:

- practitioner confidence (person–process, exo context);
- parents' reluctance to engage (person–process, intrinsic micro context);
- the ongoing impact of stigma (exo, macro and chrono context);
- importance of support from management (exo context);
- time and resources to engage families (person–process);
- direct work with mental health service users (person–process, micro–macro context);
- training of practitioners (exo–macro context) who work with other members of the family, including children (Golden et al, 2020).

By applying the framework, a more detailed application of the ecological model becomes possible with an emphasis on specifically locating the points of influence and interaction to inform actions and responses. When children are involved, the impact of severe and enduring mental illness on parents can be especially disruptive. Disruption caused by parental mental illness has implications for *intergenerational relations*, where children can take on caring roles beyond their years. *Health and wellbeing* can be debilitated by severe mental illness that has an impact not just on the parent but also on the children, partner and wider family network. Inadequacy of services and support and health inequality need to be critically considered here. *Lifecourse and transition* may be mapped by these disruptions being turning points or key moments influenced by both micro-level factors, such as the impact of a mental illness, as well as wider exo and macro factors influenced, for example, by cultural factors and societal stigma. Many themes arise in relation to *protection and support* in terms of balancing the need for parental support and risk factors faced by children and sociolegal practice within mental health legislation relating to detention and capacity practices influenced by wider exo and macro factors (discussed further in Chapter 8).

With regard to *civic engagement and partnership*, in many jurisdictions, service user representation in mental health has been strong, often drawing from collective opportunities for mobilisation to address wider structural barriers. This work has become increasingly sophisticated and integrated into service provision settings. For example, Näslund et al (2019: 1) write about 'service user entrepreneurs' defined as 'individuals with service user experience who have made a career of their engagement in mental health issues'. As discussed further in Chapter 8, working through networks of citizens helps develop a civic engagement and partnership approach to mental health based on partnerships, advocacy and rights-based practice. This relates to both micro–meso interactions within the family and wider exo (support services) and macro systems (negotiating limits of independence and capacity under the law), and takes place within the context of interdisciplinary and multidisciplinary cooperation. In the 'Tips for critical ART in practice' at the end of this chapter, the example for this theme includes suggestions about how a practice teacher could use the framework to encourage critical ART by their student to develop the points made above.

Supporting a move to alternative care for older people

An older person moving from independent living to alternative (usually institutional or group) care is often a major transition in the lifecourse of an individual and their families. Sometimes this transition is welcomed and a relief for the person and/or their family. As discussed in Chapter 6, most transitions happen through families and/or community and health services without direct social work interventions. However, many times, it is disruptive because it brings about a range of psychosocial challenges for the person and their family, and requires specialist social work support. Often the move from independence to alternative care happens abruptly from hospital or rehab where the person has had a serious illness or a stroke, and the changed circumstances mean a return home is not possible. In other contexts, it is a more planned approach. For example, dementia can be progressive, sometimes leading to a person requiring full-time care outside the home which impacts on the person with dementia, the carer and the social worker (Fitzpatrick and Grace, 2019). This could be due to the nature of the condition or the capacity of the family to continue to care. Or it may be due to lack of presence of family and social support, requiring institutionalisation for an older person as their independence diminishes. Assessing and supporting this decision-making is central to the work of the hospital or clinical social worker.

A major contribution social work makes within a multidisciplinary context is the provision of person-centred care that challenges the potentially disempowering aspects of moves to residential care that include lack of choice and consultation, speed of a move, pressure on families due to emotional impact, and/or possible guilt and loss. Social work promotes empowerment through enhanced communication and support to families as well as the individual concerned, and through recognition and understanding of the emotional as well as practical aspects of transition. Linked with this, the impact of wider exo and macro factors is addressed through sociolegal practice, advocacy, networking, multidisciplinary and rights-based practice, as discussed further in Chapter 8.

Reflecting on how the framework can help inform ongoing critical thinking, loss and grief are important themes, intimately linked to attachment. Schäfer (2020b) identifies a number of areas relating to adult development where attachment is key, including the impact of parenting style and within intimate and couple relationships. Schäfer (2020b) describes the attachment styles in adults as broadly similar to child–adult attachments, and emphasises the importance of cultural factors that influence attachment styles (for example, a very patriarchal structure in society has been linked with more ambivalent or insecure attachment patterns). Social workers need to be aware of intergenerational transmission of patterns. Theories of loss include Kubler-Ross's work (1989) on the stages of grief, Stroebe and Schut (1999) consider loss and grief in terms of mindsets and Worden (2003) focuses on the tasks involved to process the grieving process (see Sudbery, 2010).

Loss relates not only to experiences of death but also to a range of other lifecourse events, with particular attention needed in relation to childhood loss and bereavement (Talpin, 2020). Attention to cultural factors and loss are essential, as Moore et al (2020) argue in relation to clinical support with Black Americans. The role of spirituality and religion is likewise significant across many domains of social work (Ní Raghallaigh, 2011; Coulter, 2014) and comes to the fore when considering the rituals and practices of dealing with loss and bereavement. As Cacciatore and DeFrain (2015) show, in their exploration of bereavement and loss in Korea, Kenya, Brazil, Romania and Australia, with Native American communities and in the context of different religions (Jewish, Muslim, Christian), critical awareness of the interplay between personal, universal and culturally specific and indigenous responses is crucial.

As people get older, they can experience multiple losses, and a physical move to a residential home results in loss of place, attachments, connection, familiarity, friendships, proximity to family and grandchildren, and many other key factors that impact on a person's health and wellbeing. Loss can also be experienced as a disconnection from previous activities and regular routines. With reference to moving to care homes in Iran, Zamanzadeh et al (2017) describe many experiences of older people's transition as losses. These include loss of previous support systems, independence and control over routine and 'communication isolation'. There is also loss for family members, especially partners, children, grandchildren and other close contacts.

Loss caused by a move to residential care can be described as 'disenfranchised grief' (McKenna and Staniforth, 2017), a concept associated with the work of Doka (1989). This loss is not always recognised or acknowledged. Mulvihill and Walsh (2014) applied this theory in an Irish context, referring to the experience of disenfranchised grief in Ireland relating to pregnancy loss. They found that grief experiences were often not acknowledged by family members or health professionals, and this led to mothers feeling 'denied opportunities to publicly mourn the loss of their baby' (Mulvihill and Walsh, 2014: 2300). They argue that 'co-ordination of a holistic and responsive service may be the most effective use of resources and avoids the hazard of either denying or over-pathologising painful, but normal, grief reactions' (Mulvihill and Walsh, 2014: 2303). The key practice learning is the importance of not imposing our own assumptions about loss onto another person, and being sensitive to individual, cultural and family differences in dealing with loss. Particular attention should be paid to religion, spirituality, rituals and practices, taking into account both 'individual' and 'global' culture (Doughty and Hoskins, 2011).

While issues of loss and attachment are key in relation to the impact of a move to institutional care, there are many other intersecting themes from the literature that can be mapped ecologically. These include:

- The impact of trauma on the person and their family (see McKenna and Staniforth, 2017, in relation to New Zealand) (micro–meso level).
- The importance of family support (Cury et al, 2019; Scheibl et al, 2019) (micro–meso–exo level).
- The gap between physical and psychological transition and connectivity (see Koppitz et al, 2017, in relation to Switzerland) (PPCT).
- The importance of multidisciplinary and interagency working (exo level).
- The range of safeguarding issues, as discussed in Chapter 3 and developed by Starns (2018) regarding the English context (micro–meso–exo level).
- Ageism and lack of empathy reflected in policy-making (see McKenna and Staniforth, 2017, regarding New Zealand) (exo–macro–chrono level).
- Ethics of care as derived from 'feminist ethics of care' that challenges notions of 'care' associated with dependency as opposed to being 'part of our nature' (Lloyd, 2006: 1184) (macro–chrono level).
- Marketisation of care, as discussed in Chapter 1, from a neoliberal perspective, where care can be critiqued as being about pushing too much responsibility onto the personal carers in a family instead of providing public resources (macro–chrono level).

Indeed, the complexity inherent in these themes reiterates the importance of students, new graduates and experienced practitioners to have frameworks such as the one used here to map and identify, from the range of themes, what is most significant in any one situation, and how one might respond. In the 'Tips for critical ART in practice' at the end of this chapter, a summary of how the issues map onto an ecological framework in relation to the five framework themes is provided using a case example. The reflective exercise that follows, on ethics of care that impact on interactions at all levels of the ecological model, also helps to expand this work further.

Disruption caused by severe child abuse and neglect

The question of how to balance support and protection is central to many child welfare systems. The importance of social protection internationally is emphasised, for example, by UNICEF (2020) that takes particular account of the impact of child and family poverty, and is directly linked to the UN's 17 SDGs. Texts such as those from Gilbert et al (2011) and Merkel-Holguin et al (2019) provide comprehensive overviews of child welfare systems in a number of jurisdictions, showing varying degrees of orientation from support to protection within a broad children's rights framework that influence policy formation and development (see also Lonne et al, 2020). The need for an ecological approach in child welfare is well established. While each country has its own history and diversity across its ecosystem (Gilbert et al, 2011), globally the centrality of family support, prevention, early intervention and participation practices is recognised (Daly et al, 2015; Malone and Canavan, 2018). Public health approaches that emphasise multidisciplinarity, community and wider welfare responses are likewise recognised as urgently required to ensure early identification and responses to child protection and welfare issues (see, for example, Daro, 2016, 2019; Lonne et al, 2019, 2020). There is strong evidence of the need for a differentiation of responses to child welfare with regard to individual micro-level issues and wider macro-level issues, such as poverty and inequality, as discussed earlier (Bywaters et al, 2018). Child welfare responses must also have, by necessity, an intergenerational perspective that balances children's and parental rights (for example), set within a lifecourse viewpoint in recognition of the potential impact of child abuse and neglect across a person's life trajectory.

As a contribution to the wealth of analysis available, we focus here on a case inquiry report from Ireland, the *Roscommon Child Care Case*. We refer to this case to illustrate how our framework can enhance an approach to understanding and responding to disruption of development caused by long-standing child abuse and neglect. The inquiry report, published in 2010, had a pivotal impact on public and professional awareness and responses relating to child welfare and protection in Ireland (Gibbons, 2010). It related to a case in a county in the West of Ireland with a mostly rural population. Since the report was published in 2010, major changes have occurred in the Irish system (McGregor, 2014), including the establishment of the Irish child welfare system (Tusla), constitutional reform to strengthen children's rights and implementation of a range of measures to improve both family support and child protection services (Burns and McGregor, 2019). In the current Irish system, two practice models are in place aimed at mediating the balance of support and protection. The practice model, called 'Meitheal', emphasises the responsibility of everyone involved in supporting children and families to focus on working together in partnership with the child as central – the aim is for prevention and earlier intervention with families in need or at potential risk (Rodriguez et al, 2018). The model is structured to operate outside the child protection system and is being implemented alongside Signs of Safety® (Turnell and Murphy, 2017; see also Keddell, 2014), a model of child protection now used in a number of jurisdictions. This offers great potential to deliver a more comprehensive response to child welfare in terms of balancing support and protection (Malone et al, 2018), especially if developed within an ecological perspective with an emphasis on networking, as proposed by McGregor and Devaney (2020b) in their iteration of a model for practice based on 'protective support and supportive protection'. It is important that you use your own enquiry-based learning approach to examine the orientations of child welfare systems in your own context. In so doing, you can then reflect on how best the balance of support and protection can be managed, using our framework here as one example to develop practice, to specifically inform your practice and critical ART that informs this.

Reflecting back on the case provides an opportunity to illuminate the disruptive impact of neglect and abuse and how best to respond. While there have been significant changes within the system since 2010, this case still acts as a resource for learning for illustrative purposes. We recommend a full reading of the report (Gibbons, 2010) as it provides an in–depth snapshot example of the kinds of issues that come up in many inquiries in the UK and elsewhere at different moments in time. We think the detailed analysis should resonate with similar inquiries in other jurisdictions.

The *Roscommon Child Care Case* opened with the following statement about a case known to child welfare since 1989 (the birth of the first child) through the Public Health Nursing Service and subsequently the Child Welfare and Protection Service:

> On the 22nd of January 2009 Mrs A, a mother of six children, was sentenced in Roscommon Circuit Court to seven years in prison following her conviction for incest, neglect and ill treatment. The presiding Judge, Judge Miriam Reynolds, (RIP) said the children were failed by everyone around them and that she was concerned that, while the former Western Health Board had been involved since 1996, the children had not been taken into care until 2004. (Gibbons, 2010: 7)

On 5 March 2010, Mr A was sentenced to 14 years imprisonment following his conviction on 47 counts of rape and sexual assault in the Central Criminal Court in relation to these offences (Gibbons, 2010: 64).

One of the overall concerns arising from this case was the extent to which too much emphasis was placed on an (optimistic) focus on support to the family to the detriment of sufficient attention to protection of the children. The inquiry report concluded that:

> All the workers who provided services to the family were well intentioned and concerned for the family's welfare, and made genuine efforts to improve the situation in which they lived. However, in the view of the Inquiry Team, they were, with one or two exceptions constantly diverted and deceived by the parents and were unduly optimistic about the parents' ability and willingness to care adequately for their children. (Gibbons, 2010: 69)

> … an ill-defined family support approach was preferred over a child protection approach, even when there was a well established pattern of parental non-compliance and recidivism. Despite the fact that the parents would consistently promise co-operation and then withdraw it, key staff members displayed an extraordinary optimism in their ability to change and a belief that things would get better. For this reason the interventions provided were often not appropriate to need. (Gibbons, 2010: 70)

With regard to sociolegal skills, the report found that:

> … staff lacked the assertiveness to confront the parents appropriately when required and did not adequately challenge them regarding the effect their behaviour was having on the children. In general the Inquiry Team believes that staff did not exercise their statutory authority under the Child Care Act 1991 to protect these children at the earliest possible point. (Gibbons, 2010: 71)

In sum, the case shows the complex balance of *support and protection* involved in such cases and *intergenerational relations* (for example, the older children were expected to take on too many adult or parental responsibilities). The negative impact of persistent neglect is stark (*health and wellbeing*). The parents appeared to have struggled to make the transition to parenthood and the related responsibilities that go with it (*lifecourse events and transitions*). The value, but also the limits, of working in partnership is highlighted, such as the need to be critically aware of tacit compliance being mistaken for partnership working (*civic engagement and partnership*). The case can also be analysed from a power and power relations perspective. For example, the parents used their power to resist intervention using the special protection the Irish Constitution gives to married parents vis-à-vis children's rights at the time. The Irish constitutional protection of parents over children's rights was found wanting in an earlier high-profile inquiry, the *Kilkenny Incest Investigation* (McGuinness, 1993), and was revised following a Children's Rights referendum in 2012 to give more prominence to children's rights and to treat all parents, in relation to issues of abuse and neglect, equally, irrespective of marital status (Lynch and Burns, 2012; Kilkelly, 2016).

The importance of attachment emerges as a core theme. One of the issues addressed in the inquiry report was a concern about social workers' understanding, observation and interpretation of attachment relationships in complex situations such as chronic neglect and maltreatment. We know that attachment theory, and how it relates to the micro–meso level especially, is foundational for informing how we understand the nature, causes and responses to situations where harm and neglect happens within adult–adult or child–adult relationships. Attachment theory is about the nature and importance of relationships. Often in relationships affected by neglect and abuse, there is trust, love, reliance and intense connections between people spatially (in the home, for example), psychologically, emotionally and socially. Originally developed by Bowlby (1969, 1973, 1980, 1988) and Ainsworth (1964; Ainsworth and Bell, 1970) in relation to early attachment relationships, attachment is now applied across the lifecourse and intrinsically linked with identity. While childhood attachment patterns may affect adult attachments, this is not necessarily the case, and with conscious reflection and self-awareness, adults can change and adapt attachment relationships (Schäfer, 2020b). Attachment behaviour is also about protection, and can be described as secure, insecure, anxious, resistant and/or avoidant (see Howe, 1995, 2011; Schäfer, 2020a, b). The importance of a critical understanding of attachment in relation to children and adulthood (for the parents and for the future of the children concerned) is evident from the excerpts quoted below:

> Many of those we interviewed described a strong bond between the parents and the children despite all their difficulties. This was manifested for example by demonstrations of overt affection in the company of parents or great excitement upon reunion with a parent and an excessive and an age-inappropriate clinging by one child to Mr A. A contrary professional view was expressed by GP2 who felt these manifestations could be viewed as abnormal. It is evident in retrospect that the professionals involved did not recognise some classic indicators of an insecure, disorganised, attachment in the children. (Gibbons, 2010: 72)

> Children may appear to display a strong attachment to an abusing parent but, in fact, such an attachment is disorganised and insecure, as it is virtually impossible for a child to form sound attachments within a dysfunctional family. In addition, we are also satisfied that, in fact, the children were coached by the parents to give the impression to outsiders that all was well and that this was not picked up by the professionals involved. (Gibbons, 2010: 72)

It would appear from reading this that the balance of support and protection was seen to have been directly impacted by a misjudgement about the attachment bond between the children and their parents. The report has led, in Ireland, to an increased focus on training in relation to attachment, disorganised attachment (Shemmings et al, 2012) and the impact of trauma as a related concern.

While the importance of an ability to observe and understand behaviour and relationship with 'environment', and to appreciate the inherent complexity involved, is clearly illustrated in this case, many additional intersectional factors impacted on the children experiencing persistent and consistent neglect and ill treatment in respect of the wider ecological frame. This case involved an intense array of welfare concerns over the years relating to alcohol consumption, developmental concerns relating to the babies in particular, speech delay and children inadequately dressed and unsupervised. Other concerns included hygiene problems, older children having to look after younger children, children being sent to bed early in the evening, older children (pre-teens) sent shopping for alcohol and lack of stimulation for the younger children. Later in the case, concerns were also raised about the children's involvement with inappropriate (sexual) behaviour and allegations of physical and sexual abuse. The importance of interdisciplinary working is also emphasised. In this case, although many services were involved, they were found to be often working in 'silos' (Gibbons, 2010: 73). Clear connections between neglect and social inequalities were evident (see, for example, Bywaters et al, 2018).

The consequences of disruption and harm to the children involved, for large parts of their childhood, despite many resources and interventions offered over the course of the case, need to be problematised within an ecological framework. The complexity of the case shows the value of breaking down this frame not just to the PPCT levels, but also to specific dimensions of the framework. In the 'Tips for critical ART in practice' at the end of this chapter, we provide the opportunity for a more in-depth interrogation of this case for illustrative and applicable learning for adaptation to apply to other context-specific cases.

Impact of child sexual abuse on adults

Child sexual abuse poses particular challenges for services to address due to the 'secrecy, shame and stigma' often associated with this, and 'the functions of empathy, social support and socialisation, and ecological theories can offer a theoretical framework to deal with these challenges and offer improved guidance for practice' (Dolan and McGregor, 2019: 173, see also Martin and Allagia, 2013; Lefevre et al, 2019; Papalia et al, 2020). In the 'Recommended resources' at the end of this chapter, we refer you to Pearce (2019) for an up-to-date comprehensive overview of responses to child sexual abuse and exploitation. The development of multiagency responses, such as that provided by the Barnahus model (Johansson et al, 2017), is an indication of significant developments and improvements in this field.

Here, we focus specifically on the impact of child sexual abuse on adults with an emphasis on disruptions in the lifecourse. Sexual abuse was one of the many forms of abuse and neglect reported in the Commission to Inquire into Child Abuse Report in Ireland in 2009, known as the 'Ryan Report'. This report exposed the systemic abuse of children within former institutions provided by religious orders and subsidised by the state (see also Raftery and O'Sullivan, 1999). Adults who suffered abuse as children report recurring nightmares, disrupted identity issues, an impact on adult relationships and many social and emotional effects, showing that the impact of childhood abuse, throughout a lifecourse, can be profound. Reflecting specifically on the impact of childhood abuse and family violence on adulthood, this can often be linked to mental health needs, as discussed by Xiang and Han (2020) in relation to their study with Chinese social work students. Individual and unique for all, with some 'surviving' and others thriving in spite of those experiences, the need for greater recognition and attention to the impact of childhood abuse in adulthood – whatever the nature and source of that harm – is clear. This includes the need for attention at micro–meso level to empathy, compassion and commitment to direct social work and at exo–macro level to the urgent need for policies and laws that enable disclosure and closure if possible, as studies in Ireland have shown (Mooney, 2018).

Sometimes people are adults when they come forward to disclose child sexual abuse. From a lifecourse perspective, it is essential we recognise the importance of adults who experienced abuse in the past having support from the micro (practitioner empathy, attitude and willingness to support) to the exo–macro (clear and robust policies and laws), not just for their own health and wellbeing, but also to ensure the protection of present and future children. In Part I, we talked about the importance of history in understanding and critiquing the present. This is not just general history, but also people's own histories. As individuals in our respective environments, we carry our histories with us through our lifecourse, with different moments having a particular relevance at different times. Reflecting back to lifecourse mapping discussed in Part I, the importance of such an approach with adults who disclose child sexual abuse seems particularly relevant.

While prevention of sexual abuse occurring should be the priority, we must acknowledge that we may not be able to do this, but we can do a lot to learn about the range of responses available to current and retrospective disclosures (Pearce, 2019). This includes being critically aware that child sexual abuse can be one of the most disruptive experiences for an individual, often with lifelong consequences. Despite our public awareness of such a range of forms of sexual exploitation by individuals or groups (trafficking, paedophile rings, internet abuse, child pornography and institutionally sanctioned abuses), prevention, detection and criminal investigation in many jurisdictions is alarmingly lax. As on-the-ground practitioners, we should not be overwhelmed by the enormity and power of these forms of exploitation, but rather, we should identify, from each of our own personal professional positions, how we can use our micro–meso-level practices to critically engage, challenge and expose exo and macro systems that act as a barrier, or, worse still, facilitate and collude with such abuses. We do this through our sociolegal practice aimed at supporting and protecting at exo and macro levels as well as meso and micro levels. This includes interactions through legal, criminal justice systems and sociolegal practices, as discussed in Chapter 8.

Summary

It is a lifelong endeavour to keep up to date with the range of factors that can lead to disruptions that will need interventions for children, young people and adults, and we could discuss many more examples in this chapter. A critical ability to walk the 'tightrope act' between individual and structural issues is needed, as discussed by Parker and Ashencaen Crabtree (2020a: 97). Ongoing commitment to enquiry-based learning and critical ART is essential. In considering disruption as a core theme, we need to be careful not to reinforce the problem of early theories of personality, behaviour and cognition by focusing too much on the person-in-environment rather than on the impact of the environment on the person. In Chapter 8, we pay particular attention to practices at the exo and macro level for this reason. We provide a range of examples, including community and social development and sociolegal practice, with further critical consideration of the use of the ecological model with an emphasis on networking.

Recommended resources

Child sexual abuse

For a comprehensive overview of perspectives on child sexual abuse and exploitation, we recommend Jenny Pearce's *Child Sexual Exploitation: Why Theory Matters* (2019).

Links to the *Roscommon Child Care Case* are discussed in: www.tusla.ie/uploads/content/Publication_RoscommonChildCareCase.pdf

The Barnahus model (www.barnahus.eu/en) was inspired by the US Child Advocacy Centre Model (www.nationalchildrensalliance.org/cac-model). It was developed in the Nordic countries (Barnahus comes from the Icelandic word for 'children's house') and has been adapted in a number of other countries, including Ireland, where it is being implemented as the 'One House Model'. For a detailed and critical overview of the Barnahus model, see also Susanna Johansson et al's *Collaborating Against Child Abuse* (2017).

Child welfare orientations

The books listed below examine the nature and orientation of a range of child protection and welfare systems that give an insight into the balance between support, protection and children's rights:

Neil Gilbert et al (2011) *Child Protection Systems: International Trends and Orientations.*
Lisa Merkel-Holguin et al (2019) *National Systems of Child Protection.*

Tips for critical ART in practice

Learning from child abuse inquiry reports regarding balancing support and protection within an ecological context

Tables 7.1–7.3 illustrate the analysis of some sample aspects of the *Roscommon Child Care Case*. You may prefer to select a similar inquiry from your own jurisdiction and adapt the critical analysis we outline below to help inform reflection and thinking about implications for your practice. This can also be adapted to examine some of the other themes discussed in this chapter.

Four periods were identified in this case. Table 7.1 examines some issues arising at different levels of the ecosystem with reference to one of these periods by way of illustration, Period 3.

Table 7.1: Illustration of some issues arising in the *Roscommon Child Care Case* through an ecological lens

Ecosystem examples		Period 3: July 2000–02
Person		This can relate to reflections of individual issues for the mother, father, the various social workers directly involved and the impact of this
Process		Duality of support and protection (see Table 7.2)
Context	Micro	Focused on complex mediation of support and protection including a number of formal case conferences (see Table 7.2)
	Meso	Some focus on bonding and attachment in assessments and observations
	Exo	Issues raised about organisational recording of key decisions relating particularly to the decision to change from a Care Order to a Supervision Order (see Table 7.2)
		Many intersecting issues being addressed, although none directly in relation to treatment for the alcohol issues until Period 4, when the parents agreed to engage with an addiction counsellor (Gibbons, 2010: 65)
	Macro	Use of the Constitution to defend rights to family privacy – highlighting the Irish societal imbalance of parents' rights (based on marriage) over children's rights
Time	Chrono	A greater prominence of children's rights was developing in policy and practice during the course of this case
	Moments	The inquiry report highlights many moments of interventions by social workers and/or case conferences where a more direct focus on a particular issue (eg protection needs or alcohol treatment interventions) might have resulted in a different type of intervention

Notes

Table 7.2 maps out some of the processes applied in the four main periods of the case as presented in the inquiry report (Gibbons, 2010), with regard to the balance of the duality of support and protection. The case shows how the emphasis between protection and support changed during the different periods of the case. Some details are inserted from the report for Period 3. This is not a complete analysis of this period but rather, examples are provided for illustration. When reviewing the report, you can complete other sections of the table that are blank to develop your own analysis.

Mapping the case onto the other five framework themes, and by way of summarising and concluding this section, Table 7.3 highlights important key issues to inform critical thinking.

Table 7.2: Duality of support and protection: illustration of the process of balancing support and protection in the *Roscommon Child Care Case*

Period	Practical/social support Family support interventions	Sociolegal mediation	Court system/criminal justice system
1 1989–95			
2 1996–July 2000			
3 2000–02 (this period shows the greatest vacillation between support and protection)	Home help services	Response to further allegations of neglect from concerned neighbours/relatives, concerns regarding care of the children, high alcohol consumption, inappropriate behaviour involving the children	High Court challenge to 'voluntary' shared parenting
	Home management advisory service		Parents argue it is being imposed on them
	Public health services	Planning for shared parenting (voluntary) with relatives (parents told if not possible, Care Orders were the alternative)	Supported by organisation to pursue issue under Irish constitutional primacy of (married) parents' 'imprescriptible and inalienable' rights
	Speech and language	Childcare worker support	
	Assistance with housing application	Relatives approved for kinship fostering in 2001	
		Allegation of child sexual abuse from someone outside family made – investigation found child sexual abuse had not occurred	
		Legal confusion over right to pursue District Court Care Order and awareness of challenge of evidencing neglect for Care Order (Gibbons, 2010: 50)	
		Case conference in February 2002 notes improvements in overall situation, withdraws Supervision Order application	
		Follow-up case conference in September 2002 confirmed the partnership needs-based approach was continuing	
4 2003–04			

Table 7.3: Mapping the themes from the *Roscommon Child Care Case* onto the framework

Theme	Example
Duality of support and protection	Complex process of balancing provision of support to the family and the assertion of protection of the children
	Balance at times was too much in favour of ongoing support even though significant changes in the family circumstances occurred
	Shows the complexity of the law, further complicated in Ireland by the constitutional protection of the married family at the time, and the importance of sociolegal skills in mediating support and protection
Intergenerational relations	Role of maternal grandmother and relatives
	Children expected to do tasks an adult should have been doing (eg buying alcohol, young children babysitting younger children)
	Lack of generational boundaries relating to parental responsibility and children's needs
	Too much responsibility on eldest child to report concerns leading to Care Order
Health and wellbeing	Developmental delays in speech, physical development and emotional trauma
Life events and transitions	Engagement in main life events disrupted due to persistent neglect
	Move of children to care and public awareness of the case
	Transition to parenting did not seem to happen for the couple after the birth of their first child
Civic engagement and partnership	Scope for this was limited mostly because of resistance of the parents to intervention (and some outside support in doing this also focused on the legal rights of family privacy), but there are points in time where cooperation did occur
	While the inquiry report refers to the views of the children, the context of practice preceded the Children's Rights referendum and the many developments since then relating to enhanced participation of children, young people and families in child welfare and family support. For example, the inquiry report findings stated that: 'A significant contributory factor to this failure was the absence of meaningful engagement with the children directly and an over-reliance on parental accounts of their well-being' (Gibbons, 2010: 69)
	Note in the inquiry report about the amount of referrals from concerned neighbours, relatives and a community welfare officer showing community-level concerns. The inquiry report found that these concerns were not treated with sufficient gravity (Gibbons, 2010: 72)

Critical ART relating to move to institutional care: a case illustration

In the following, we provide a summary of how the issues map onto an ecological framework in relation to the five-theme framework using a case example relating to a move to institutional care. We incorporate critical reflection on the ethics of care that affects interactions at all levels of the ecological model.

Case example

Afreen and Inaya are a Muslin couple living in Ireland with Afreen's mother, Kalima, who has dementia. Inaya has no direct family support as she is an only child, and her parents have died. Afreen is from a large family from Saudi Arabia. While managing the dementia for many years at home, and also caring for their own three children, they have come to the point where they can no longer manage Kalima's needs. A residential place has been found, but Afreen is under pressure from his family to maintain Kalima at home. They are both devout Muslims and are strongly influenced by the teachings of the Quran in relation to a duty of children or the young for care for their elders. Afreen's family in Saudi Arabia are against their mother being placed in residential care. They have fallen out with Inaya, who they see as the woman in the family and the person primarily failing in her duties. This has caused relationship difficulties between Inaya and Afreen, and they are in crisis as to what to do. The social worker for the hospital, where Kalima is presently in, due to a fall after going out on her own in the dark, is working with the family to support the transition to residential care.

Reflecting on this case, Table 7.4 highlights some considerations from the point of view of the framework, highlighting issues ranging from the micro–meso (relationships within the family) to macro–chrono (religious beliefs and customs). Critical ART in relation to these issues should help ensure that the assessment and intervention is carried out with the range of eco issues in mind and with attention to the disruption in lifecourse for Kalima, Afreen and Inaya, and their relations with their wider family network.

Table 7.4: Critical ART using the framework in relation to supporting transition to care

Theme	Critical ART considerations
Duality of support and protection	Need for protection and support for Kalima is evident and social and family support is no longer sufficient to address this. The risk of harm has been deemed to outweigh the potential for support in the community and institutional care is deemed necessary by the health team ADD other issues:
Intergenerational relations	Afreen and Inaya feel obliged, as the son and daughter-in-law, to continue to care for Kalima. The family also reinforce this obligation influenced by micro–meso factors and macro–chrono factors, all influenced by dominant beliefs based on religion and culture. There is a need to consider the intergenerational relations within the family system as well as critically considering the wider social views on intergenerational relations in accordance with the Quran ADD other issues:
Health and wellbeing	The health and wellbeing of Kalima, Afreen, Inaya and their children need to be considered. Health and wellbeing connects with protection and safety. The dominance of the expectation of care from Inaya especially seems to outweigh her wellbeing and interests. Ethics of care can be used to think critically about the gendered nature of caring (Lloyd, 2006) reinforced by religious beliefs that construct the normative role and responsibility of caring as Inaya's responsibility. This is reinforced from the micro (eg relationship with Afreen) to the meso (wider family views) to the macro and chrono (cultural and religious beliefs). How the institution identified can respond to the caring needs of older Muslim people, who will be a minority in an Irish context, needs to be explored ADD other issues:

(continued)

Table 7.4: Critical ART using the framework in relation to supporting transition to care (continued)

Theme	Critical ART considerations
Life events and transitions	This is a disruption for Kalima that is also disrupting Afreen and Inaya's relationship and their relationship with their wider family network. While Afreen and Inaya are going through what we may call a 'natural' lifecourse change, which many Irish families experience, the particular cultural and religious considerations in this case require specific attention ADD other issues:
Civic engagement and partnership	Afreen and Inaya are from a minority ethnic group in their Irish community. While they have friends with older parents experiencing similar issues, they do not have Muslim friends and feel isolated and misunderstood when sharing their concerns with their peers. The lack of opportunity to critically discuss issues in the context of the Quran, for example, could be addressed through exploring networks of support for Muslim families. Networks for Inaya are especially important as she seems to be isolated within the wider family network and her small informal network. Critical reflection with Inaya, with particular attention to gender perspectives, needs to be done in partnership ADD other issues:

Parental mental illness

Case example

Mian and Dave live in rural Scotland. Mian has schizophrenia and regular periods of hospitalisation. Dave cares for the two teenage children, James and Jane, but they have all been acting out recently. The family do not talk about the mental illness outside the home. There is a great deal of embarrassment from Dave and his family, and the children have internalised this. Mian is violent when she is ill, and all of the family have experienced beatings but they keep this to themselves, knowing that it is not her but the illness. When Mian is hospitalised, they tell their school and friends that she has cancer.

Complete Table 7.5, or apply it to another case of your choice.

Table 7.5: Case illustration of parental mental illness

Persons	Support and protection	Lifecourse and transitions	Intergenerational relations	Civic engagement and partnership	Health and wellbeing
Dave	Needs parental support	Regular disruptions	Has Dave wider family/parents/siblings? Impact of role of carer on wife and children	How can he engage in wider society for own wellbeing, eg parenting group?	Attend to possible stress, sleep deprivation, own mental health
Jane and James	Need support and protection from risk of harm	Regular disruptions	Greater responsibility from a young age. Are there other support figures?		
Mian	Support regarding ability to protect and parent when home	Regular disruptions	Impact of dependency and its effect on relations with the family		
You	Your awareness of responsibilities to balance support and protection – eg beatings have been disclosed but not reported	How can you help to support management of disruption using lifecourse tools?			
Critical ART	Place reflections in an ecological context. Analyse the dynamics, risk and protective factors	Reflect back to theories and evidence about lifecourse and disruption	Think about the impact on children with parents who have schizophrenia – what does the research say helps?	What is different about civic engagement and partnership in other contexts? Reflect on how each person can maximise their citizenship in society – not just development and protection but active participation	Many factors affect health and wellbeing of families with parental mental illness as this chapter discussed. Think about stigma in particular, analyse findings relating to this and think about how you can address this in this case

8

Activating the framework at exo- and macro-level interactions in practice

Introduction

In this chapter, we focus further on activating our framework specifically with exo and macro levels of the ecological context. With regard to wider engagement with the exo and macro levels, we begin with a discussion about our well-established and advanced practices in the fields of community work, community development and social development from which we can draw. We then consider some of the opportunities and challenges to developing expertise in sociolegal practice within the areas of mental health and criminal justice practices (by way of illustration) as a means of mediation and interaction with exo- and macro-level concerns. We then recap on the ecological approach, and propose networking as a particularly useful approach to help move from more general to specific interactions across exo and macro systems. The overall intention of this chapter is to expand and enhance the capacity for social work to operate effectively in interactions across the ecological system levels.

Community and social development as exemplary practice

Community and social development, community work and community education are core strands of social work alongside individual and group work approaches. We use the term 'community and social development' here, although note the important critical differences between community work, education and development and their complexity. Larsen et al (2013) provide a thought-provoking discussion on community work and participation specifically, and how this has developed historically. They remind us that community work and community organisation is an age-old practice across many societies, which social work and related professions became involved with from the mid to late 19th century onwards. The beginnings of community work in social work are often associated with Jane Addams in Hull House in Chicago (www.hullhousemuseum.org/about-jane-addams). Larsen et al (2013) also highlight the central role of Paulo Freire's *Pedagogy of the Oppressed* (1968) in terms of influencing emancipatory participation practices. Citing Sewpaul (2013), they argue that his contribution has been particularly significant in linking micro-level educational methods with wider social change. Using Freire's work, Larsen et al (2013) assert the fallacy of disconnecting the micro from the macro. Other important international influences identified are Mahatma Gandhi in relation to practices in India and more broadly in Asia, and Nelson Mandela in relation to practices in South Africa.

Community and social development is diverse and multidisciplinary, and involves both professionally qualified practitioners, laypeople and volunteers. Social work makes up some of this workforce to different degrees across jurisdictions. For example, in Ireland and the UK, it is less dominant as a site for social workers to practice, whereas in South Africa, South America and in some parts of Asia, it is prominent. This is an immense field of practice and expertise in its own right that we expect students will be studying in different modules and across programmes. Here, we briefly comment on how the principles and practices of community and social development are so central to informing the advancement of practices across all domains of social work to inform how we interact more assertively with the exo and macro contexts of the individuals and families we are working with.

As discussed in Chapter 9, one debate about community work and development and social work is the scope there is, especially in jurisdictions where it is the minority strand of practice, to achieve the ideals and principles of community work within the realities of practice.

Cheetham and Hill (1973: 346), for example, reflected on this many decades ago in the UK context, and concluded that:

> The community worker, like many other social workers, may be committed intellectually to fundamental political changes and yet be unconvinced of the likelihood of these. His contribution may therefore be limited to improving marginally the circumstances of some of the most deprived, and this often only by compromise. Inevitably, he is faced with a gap between his personal ideology and his working principles. It is possible that the problems of living with the gap leads community workers to hope for more from their activities than is realistic.

This comment remains relevant in the present day, and resonates with other arguments we have made in the book about the extent to which social work can address the wider structural factors that are so impactful on people's lives. Community and social development offers principles and ideologies, as well as concrete practices, that can be applied in mainstream social work. There are many examples of successful social work practice within the field including practice led from academia. For example, Westoby et al (2019) report on a partnership between academics and social and community practitioners that led to the development of a Popular Education Network (PEN). They argue for the radicalisation of community development through 'combining education, organising and linking to progressive social movements' (Westoby et al, 2019: 2207).

Community and social development as a method provides an excellent example of the necessity for international co-learning and cooperation to observe where it has been most effective and influential. As Sewpaul argues: 'effecting change will depend on our ability to build alliances and bridges across similarities and differences; to network across borders; and on joining and supporting global social justice movements' (2013: 226). In doing this, as highlighted by Sewpaul and Larsen (2013: 233), we need to remain mindful of the 'North–South power dynamics' with regard to Eurocentric and 'Western' knowledge forms versus other global, local and indigenous knowledge (discussed further in Chapter 9).

With regard to the 'mainstreaming' of ideas, specific attention to community and social development principles enables wider critical application of our framework. For example, in relation to *support and protection*, a community and social development approach allows for greater attention to doing this work through harnessing informal (for example, mentoring) and formal (for example, community services) supports and partnership working (for example, with the police and local court services) in also protecting and addressing justice issues. Sociolegal practice has scope for further development within a community development context, although we have further work and research to do to advance this element. In addition, the networking approach, adapted from McGregor and Devaney (2020b), which we discuss below, aligns with the community development principles of collaboration and partnership working. Communities follow *lifecourses*, and much of social work operates in contexts where communities and societies are in *transition* due to influences such as conflicts, wars, civil unrest or corrupt governance. It is often through community-level engagement that *intergenerational relations* can be best addressed. For example, Cramer (2019) explores intergenerational trauma in the context of Rwanda. Chaskin et al (2018), in relation to the UK and Ireland, highlight a sense of disconnection between marginalised youth and adult-designed and operated systems. As McGregor et al (2020) comment, reporting on this study, 'Young people are frustrated with not having more influence on decision-making and with being treated more like citizens in the making rather than active citizens with important and insightful contributions to make' (2020: 965).

Regarding *health and wellbeing*, community approaches to health inequality are far-reaching in community and social development as well as in the field of health promotion. Backwith and Mantle (2009) demonstrate how community-oriented social work relating to health inequality in Cuba was relatively more successful in maintaining health than has been the case for social work in more wealthy countries such as the UK. Moreover, with regard to *civic engagement and partnership*, the core of the approach is underpinned by principles of community engagement, cooperation and cross-disciplinary practice. Citizenship practices are key here. As Lister (1998: 16) has argued, the 'concept of citizenship offers social work a framework which embraces anti-poverty work, principles of partnership and an anti-discriminatory or oppressive practice, and an inclusionary stance'. McGregor et al (2020), reflecting on how social work can become more focused on citizenship-based social work, argue that civic and political engagement 'can be mainstreamed as a specific transformative approach to practice ... in different social work settings such as community work with greater focus on the notion of citizenship and use of outreach and street social work practices' (McGregor et al, 2020: 964; see also Hill and Laredo, 2019).

In Chapter 9, when reflecting on the paradigms for social work, we will return to the discussion on community and social development, which has most often been presented as offering the best mechanism for more radical-oriented approaches in social work. What follows in advance of this is a discussion of other ways to advance our critical interaction with wider exo and macro factors by revisiting our discussion on sociolegal practices. As we have already argued, sociolegal practice includes mediation between the meso–micro-level contexts and interaction with the exo (for example, organisational policy) and macro (for example, legal system).

Revisiting sociolegal practices in mental health and criminal justice

Parton (1991) described the historical development of child protection and welfare social work as representing a shift from 'medicosocial' to 'sociolegal' from the mid-20th century onwards. This history also relates to medical and psychiatric social work that was one of the earliest strands of social work to professionalise in Ireland, the UK and the US in particular (Skehill, 1999). The medical and psychiatric social work role involves mediation between social models and medical and psychiatric models of intervention. Mental health social work practice fits well into a socio-ecological frame (Reupert, 2017) taking into account a range of social factors (Golightley and Kirwan, 2017). Social workers often carry an explicit mandate for sociolegal practice under mental health legislation relating to detention and decision-making capacity, although there is great diversity globally regarding who carries this role and how it is integrated with clinical and support services. There has been much debate for many decades about the ethics and dilemmas of involuntary admission to psychiatric hospitals (Szasz, 1975), and the implicit social control function associated with detention and capacity has, in some jurisdictions, meant social workers have been reluctant to engage (see Butler, 1995, in relation to the Irish context). This field of practice is well established in the UK. The role of approved social worker in mental health has existed since 1983, and was extended in 2007 to other approved practitioners, including psychologists and nurses (Stone, 2019). The best interests assessor is a related example of an explicit sociolegal responsibility (Hubbard, 2018). Morriss (2016) asks whether this legally obligated work is 'dirty or prestigious'. She highlights the assumption that the role of social control inherent makes this 'dirty work', but through her study with social workers, she shows a much more complex and nuanced understanding of the care–control role emerging. This concern shows the importance of thinking about practice with regard to power and power relations. The idea of 'dirty work' suggests a focus on the negative views of power as opposed to considering how power can be used creatively, positively and assertively in the practice of sociolegal work.

Reflecting back to the framework, awareness of the complexity of sociolegal practice can be enhanced. *Support and protection* can be framed in mental health legal interventions within the theme of coercion balanced with the promotion of civil freedom. Knowing the risk of dehumanisation of the person with mental illness and the stigma attached when it comes to detention, the importance of practices that promote *civic engagement and partnership* in a holistic way is key. As Wilberforce et al (2020: 1324) found in relation to mental health service user perspectives on social work, one of the positive qualities identified was that 'the social worker thinks about my whole life, not just my illness'. Recovery and strengths–based approaches that underpin mental health social work focus on *health and wellbeing* while acknowledging serious mental illness and its effects. *Intergenerational relations* can be considered in terms of infantalisation of those who have diminished capacity, and the way in which roles as adults, parents and partners can be eroded with policies of restriction. The experiences of mental health coercion can have a life-changing impact on *life transitions* – those who are detained often experience stigma and exclusion that sets them on a new path, which is sometimes difficult to come back from and into 'mainstream' society.

The decision-making role of social work in this context is complex (McDonald, 2010). It is often shared with multidisciplinary groups such as psychology, occupational therapy and nursing. It also interfaces with powerful psychiatric and medical discourses and discourses of the law and legal system. Stone (2019) examined practices in relation to the Mental Health Act 2007 in England and Wales that introduced interdisciplinary responsibilities relating to the law. In comparing social workers and nurses, he found no marked difference in decision-making (for example, in relation to detention), and suggested the differences found may be as much due to individual differences as they were due to professional training and identity (Stone, 2019: 83). Even though not always a social work role, the discipline-specific sociolegal practices and values of social justice, human rights and freedom have much leadership to contribute (James et al, 2017). Even in areas where the social work role is still being developed, as discussed by Negroni et al (2020) in relation to Puerto Rico, the sociolegal expertise of social work in shaping and advocating for practices of least restriction is key. This involves balancing support and protection and engaging with legal systems such as the European Court of Human Rights as well as other national and international frameworks.

When it comes to probation, the sociolegal role is even more pronounced. Probation practice is a stand-alone area of expertise in its own right, as illustrated in the range of themes explored within journals such as *Probation Journal* (see, for example, Carr, 2020). The close relationship between probation and sociolegal social work is significant and long established. Hardiker wrote about social work ideologies in probation practice in 1977 and illustrated, albeit in different terminology, the care–control role that underpins practice. She argued that no ideologies are applied puristically in practice, and that instead:

> Ideologies appear to be mediated by the exigencies of practice, and this may be one reason why notions about "responsibility" and "treatment" appear to exist side by side in social work. Once we examine the context in which social workers practice, it seems we can no longer argue that they go around applying a seductive casework model in a blind and global way. (Hardiker, 1977: 153)

Smith (2005), a few decades later, reviewed the themes of probation covered in *The British Journal of Social Work*, and concluded that 'effective probation practice is likely to be informed by values and skills that are recognizable within the tradition of social work' (2005: 621). Raynor and Vanstone (2016) discuss the separation of probation and social work in England and Wales, and argue for greater alignment of probation and social work, more in line with Scotland and Jersey. In other countries, such as Slovakia (Lulei, 2010) and Romania (Tomiță and Goian, 2009), probation is emerging as a relatively new form of practice, and social work as a discipline is being looked to as a parallel in relation to skills and expertise.

One of the areas of expertise in probation work is professional judgement. Mullineux et al (2019, 2020) examined social workers in criminal justice and their decision-making processes in Northern Ireland. Their study demonstrated the 'value of a psychosocial rationality model of professional judgement, embodying elements of both statistical knowledge and "explanatory" judgement processes' (Mullineux et al, 2020: 813), reinforcing again the sociolegal dimension of practice. The study also shows an in-depth process of decision-making applied in criminal justice social work in a context of the pressure for risk assessments to be as 'certain' as possible. As in the case of practice in other sociolegal fields, they conclude that 'assessment tools need to take into account, not only actuarial measures of risk factors but also the ways in which the probation officer conceptualises the risks in everyday practice' (Mullineux et al, 2019: 56).

Raynor and Vanstone (2016) are critical of some discourses in England and Wales that question the professional value base of social work that informs decision-making, and propose a more simplistic notion of punishment or welfare orientations (see, for example, Narey, 2014). Referring to social work more generally, Maylea (2020) asks a similar question about the social control function in relation to the Australian context. From our perspective, this belies the necessarily sociolegal nature of practice that mediates between subjective potential and objective behaviour (Philp, 1979), and implies a misunderstanding of some fundamental common features of social work and related practices. Conversely, we would argue that probation, criminal justice or youth justice social work is the epitome of sociolegal practice, given its core function of mediating people's subjectivities and potential to change alongside objective criminal behaviours and the advancement of restorative justice (Marder, 2019).

The range of dimensions at micro–meso and exo–macro levels embedded in sociolegal mediation in probation is immense. For example, the way in which parents – mothers (O'Malley and Devaney, 2016) and fathers (Bartlett, 2019) – experience incarceration is important to consider from the point of view of care and control or regulation; intergenerational relations; the impact on children of having parents imprisoned; and the gendered nature of interventions. The experience and higher incidence of certain population groups in prison requires critical interrogation, such as Travellers in the Irish prison system (Gavin, 2019) and people with a disability or mental health issue (Houston and Butler, 2019). The challenges of transition from youth to adult justice systems is another important consideration (Price, 2020). Practice is enabled and constrained by the policies and perspectives of different governments in relation to crime prevention, punishment and control, highlighting the importance of understanding and interaction with the macro level. Where different departments govern social work – this could be Justice, Education, Health, Social Services and/or Social Care – the specific political influences are likewise shaped.

Reflecting on probation and mental health and chrono-level concerns, we need to critically engage with the conceptual and historical debates from criminology, politics, sociology, gender studies and politics. These include debates about the nature of justice systems, prison structures, surveillance and contradictions between care and controlling practices (see, for example, Foucault, 1977). The power dynamics and discourses of professions, including social work, as they sought to develop expertise and authority is another consideration (Cohen, 1985; Rojek et al, 1988). Currently, the greatest potential for transforming sociolegal practice is work that aligns with service users in the proliferation of legislation that, on the one hand, promotes freedoms and rights, and at same time, often fails to deliver in terms of services (Negroni et al, 2020).

To do this, we are reminded of the importance of an ecological perspective that captures chrono themes such as those discussed above, and how these influence interactions across the contexts of micro to macro. At this juncture of the book, we wish to review the potential and limits of the ecological model to help advance our thinking to ensure this layered framework for critical ART enables us to both 'see' (assess), 'respond' (intervene) and critically evaluate at the right point in time and in the person's ecosystem.

The potential and limitations of the ecological model

Throughout this book we have discussed the importance of practice that takes a broad ecological approach. To recap, the following are some of the main points we have made thus far:

- A lifecourse perspective aligns with emphasis on the bio-ecological model, especially with regard to a focus on time.
- The need to challenge the 'neatness' of 'nested dolls', as presented in the original ecological model, has been exemplified by the fact that, in many instances, the 'context' for individuals can mean overlapping or multiple contexts.

- Culture needs to be applied to all dimensions of context.
- The 'environment' of the ecosystem includes not just social but also physical and material elements.
- Aligning the ecological approach with a lifecourse perspective has allowed for more in-depth consideration of the person, for example with regard to the past, present and future.
- Influences such as digital and electronic technology and issues relating to the environment and sustainability are also significant, not just for consideration at the macro or chrono level, but also throughout the context.
- We have used the approach to help us to think more deeply and critically about interactions influenced by transition, disruption and change across context.

Yahya El-Lahib (2020) explores the experiences of people with a disability and immigration, and identifies macro-level factors such as 'ableism, racism and colonialism'. He suggests that 'social work as a profession is implicated in facilitating the operation of such discourses through efforts to actualize opportunity' (El-Lahib, 2020: 1). This relates back to our argument about social work being contested and contradictory. Here is an example of social work being part of the problem within a person's ecosystem rather than offering a solution. We would argue that the ecological approach needs to be explicitly used alongside critical anti-oppressive and anti-discriminatory approaches. This means extending our capacity for promoting advocacy, human rights and social justice in practice. To do this, we need to recognise 'superdiverse' factors throughout the system, such as race, ethnicity, culture, religion, gender, sexuality, class, identity and politics. It is rarely possible for social workers to tackle such complex issues alone. Instead, we need to consider how we can build networks and use networking more extensively in social work practice.

Networks and networking

In this section, we begin by connecting networking to our framework, and then discuss relevant theories and skills associated with this. We provide one example of social network mapping, and discuss networking and social policy and advocacy practice. We then consider e-networking and connections with social capital.

Connecting networking to our framework

Frost (2017) refers to social work as a networked profession. Golightley and Holloway (2020) summarise the many challenges for social work in often-hostile environments. They argue for the building of 'partnerships and supportive networks and seeking out of friends and allies' (Golightley and Holloway, 2020: 303–4). Greater attention to networks and networking can add further critical capacity to the use of the ecological model in practice, especially in relation to maximising the five themes of the framework from a lifecourse perspective. We have already made connections between networking practices and community and social development. Here, our focus is on the use of networking across the wider domains of social work. *Support and protection* practice can be advanced through collaboration with others in our network with whom we are working (formally and informally). A focus on networks with *life transitions* in mind recognises the importance of present, past and future networks that are key to a person's identities and personal resources. This enables the harnessing of *intergenerational relations* and connects with the promotion of *health and wellbeing*. Our overall approach must be framed with a commitment to *civic engagement and partnership*. Networking practice includes:

- formal networking (with other professionals, disciplines and organisations);
- networking through virtual mediums;
- harnessing informally occurring networks that occur through a range of structures;
- networking as a core practice in social work, linked to social support and social capital;
- integration of networking as a core skill for social work.

McGregor and Devaney (2020b) developed a model for practice and supervision in relation to protective support and supportive protection. Their intention was to inform child welfare practice, but we argue it can be used across other domains of social work. They emphasise the importance of:

- context-specific approaches;
- the relevance of a range of actors, practitioner and supervisor expertise through experience;
- proactive partnership-based engagement with children, families and relevant communities in all aspects of service delivery, including evaluation.

Social network theories and skills

McGregor and Devaney (2020b) propose the use of network theory and practice to address the limitations of the ecological model. Social network theory has a wide application in social work and social care (Sharkey, 1989; Timms, 1990; Kadushin, 2012). There is a diversity of areas where social networking is successfully used to support social work interventions, and the following are a few such examples. Francis et al (2020: 122) argue that 'working with women in recovery from substance abuse, actions to build recovery-supportive networks can provide a focus for clinical work to help them become integrated into their communities'. Webber et al (2019) demonstrate how the Connecting People Intervention, based on networking and social capital, can improve social outcomes in the fields of mental health and disability. Colvin and Miller (2018) demonstrate the benefits of interorganisational networking in relation to child welfare. Another study in

Hong Kong, focused on older people, found that social networking helped to overcome stressful life events relating to ageing: 'persons who were continuously active throughout the intervention period experienced considerable increases in self-esteem and sense of belonging' (Chow and Yau, 2018: 907). Herrera-Pastor et al (2019) provide an in-depth illustration of socio-educational network practices in Los Asperones, Spain, to demonstrate the mechanisms involved in the leadership of a network aimed at addressing a range of intense socioeconomic circumstances at exo and macro levels affecting a community living on the outskirts of Málaga in an under-resourced and marginalised community setting (see also Ruiz-Román et al, 2019). Through networking, social workers can enhance culturally sensitive practice through working with intercultural mediators (Genova and Barberis, 2019).

While there are many evidenced benefits of taking a social networking approach, there are also challenges to collaboration through networking. As McGregor and Devaney (2020b) summarise with reference to Turba et al (2019), professional and bureaucratic authority can cause irritation and difficulties of engagement between different actors. Implicit in examples of networking practices is the need to be critically conscious of power and power relations between different organisations (for example, statutory and third sector organisations), professional groups, individual leaders, lay representatives and the public and community leaders. McGregor and Devaney (2020b: 9) also argue: 'Practitioners need a wide range of skills to identify and protect and support directly through therapeutic or sociolegal work as well as indirectly through agency and organizational structures and related organizations.' Such networking skills include:

- collaboration;
- mediation;
- sociolegal skills;
- advocacy;
- interdisciplinary working with a range of social, welfare and justice services;
- managing power and power relations;
- enhancing public awareness and public engagement;
- social policy practice;
- building social capital.

McGregor and Devaney (2020b) argue that a commitment to developing networking skills also requires the advancement of practice research in social work to engage practitioners more actively in applying and testing different approaches to practice development (as discussed further in Chapter 9). Collaborating together and within the profession to progress knowledge for practice is essential:

> When practitioners form networks, they can develop the perspectives, concepts and categories that are relevant to their needs: By generating knowledge gained from different perspectives, such research would be

> reflexive and well-grounded in specific practices rather than presuming to produce the one right answer to address one pre-described category of problems or methods. (Rasmussen, 2012: 47, cited in McGregor and Devaney, 2020b: 13)

Network mapping

McGregor and Devaney (2020b: 10) argue that an 'emphasis on networks enables the location of specific network activity between workers and service users (micro–meso) and exo and macro "nodes" to address some of the extrinsic factors that have such a great impact'. They provide the map below (see Figure 8.1) to

Figure 8.1: Sample discussion tool for practice development and supervision: networking

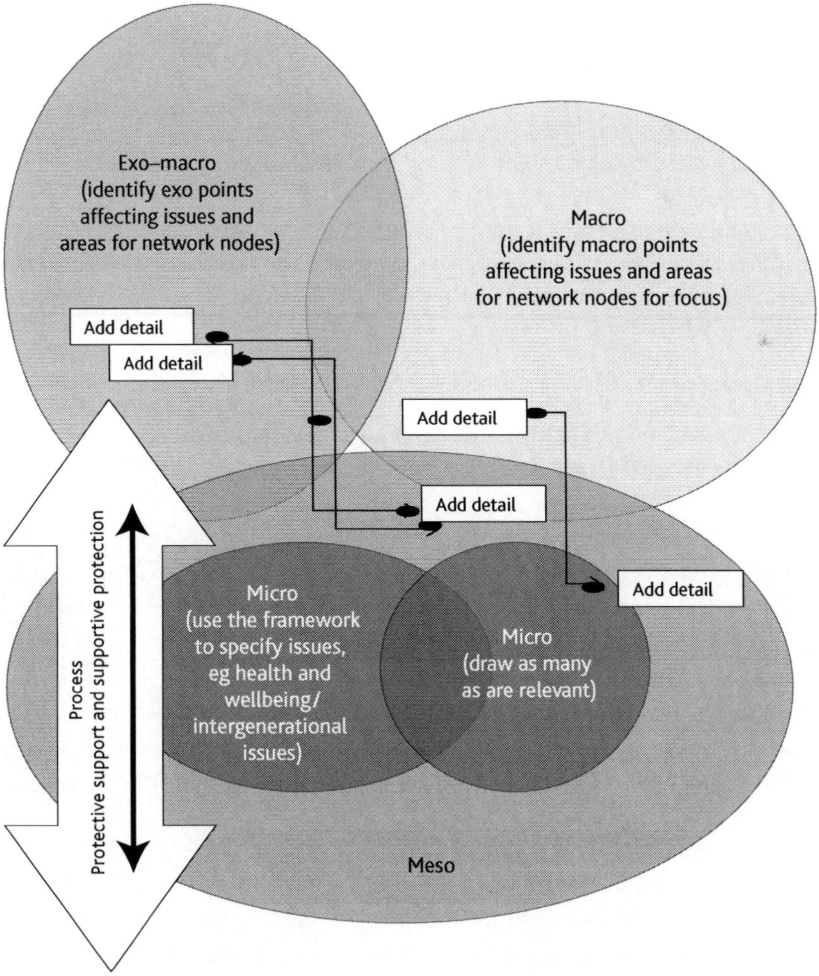

Source: Adapted from McGregor and Devaney (2020b: 15), reproduced under Open Access Creative Commons CC-BY 4.0 license

develop a network plan that 'can be used to target the relevant organization, formal network, campaign group, service user group, and so on to engage with' (2020b: 10). In using this mapping with service users, specific nodes for targeting networking can be identified to advocate, collaborate, seek a service, challenge decisions and so on. Each plan can be drawn specifically, and in partnership, for the individual or collective issue. By specifying key nodes, and prioritising those most connected with the issue at hand, a more focused intervention is possible. This involves critical analysis, reflection and thinking about both causes and possible responses to the presenting issue being dealt with from the perspective of the person(s) you are working with. It should be used as an adaptive and collaborative tool. Networking practice must go beyond critical ART. We cannot just analyse, reflect and think about it; we have to have skills to 'get out there' to do the networking, using, for example, practices of street–level and spatial social work or 'liquid social work', as discussed by Ferguson (2008b). In the 'Tips for critical ART in practice' at the end of this chapter, we revisit a case study from Chapter 6 to consider how use of network mapping can be applied.

Networking, social policy and advocacy

Networking skills include advocacy and social policy practice. In addition to applying and implementing policy and law, social workers use their judgement and professional powers to interact with policy delivery, formation, organisational culture and practices in the development of law and other macro contexts. Southall et al (2019: 8) emphasise the important role of social work in leading policy practice to highlight the 'gap between the profile of the service user in policy and the reality of the people that social workers are supporting in practice'. Montgomery and McKee (2017: 204) provide an example from adult safeguarding in Northern Ireland that highlights some of the features that enhance a social policy approach, which include 'clearly developed local solutions', 'a history of local partnership working and strong affective relationships' and shared ownership and responsibility.

Social policy involves getting actively engaged with policy formation and developed through, for example, the life cycle approach to policy-making, discussed by McGregor and Millar (2020: 2348): 'Through networking and policy engagement at various stages of the lifecycle, the opportunity to speak up, influence up, ask questions and contribute to framing and challenging misframing opens up further the possibility of collective action towards greater social justice.'

Using the generic policy life cycle approach (Cairney, 2012), McGregor and Millar (2020) argue that there is an opportunity for all social workers in practice to engage at some stage of the policy formation process. This ranges from agenda setting (framing an issue) to active participation in implementation depending on where they are working and what role they have (for example, as an on-the-ground practitioner or team manager). Networking through policy practice and advocacy needs to take place through practices of partnership and civic engagement. This can be done through interaction with existing organisations and movements in place to promote the rights and interests of user groups, as Carr (2020) demonstrates in relation to mental health service users. A critical approach to the involvement of service users in service development, planning, design, feedback and knowledge building is essential, as highlighted by Beresford (see, for example, Beresford, 2000, 2009; Beresford and Croft, 2001, 2019). There is a clear need for more alignment of user engagement and participation with practices of civic and political engagement that emphasises citizen-based social work, as discussed earlier. Risley (2014), for example, shows how, in the context of Uruguay, despite many structural political and nation-state factors that limited the potential for civic engagement, child welfare advocates were successful in using civic engagement to advocate for and achieve rights-oriented changes to child protection policy and law. Risley (2014) found two important ingredients to this success: building successful alliances through which advocacy work could be developed, and a focus on how issues were 'framed' within the specific sociopolitical context.

E-networking

The potential of networking through e-processes and digital mediums requires particular consideration. The COVID-19 pandemic in 2020 and 2021 has led to a massive shift towards online and digital practices (Lavalette et al, 2020). This remains a relatively new challenge and opportunity for social work (Kirwan, 2019; Somerville and Brady, 2019). There are clear concerns about the risks of the use of social media, especially regarding children and young people (Willoughby, 2019). However, the benefits are also immense. Chan and Ngai (2019), with reference to social work in Hong Kong, illustrate the benefits and challenges of using technology to network and support based on their research with service users. For example, they found online communication led to a 'disinhibition effect' and online 'status indicators improve service accessibility'. They also found that communication was facilitated especially through facilitation of 'feedback loops'. At the same time, communication was affected by 'incomplete communicative modalities' that 'may cause misunderstanding' (Chan and Ngai, 2019: 157).

LaMendola (2019), discussing the work of husITa, an international virtual association, demonstrates how effective social technologies can also be used to sustain community development in social work. Brown and Dustman (2019: 185) refer to the 'nearly unlimited opportunity to foster networked relationships using technology to connect adults and youth, neighbours and community partners, services and clients'. They make a compelling case for the proactive use of technology as a tool to enhance networking practices and community mobilisation. The potential to create more public awareness about social issues, such as domestic violence, is another key practice of networking that the use of social media could enhance (Nistor, 2019).

Social networking and social capital

Social network theory has wider applicability linked to theories relating to social support, as discussed earlier, and to social capital (Houston, 2019). Regarding social capital, this relates to social connections and networks between people (membership). It is based on principles of shared norms, trust and reciprocity. Early definitions described it as 'the ability of actors to secure benefits by virtue of membership in social networks or other social structures' (Portes, 1998: 6). Social capital is created by people's actions, and is not located in individuals, organisations, the market or the state, although all can be involved in its production (Bullen and Onyx, 2005).

Social capital is conceptualised as a resource to action, rather than the action itself, and has been closely connected to a wider understanding of the connection between social networks of support and resilience building (Dolan, 2006, 2012). By using the concept of social capital, we can explore further the benefits of models of civic engagement, which entail individual and collective actions to address issues of public concern. Sometimes, because people are viewed as living with adversity, it is assumed that they are not in a position to contribute to society but a commitment to a civic engagement approach belies this. Civic engagement in youth who are experiencing adversity has been found to be particularly effective. This was highlighted in the UN *World Youth Report* of 2016, where youth civic engagement was classified as beyond just political engagement but also included social, economic and even positive moral/ethical civic engagement (Dolan and Brennan, 2016; see also Chaskin et al, 2018).

The benefits to youth who are active citizens or leaders is well proven (Redmond and Dolan, 2016). It can provide respite from their own problems, and provides positive reinforcement that despite experiencing challenges, the young person is a valuable asset to society. It highlights how the young person can contribute to supporting the plight of others, thus becoming aware of how others face issues in their lives. While civic engagement has been measured strongly within the model of positive youth development, its resonance for working with younger children as civic actors should not be overlooked; many emerging models on child participation connect this (Lundy, 2007). Equally for adults under stress, the benefits of their potential for volunteering, getting involved in projects and enterprises, and being civically engaged in their communities are immense.

By using the concept of social capital, we can move to the notion of civic engagement that involves individual and collective actions to address issues of public concern. This approach promotes a partnership practice. Two types of social capital relevant here are bonding and bridging. *Bonding* is characterised by dense, multifunctional ties and strong but localised trust. The effects of bonding social capital in a community may be both positive and negative – by keeping the community together, but preventing people from networking with outsiders. *Bridging* is characterised by weak ties and a wary, limited trust of strangers. Studies such as those by Granovetter (1974) have shown that it is 'weak ties' with strangers that are more useful in job seeking than the strong ties of family and friends who tend to know the same information as the job seeker. A study by Sabatini (2006) showed that stronger bridging and linking social capital was associated with higher incomes. It is therefore important to distinguish between the different types of social capital and what they are needed for. Woolcock and Narayan (2000) argue that localised bonding social capital operates as defensive strategies against poverty, but that real development requires a shift to looser networks. A shift from 'getting by' to 'getting ahead' requires a shift from bonding to bridging networks. In relation to the connection between social work interventions and aligning social work practices with a strengths–based perspective (Saleebey, 1996), a key function for the social worker lies in distinguishing between these two positions. Within the model of resilience building, 'getting by' social capital connects to *surviving*, and may be the best option for an intervention at a given time, for example in the immediate aftermath of a family crisis. The 'getting ahead' approach connects to being resilient and *thriving*, and entails social work support that enables not just overcoming a crisis but also doing better than expected and over time (Masten, 2001).

Summary

We have considered a range of approaches that can be used to direct interactions and action at the wider exo- and macro-level system. While some forms of practice will be directly designed to operate within this space, such as community and social development, practitioners across the domains of social work can be more proactive in their engagement with the environment within which the people we work with live, often within contested and complicated relationships and interactions.

Recommended resources

For further reading relating to participation and community development, we recommend Anne Karin Larsen et al's *Participation in Community Work: International Perspectives* (2013).

For further information on networking, we recommend Caroline McGregor and Carmel Devaney's 'A framework to inform protective support and supportive protection in child protection and welfare practice and supervision' (2020b), and encourage readers to review the appendices in particular to inform your own practice reflections.

Tips for critical ART in practice

Advancing Amira's case study using the networking discussion tool

Return to Amira's case study in Chapter 6. In this, we proposed that readers could develop this exercise or use one from their own context. In addition, we suggested:

- *Preparation*: use an enquiry–based approach to collect basic information about the Syrian conflict, the resettlement programme referred to, the local Direct Provision centre and other relevant information.
- Focus on Amira and Jamal, the *people* affected by this.
- Recognise your role (*process*) as offering support and protection.
- Reflect on *context* to determine the most significant interactions or needs for support to address (see Table 6.1).
- Focus on *time* to appreciate the key moments in the family's life that may have been significant (for example, time spent in a previous refugee centre).

Table 6.1 outlined issues to consider at each level of the ecological map. Take the 'new beginnings' section for illustration. Use the mapping process to specifically identify the supports that are needed. Note them on the network map. Discuss the interactions you will engage in, with the family, to access the support service identified. In relation to 'mediating' the support organisations, specifically name the organisation and people you can engage with to support Amira and Jamal. Can you physically go there to meet someone?

The eco map identifies but does not problematise the Direct Provision conditions or the fact that the family were referred to child protection when it was more of a case for support in extreme conditions outside the family's control. Draw your own version of the discussion tool. The following are ways to consider using this to specify and clarify actions:

- A network node to specify at the exo level is interaction with the manager who referred the family, to inform him of the outcome and to ask about conditions and possible changes in this.
- At the exo level, direct engagement with the resettlement programme provides a scope for advocacy for this process to develop.
- Making contact with a specified person within an advocacy group who speaks out about Direct Provision is another possible exo contact:
  - for Amira and Jamal to raise critical awareness of their experience; and
  - to connect them in interactions to facilitate their own possible engagement in advocacy through an organisation.
- This could also lead to the creation of networks with others experiencing similar situations, and collaboration in relation to addressing this.
- The macro level may seem far away, but for the asylum-seeker, the legal processes that control their daily existence, such as long delays in Direct Provision, have immediate and intense effects. Either through the advocacy agency, or directly, identify a route through which the family can be supported to express concern about processes and delays, how they can be made aware of their rights in accessible and understandable language rather than distant and often difficult to understand official terminology (even if they are familiar with the English language).

- Also at the macro level, find out if the relevant department – for example, the Department of Justice – has policies relating to anti–racism, dignity and human rights. Is there a person designated as responsible for this? If not, ask why not. If so, find the policies, and share and discuss them, and identify an action node in the network. What other agency (for example, the Refugee Agency or Council) can be contacted by the family or by you?
- Remember that for this family, there are overlapping networks, the 'new beginning' and the home that was left behind in Syria. There is reference to broken networks with friends left behind. This is likely to be having a detrimental impact on their health and wellbeing, which can, in turn, affect the ability to parent and support. With digital technology, it may be possible to re-establish those connections and facilitate regular online video or phone calls. If necessary, seek out digital support such as a phone or laptop. Find a network node for this:
  - Can the organisation provide this? Who will you contact?
  - Ask the manager, does the Direct Provision centre facilitate communication? If not, why not? Can it? Will it?
  - Is there a local charity that assists with technology for those who cannot afford it?
  - Is this a small campaign you could instigate to raise funds locally or seek contributions of devices from family and friends?
  - Is there a public awareness job (a letter to the local newspaper to raise the issue – is there a local journalist who shows an interest?) to highlight the challenge for families in Direct Provision with almost no income of their own, to have a basic tool of communication to stay connected with family and friends in their home countries?
  - Ask questions about who is responsible to help maintain basic rights to family life for people in Direct Provision. Do some research about this and highlight it to supervisors, colleagues, peers and advocacy groups.

Reflection on the framework

As the final chapter in Part II, we encourage you to reflect back on the framework from your own experience. Table 8.1 summarises some key considerations to connect to your own practice examples.

Table 8.1: Key considerations to connect to your own practice example

Theme	Summary	Select a practice example – how can you apply this in your critical ART?
Protection and support	Sociolegal practice is fundamentally about balancing protection and support in the context of the law, policy, person and processes of interventions	
	Networking as a practice can create a wider range of opportunities for support and protection, ensuring the focus is not just on micro–meso–level interactions or individual rather than wider sociostructural factors	
Life transitions and events	Sociolegal practice is often most central at points of change in a person's life	
	Social networking is an approach that can be used to maximise interactions and support as well as to advocate, challenge and collaborate with key organisations, people and resources to support transition and life event challenges	
Intergenerational relations	Importance of attention to complex intergenerational relations in sociolegal practice	
	When network mapping, bear in mind the maximisation of interactions across and between generations	
Health and wellbeing	If practice can be developed to interact more proactively within people's contexts and networks, the potential for greater wellbeing is clear in terms of helping to overcome structural barriers such as poverty and marginalisation and to work on partnership	
Civic engagement and partnership	Practice must be underpinned by this. While in the past, we may have relied more on theories that impose analyses on a person's life (discussed further in Part III), in the present, the 'theory' and 'target' of intervention should come from partnership working and a commitment to maximising an individual's citizenship rights and engagement	

PART III

Bringing it together

Part III has two chapters, as listed below. Its intention is to bring the learning together and to offer a revised commentary on frameworks for social work theories and their application to practice and the process of learning developed in the book and used in the module associated with it.

Chapter 9 explores practical ways forward for social work knowledge and theory. We critically review the wider context of social work theories and knowledge production and application. We discuss the theory and paradigms of social work, and reflect on the reality that no amount of academic theory and knowledge development alone will address some of the profound structural factors that impact day-to-day practice, past, present and, most likely, into the future. We have sought in the book to offer a framework that can give a holistic frame for critical ART, and suggest that this could become a constant that can be used to frame whatever paradigm, approach or method is being used. However, we recognise that this is insufficient – there is a need for more active participation of practitioners and service users or members of the public in developing theories and frameworks informed by experience and practice. Those who use and deliver services are ethnographers of their worlds, and we urgently need to rebalance our knowledge production to give more space and power to these domains. We conclude with a suggestion that it is as much the mode and principles of learning that we bring to this process as it is the processes involved that will affect the level of transformation possible.

To bring the learning from the book together, and identify ways forward, Chapter 10 begins with a commentary under the theme of critical ART that binds the book back to the opening chapters, and emphasises the role of the learner and the practitioner in critical ART in practice. We reflect back on our framework to provide signposts of where we need to go next in relation to the quest for ongoing critical analysis, reflection and thinking about social work. We consider how we can maximise your practical application of the framework to aim towards best outcomes for children, young people and adults. We discuss the leadership role social work can play in response to this commentary. We end with our own final reflections and acknowledgements, and set out some signposts as to the direction of our own future learning.

9

Practical ways forward for social work theory and knowledge

Introduction

An underpinning assumption in this book is that social work is necessarily a complex set of dualities. It seeks to regulate and liberate. It is perceived as a beacon of rights and justice and as a regulator and reinforcer of societal norms. It has moments of great achievements in the past, alongside 'horrible histories' (Ferguson et al, 2018). The dilemma of social work is that it is a socially constructed phenomenon that promotes itself as committed to progressive social change while it draws from conservative intellectual sources (Witkin, 2017). Social work operates within a context of neoliberalism that can turn potentially progressive notions such as empowerment into an individualised rather than a structural focus. Conversely, the movement towards greater emphasis on civic engagement, partnership with service users and democratisation of knowledge within current postmodern conditions has opened up greater scope for social work to critically engage at both individual and structural levels towards transformative practice.

In social work literature, questions are asked about whether social work is more about being 'servants of a "sinking titanic" or actors of change?' (Jönsson, 2019), and 'is social work at war, and if so, who or what is the enemy?' (Golightley and Holloway, 2020: 304). Alternatively, 'is it about protest?', as Shokane and Masoga (2019) ask in relation to social work in South Africa. The question of whether we are at the 'end of social work' has also been posed (Maylea, 2020). While these are important questions to ask, we are of the view that they give insufficient attention to the fact that balancing the duality of 'care' and 'control' in social work is the very *nature* of the strategy. As discussed throughout the book, this duality has many manifestations and is associated with the question of the extent to which social work regulates (to protect, for example) and supports. In terms of individual interventions, we have discussed how social workers are typically faced with an objectified individual – such as a person who has criminally offended – with an objective legal mandate to intervene. Alongside this, they have the job of promoting the subjectivity of that same person, for example assessing the person's capacity to not offend in the future and understanding the factors that led to the offending behaviour. Philp (1979) calls this the 'creation of subjects' or identifying 'potential sociability'. To advance this duality, we have used the ecological model to break down the 'social' so that we can identify different levels and interactions to guide and target our mediation with individuals and the social environment (ecosystem). It also places the subject more assertively in the context of their wider environment through a lifecourse lens. We have proposed networking specifically as a way to ground and advance this work as a means of harnessing specific points in the ecosystem to target for support, advocacy or critique and challenge.

Keeping with the assumption of social work as being about 'mediation in the social', this implies social workers have expert knowledge – sometimes referred to as 'psy expertise' (Ingelby, 1985; Rose, 1985, cited in Skehill, 2003). It has been argued that this 'expert knowledge' 'ascribes the social worker certain powers to mediate and govern within their particular space in the social' (Skehill, 2003: 142). As Philp (1979), Cohen (1985) and Foucault (1977) argue, professionals, such as social workers, have the power to 'classify' a social problem and an ideal response. This important classification of social issues and responses 'is arguably one of the purest power deposits at the disposal of professionals such as social work' (Skehill, 2003: 153).

As we suggest and discuss below, we need further critical ART on the nature of knowledge and theory for social work to find new ways of classifying, understanding and responding to social issues. We can reflect on how we can use our power positively to influence future knowledge production for social work (for example, testing and critiquing different methods and theories). Specifically we believe there is untapped potential for the profession to move away from defensive approaches to expand the scope for practice and public-generated knowledge and theory, not just to the benefit of social work, but as a matter of social good.

With this in mind, the next section examines the theory and paradigms of social work. We highlight the dilemma that no amount of academic theory and knowledge development alone will address some of the profound structural factors that affect day-to-day practice past, present and, mostly likely, into the future. We consider how we can advance knowledge in and for social work through more active participation of practice educators and practitioners, and following this, the co-production of knowledge with service users or members of the public. We conclude with a suggestion that it is as much the mode and principles of learning that we bring to this process as it is the processes involved that will affect the level of transformation possible, with reference back to our framework.

Theory about and for social work

Theory and practice

As stated from the outset, we should not look to 'theory' to guide practice, but rather reach from practice towards different 'theories' that can be used to inform this work. In order for theory to be effective, it has to translatable and usable in the day-to-day working life of a social worker. Using our framework to scaffold how we approach practice, we promote respect for the lifecourse of each person as unique, connected between generations and ecological systems. This implies a strengths–based approach that promotes health and wellbeing, and an approach to partnership working based on concepts of citizenship and civic engagement. It recognises the many ethical challenges and dilemmas involved in support and protection, and places the value of empathy centre stage. It also connects to social work as mediation in the social, in that people's subjectivity can best be promoted if we can empathise with that person and see them as 'subjective' in the context of their own objective behaviour and/or context. This empathy also enacts awareness of a moral responsibility to mediate between individuals and the systems that affect them. It enables differentiation, for each individual moment of interaction, between the need for mediation at an individual level and the need to focus on wider, specific, social factors. This leads to a requirement to consider what specific mechanisms we have to address social factors through practices such as community and social development, social policy practice, networking and sociolegal practice (as discussed in Chapter 8).

A theory, put simply, attempts to explain something. We have focused a lot in this book on 'knowledge theories' that explain about people in their environments. This has included some familiar theories, such as ecological and attachment theory, as well as lesser-used theories, such as transition theory, cultural presence theory and power theories. It is important to have a critical ART approach to social work theories as they are constantly evolving, so we can gain greater knowledge and understanding from research, service user and public engagement and critical applications by practitioners.

Philp (1979: 84) argues that 'beneath the apparent theoretical freedom in social work there is a form, an underlying constitution to everything that is said. This form creates both the possibility of a certain form of knowledge for social work and also limits social workers to it.' He challenges the idea that any knowledge can be individualist and idealist. Instead, knowledge always exists within a specific framework that gives the person or group the possibility to speak about it (Philp, 1979). This is similar to our point about 'scaffolding', to suggest the parameters that shape and inform our critical ART. Paradoxically, Philp suggests, just as individual knowledge does not stand alone, neither does the idea of 'structure' that is related to economic, social and political forms and subject to 'ruptures and discontinuities', as described by Foucault (Philp, 1979: 85). This framework needs to be clearly contextualised within our assumptions about social work theory in as explicit a way as possible.

Paradigms of social work

Social work theories help us to understand *and* respond to issues arising in practice – such as theories about assessments, interventions and outcomes. Different social work theories give rise to different methods. Often influenced by wider social or psychological theory, social work theories imply *a position and a particular belief system*. Resources for 'theory' for social work are immense. They range from core textbooks, such as *Modern Social Work Theory* (Payne, 2016), to books that apply different critical theory or theorists to social work (Gray and Webb, 2009; Garrett, 2018), to the development of practice guidance and to bridge knowledge, values and practices (Houston, 2015). The discipline has a wide range of core theory and methods for social work texts to draw from that is far beyond our coverage in this book, so we encourage you to bring the most relevant core textbooks for social work theory and practice to frame from your own context, to inform your reading and critical ART in this chapter.

The organisation of theories for social work has been a major programme of work for many writing about social work theory, to offer ways to 'organise' and explain different perspectives (McGregor, 2019). When it comes to understanding the core purpose and function of social work, *Social Work: A Reader* (Cree, 2011) is a valuable resource. Viviene Cree (2011) reproduces some original works about social work that are foundational. This includes a chapter from Malcolm Payne (1996) who asked 'What Is Professional Social Work?' He offered a triangular explanation where he put forward a view of social work as either therapeutic (reflexive), social order (individualist/reformist) or transformative (socialist-collectivist) (cited in Cree, 2011: 12). Mark Doel (2012) provides another comprehensive commentary on social work in terms of its past, present and future, providing great insight into early understandings of social work in context. David Howe's *Introduction to Social Work Theory* (2017, 3rd edn) very astutely situates social work within its wider context through the use of the paradigm, as developed in the first edition in 1987. Howe organises theory in terms of its view of social problems, its view of social work (methods) and its view of society. His paradigm framework of theories, derived from Burrell and Morgan (1979), has been influential in contributing to how we understand and differentiate between different social work theories and methods. McGregor (2019) reviewed this paradigm framework in the context of 21st-century social work.

In relation to 'paradigms' for social work, a distinction is often made between 'traditional' and 'radical' approaches or individual or collective action. A range of methods is placed within certain paradigms depending on their orientation. McGregor (2019) calls this 'reform/maintain' or 'transform'. The origin of the paradigms of social work can be traced to efforts to 'organise' social work theory as it grew and diversified from the 1970s onwards. For example, community work is traditionally considered to have more potential to be radical, whereas individual casework is considered to be more about maintenance and individual reform. In the 1970s, the way these paradigms emerged from separate ideologies is instructive. For example, on the one hand, in the UK *Case Con: A Revolutionary Magazine for Social Work* strongly criticised the casework model of social work and called for more critical engagement in radical and revolutionary perspectives (https://libcom.org/library/case-con-magazine-revolutionary-social-workers). On the other hand, social work casework leaders such as Helen Perlman criticised social work for claiming community work practice, describing it as the '"naive megalomania" which has gripped those caseworkers who have "oversold their powers and their purposes", thus, albeit unintentionally, seriously misleading or disappointing their clients and their employers' (Cheetham and Hill, 1973: 331).

We can go back to earlier histories of social work in the UK and US to reflect on the tension between a focus on individual versus wider social context. For example, the dual development of the COS and Settlement Movement, mentioned in Chapter 1, drew from different perspectives on the person–in–environment in relation to cause, effect and response to social and private issues. The argument McGregor (2019) makes is that, on the one hand, these differentiated paradigms remain crucially relevant for the present day. However, they should not be presented as necessarily oppositional and mutually opposed. The following points are developed from McGregor's paper to inform our discussion here:

- While the value of a paradigm framework for social work continues to be relevant to the present day, there is a need for more 'fluidity' between paradigms, as Rojek (1986) and others have argued. This helps to avoid what he calls the 'gladiatorial' rivalry between 'traditional' and 'radical' perspectives' (discussed more below) while still maintaining the coherence of the paradigms.
- All paradigms are open to critique and contradiction. For example, an intended 'radical' approach may deny recognition of individual psychological needs for support. A therapeutic (for example, maintenance) approach should be challenged if individual interventions are offered when wider social factors are clearly the presenting problem.
- While certain methods fit within certain paradigms, this does not mean their intention or potential to transform is fixed. For example, the role of social work as 'maintenance' features as a core critique of individual approaches (Davies, 1994). This holds sway if the actions of maintenance are about 'putting up with' unacceptable social conditions such as poor housing, homelessness, severe poverty or discrimination. But if 'maintenance work' is the approach being used to enable a parent with severe and recurring mental illness to stay out of hospital, continue to parent, live independently and avoid disruptive phases of hospitalisation, this is potentially transformative practice.
- Irrespective of method or paradigm, there are certain constants in social work, such as anti–discriminatory practice, anti–oppressive practice, values, ethics and social policy practice. McGregor (2019) encourages readers to add to and identify from their own practice perspectives further 'constants'. We suggest our five-theme framework within an ecological and lifecourse perspective is another 'constant'.
- It is important to identify the 'constants' as it helps delineate knowledge that pertains to specific methods and approaches vis-à-vis knowledge that is core to the overall mission and purpose of social work.
- While paradigms are more diverse and complex in the 21st century, the value of a paradigm framework persists as long as certain conditions are met. These are:
  – local context must be emphasised;

- it is necessary to broaden the scope away from a predisposition to Western-dominated ideas to take account of indigenous social work globally (Yellow Bird and Chenault, 1999; Gray et al, 2008, 2013);
- include space for certain constants in social work;
- recognise the role of critical reflexivity in activating theory;
- the duality of 'individual versus collective' or 'reform versus transform' needs to be problematised to be less oppositional, as discussed further below;
- it also needs to be revised more significantly to take account of new forms of knowledge from practitioners and the public, also discussed further below.

Beyond 'gladiatorial' positions in social work theory

The critique by Rojek (1986) and McGregor (2019) referred to above resonates with the earlier argument from Philp (1979: 84) regarding competing social work theories: 'Each argues that the other has failed to grasp what social work should really be about. In doing so their stance is essentially idealist for not only do they fail to question their own objectivity, but they also fail to ask what social work actually is.' This tension continues to be a challenge in the present day. For example, McGregor and Millar (2020) argue that:

> One step towards greater clarity is to move beyond the bifurcation of social work between "traditional" and "radical", "individual" or "collective" or "critical" and "non-critical". The division seen in some literature (see, for example, Webb, 2019; Payne and Reith-Hall, 2019) seems to falsely divide present day social work. (McGregor and Millar, 2020: 2338)

Frost (2019) makes a similar argument to exercise caution relating to: 'unhelpful and misleading dichotomies' such as 'agency or determinism; practice or theory; sociology or psychology; the internal or the external; the knower or the known' (Frost, 2019: 117, cited in McGregor and Millar, 2020: 2338). The question for this section, then, is how can we progress social work theory beyond the 'gladiatorial' and yet avoid it falling into unhelpful, over-generalised eclecticism?

It is well established that current global social work demands an approach that draws from multiple layers of knowledge, each valid and significant, from practice, experience, policy and local experience. The paradigms for practice, such as explicit radical social work, remain essential. For example, Kamali and Jönsson (2019) show, in a special issue on revolutionary practice, how the profession maintains a role of operating critically in relation to political, social and environmental challenges. The journal *Critical and Radical Social Work* provides many examples of proactive and politically engaged practice. The scope for radical practice is largely influenced by the context a social worker is operating within. A person working in a policy context can make use of the practices of lobbying, advocacy and political action. A person working in a clinical context may use the philosophies behind radical approaches regarding social disadvantage and the need for social and political change, but their scope for practice will be different. For example, it could include taking advantage of service user mobilisation, networking and partnership with other disciplines to engage community organisations in order to address wider socioeconomic issues. Mulally (1993, 2007) very helpfully distinguished between structural (radical) practice from the point of view of 'inside the agency' and 'outside the agency', which provides a useful distinction to denote the scope and potential for practice depending on the context from which it is being delivered.

Ferguson et al (2018), discussed in Chapter 1, contribute significantly to helping us to move beyond oppositional approaches when thinking about radical practice. Their approach is reminiscent of the influential work of Bailey and Brake (1975), which emphasises humanism, engagement with communities and individuals on the ground and enhancing commitment to promoting human rights and social justice in all domains of practice, both individually and collectively oriented. For example, reflecting back on the discussion in Chapter 8, the emphasis on networking includes scope for the clinical practitioner to collaborate with social workers and a wider range of social and community professionals, activists and volunteers to address wider sociopolitical or economic issues. We need to get out of 'silos' in social work methods and paradigms to recognise the value and importance of principles of community and social development in individual as well as collective practices. The same point must also be said about the importance of interpersonal skills, many developed within individual methods of social work. For example, the importance of relationships, long established in traditional casework (Perlman, 1979), is now recognised as essential across all levels of practice, as reflected in the Global Agenda for Social Work, discussed in Chapter 1. The ability to engage through a range of methods with individuals and groups is essential to inform wider community practices as all involve mediation between person-in-environment from different vantage and engagement points.

Does this position risk neutralising the debates, leading us to a bland form of 'eclecticism'? We would argue, no. It is crucial that we don't see the debate as another gladiatorial event. Instead, we need a blended approach that ensures an adequate use of usable theory, coupled with best practices and programmes all encircled and underpinned by relationship-based working. Frost and Dolan (2021) reinforce this perspective and argue for direct humanistic relationship-based practice that draws on theory that is supported by evidence as the way forward for social work. They further suggest that a more flexible approach that moves away from an over-focus on proven programmes and/or use of rhetoric will lead towards a more purposeful eclectic model of reflective practice and responsive professionalism.

Through our critical ART, we engage with the paradoxes social work poses and experiences to develop a greater sense of community, respect, shared learning, space for debate and a common purpose. We have to acknowledge in this process that the conditions of social work have been continuously problematic and often oppositional. In the 'Tips for critical ART in practice' at the end of this chapter, we outline a number of critical points to consider and debate in relation to supporting students in particular to develop their own approach to theory and its application to practice. This critical engagement is essential because one thing we have to accept is that, despite all the theory and application to practice available to us and to you, we are still grappling with how to address the wider structural and sociopolitical factors that affect so many aspects of day-to-day social work practice. The examples of poverty and neoliberalism are discussed below by way of illustration.

The impact of poverty in a social work context is often merely observed rather than focused on as the target of interventions (see also Keddell and Davie, 2018). McCartan et al (2018) refer to poverty in child welfare as the 'wallpaper of practice'. Boone et al (2019) outline how the work of Nancy Fraser, especially in relation to parity of participation, can critically inform social work practice in relation to poverty. Roets et al (2020) outline ways in which educators can enhance poverty awareness among students. They emphasise the importance of promoting a social justice approach that actively 'takes a stance to their environment and the wider historical and socio-political circumstances' (2020: 1495). They promote a lifelong learning approach that recognises that 'poverty-aware pedagogy requires collective and long-lasting supervision on the frontline individual, organisational and socio-political circumstances' (2020: 1495).

But if we look back to historical discussion on poverty and social work, such as Holman's (1973), it is somewhat alarming for the profession to face the fact that his description of the challenges for social work are so consistent with current debates. For example, Holman argued that:

> The social workers find themselves, unwittingly, in a double-bind situation. They want to relieve poverty but the powers of their departments and their present skills are not sufficient to help in any significant way. The limited role they can perform may bring some comfort to the poor, but at the same time they function to humanize poverty, making it more acceptable to the deprived and to the rest of society. (1973: 442)

Holman's three objectives for social work set out in 1973 ring true for the present day as themes to inform taking a stance and engaging in long-lasting supervision, as Roets et al (2020) suggest above. The fact that these objectives are largely unmet in social work in the 21st century is a stark reminder of the paradoxical nature, scope and limits of social work to practice, as Holman has suggested. The complex and contradictory nature of policies relating to poverty are such that the values and practices of those governing services, vis-à-vis those delivering services, are often at odds. Marthinsen (2019), referring to the problems faced in the present due to neoliberalism, scribes a similar dilemma. Neoliberalism, he says, cannot be blamed for 'all ills' notwithstanding its 'subtle nature' within historical organisational and managerial contexts. Linking back to the discussion in Chapter 1, Marthinsen (2019) acknowledges that this is not simply a matter of conflict between managerialism and professional values. He argues that neoliberalism has compromised social work even more than past welfare state ideologies, because it challenges the very concept of the welfare state by being concerned with investments: 'all investments in people, such as social policy, education and health services, become areas of investment with expectations of return, in line with economic investments as such' (2019: 352). He frames social work in the context of governance in the social, and concludes that:

> In our society social work is one of the expert areas concerned with governing the family, the child and the "social" in general. The paradox of social work becoming increasingly important is that this task does not seem to have the requisite conditions to perform best practices. This is caused by management of these organisations increasingly being preoccupied with systems drawing attention to parts of the work and activities not necessarily relevant to doing good social work. This seems to leave social work in an ambivalent position. (Marthinsen, 2019: 359)

A shared challenge for the profession is how we can avoid a debate in the future that bemoans how 'conditions to perform best practices' continue to elude us. We have already referred to a range of progressive developments throughout the book that continue to strive to rise to this challenge. The importance of critical and radical practices that are focused on achieving structural change mentioned earlier are intensified. Alongside this, as discussed in Chapter 8, other important strategies include community and social development, advancing sociolegal practice, social policy practice, advocacy and networking. Whatever strategy we use, one thing seems clear: to advance social work knowledge that can directly inform transformative practice, greater practitioner and public engagement in knowledge production and analysis is needed within our profession.

Advancing social work knowledge through practitioner research and knowledge production

Practitioners' views about social work in the 'social'

The study of how practitioners in New Zealand perceive their position in the social, based on the work of Hyslop (2013), advances the thesis about social work in the social drawing from work such as Philp's (1979). Hyslop (2013: 201) concludes that the 'key implication of this analysis is that social workers, in their role as mediators in the social, develop insight, and apply knowledge, which is informed by experientially generated understandings of the social nature of knowledge in a particular social and economic context'. In this context, social work is viewed as a 'socially engaged and politically situated balancing process' (Hyslop, 2013: 221). Based on the findings, Hyslop (2013) concludes that practice knowledge comes from social engagement and is 'influenced by the socio-political positioning of social work and social workers' (2013: 199). He argues that social work occupies an 'intermediate/intermediary location' that involves 'mediating, juggling, balancing, bridging' through 'relational engagement' (2013: 199). He also concludes that 'knowledge formed through this process of relational engagement is generated in dialogue with those who are constructed as clients' (2013: 199).

The following section reflects on how we can broaden the knowledge bases in social work more widely to think about how practitioners can contribute further to knowledge production and development.

Enhancing the power of knowledge production by practice educators and practitioners

We know that the professional landscape for social work is in a constant state of change (see Grant et al, 2020) with many challenges for social work education, practice and research (Lorenz and Shaw, 2019). There is pressure on the profession to be seen as responsive to the new and changing needs of the public (and those who experience adversities in particular), communities and societies. Practitioners are effectively natural ethnographers of practice, given that they are closest to these changes and often best placed to evaluate the types and forms of approaches that are most relevant at different points in time. In social work education, practice teachers specifically lead the crucial role of mentoring, supervising and teaching social work trainees and students, enabling them to translate knowledge into practice and educating them about how to look from their practice for different forms of knowledge to inform this. It is within practice education and practice development that our framework has the greatest potential to be applied, critiqued, developed and expanded. The specific expertise of practice teaching and practice learning is an essential additional set of knowledge you need to engage with to complement your learning in this book (see, for example, Doel, 2010), and you should consult those recommended within your own context as essential reading. The depth and range of considerations, way beyond our scope in this book and our expertise, is reflected, for example, in the work of McGovern (2016, 2018), who provides a series of seven books on practice learning entitled *Social Work Placements: New Approaches. New Thinking*, six of which are freely accessible.

In this section, by way of illustration, we wish to focus on our observation that while playing such a crucial role in social work education, it is less typical for practice teachers and educators in our experience to engage in actual research about social work methods and theories, new knowledge production and its dissemination. Throughout the book, we refer to social work educators, which encompasses those mostly teaching within university and college contexts, those teaching within the field as practice teachers and educators and those working across the domains. This includes lecturers, practice educators, tutors and professors. However, we must also acknowledge the inherent power differentials that can continue to exist within and between social work educators in 'academia' and in the 'field', caused by both structural and individual factors. Structural factors relate to the traditional dominance in many contexts – including our own – of academic university or college-based knowledge power over practice and public knowledge production. Individual factors can include our own biases, often based on our own experience of education, between the power of academic knowledge and expertise vis-à-vis experiential and practice-based knowledge and expertise. At a practice level, the desire for a changing nature in social work coming from within the profession is typically more 'organic', built on differing rationales that can range from social justice – the right thing to do – to better practices – doing the right thing in a better way. However, it can be a problematic and contested space, too, because of the demand for more effective practices that comes from public disquiet, policy-makers or media pressures. There are also time demands as practitioners are rarely afforded much time and space to write and research within their practice. This limits and enables the scope for practitioners to be more actively involved in new theory and method developments. We need to find ways to further enhance the power of knowledge production by practitioners and service users to lessen the gulf between the dominant orientation of 'academic' knowledge in texts and peer-reviewed articles and knowledge produced 'outside' academia. While this 'gulf' has, in many contexts, lessened, with greater emphasis on the importance of the impact of knowledge in practice and contribution to community by universities, the work needs to be ongoing in this direction, and for academics within social work, we need to use our power positively to advance this work.

Rasmussen (2012) articulates this challenge well in relation to Nordic social work practice research, making the argument that two 'modes' of knowledge production can be identified in social work. Mode 1 relates to traditional academic knowledge; Mode 2 relates to processes based on a wider range of knowledge sources, including those who practise day to day and those who receive services at a moment or throughout their lifetimes (see also Marthinsen and Julkunen, 2012; Uggerhoj, 2012). It is not that Mode 2 should debunk Mode 1, but rather that we find a way to give more balanced power to the knowledge emerging from practice and service users to inform ongoing theory development that has been predominantly, up to this point, generated within an academic domain. This is not a new issue for social work. Throughout the history of social work education there has been recognition that this education needs to include *both* academic *and* practice elements, and we most commonly refer to it as education and training for that reason. There are many ways that these elements are combined, and we argue the more blended and complementary they are, the better the scope for integrated learning. In the past and present, we have a range of viewpoints about the *extent* to which social work education is balanced towards one (academic learning) or the other (practice learning and training).

The reality is that they are symbiotic – one cannot exist without the other. To attempt to educate social workers by theoretical knowledge alone is as inadequate as attempting to educate social workers in a 'practical way' without this theoretical knowledge. Because social work by its nature is a practical activity, it might be assumed that it can be simplified to focus on basic practical actions, and that education can somehow be fast-tracked to achieve these practical skills. This completely misses the essence of professional social work, where experienced practitioners have had to absorb a range of critical knowledge and perspectives to inform their day-to-day practice. In the application of that knowledge, they skilfully translate it to work in a way that is natural, grounded and practical (that is, usable). Students often return to placement discussing their observations of their practice teacher making the work 'look easy', but this 'ease' comes from the sophisticated integration of various forms of knowledge into their work. For practice educators, having a student is often seen as bringing the benefit of taking time to reflect, to make more explicit the implicit theories, values and knowledge that informs practice. This can likewise be the experience for ongoing supervision that maintains a focus on personal and professional development alongside task-oriented case management and review (Morrison, 2005). Ideally, this process creates safety (McPherson and MacNamara, 2017) for the student or social worker to engage openly, honestly and critically on their practice development that is necessarily informed, explicitly or otherwise, by complex sets of knowledge and theory at all times. As said earlier, we defer to colleagues leading on the specific expertise of practice learning and education to explore this in greater depth.

Here, we want to maintain a focus specifically on the role of practice educators and practitioners in being more involved in active research in their practice. Our interest is in relation to contributing to the ongoing development, testing, analysis and critique of methods and theories for social work practice. Social work, in many jurisdictions, is already well advanced in engaging practice-based research. For example, in Helsinki, Finland, the Heikki Waris Institute 'is a home for innovative practice teaching, research and development of the social welfare sector and social work service practices. It provides a creative, dialogical cooperation arena for students, practitioners, researchers, teachers and service users' (see https://blogs.helsinki.fi/heikkiwaris/what-is-it).

Leading academics associated with this Institute, such as Professor of Practice Research, Mirja Satka (2013; Muurinen and Satka, 2020), have been progressing the field of practice research for some decades. The Salisbury Forum Group published 'The Salisbury Statement' on practice research in 2011, which asserts that:

> A major problem is a mainstream assumption that research leads practice. But research also needs to be practice-minded in order to better study and develop knowledge which emerges directly from the complex practices themselves. Practice research, involving equal dialogue between the worlds of practice and research is important as a concept, since it seeks to develop our understanding of the best ways to research this complexity. It is important at this time in history given that concerns with new accountabilities now converge with

doubts about the adequacy of scientific knowledge as a sole basis for improving practice. (Salisbury Forum Group, 2011: 4–5)

Indeed, social work practitioner research has advanced globally in the 21st century (Serbati et al, 2019; Joubert and Webber, 2020; Shaw, 2020), demonstrated in the evidence of more practitioners doing PhDs and remaining in practice, the organisational development of specific research offices and programmes within their services and increased evidence of partnerships between academic and practice domains reflected in joint publications and research programmes. Connections are being made between participatory research and its impact on social and political change, as demonstrated by Donnelly et al (2019), for example, in relation to working with refugees and older people in Ireland. But more needs to be done. McGregor (2019: 2112) concluded her analysis of paradigms for social work in the 21st century by arguing for 'the need for further global and local research studies that systematically test and interrogate the range of social work theories and practices to progress this project is emphasised' (see also Cox et al, 2021). The implication is that we need to open up more space for critical dialogues. We need to share the power of knowledge with a range of stakeholders, especially practitioners and service users, to advance theories and methods in and for social work practice. Reflecting back to a statement by Olive Stevenson in 1971, we support her view that it is not about acquiring a static 'body of knowledge', but about creating different 'frames of reference'. She argues that:

> It is vitally important that we should not be talking at this stage in our development as if the knowledge upon which we can draw had a shape and clear-cut boundaries – which is what the phrase conjures up in my mind. To change the metaphor; to try and build a social work house on the shifting sands of social science theory is asking for trouble. Social work should probably concentrate on erecting strong, portable, flexible tents rather than houses. (Stevenson, 1971: 225)

Over 50 years on, this requirement remains a priority for the profession, not just in relation to engaging practitioners more in creating, testing and critiquing theory for practice, but also in relation to engaging the public.

Engaging the public in knowledge production

Through a commitment to partnership research and civic engagement, greater scope for research with the public emerges. Citizens must be included in services at a number of levels other than as service users and carers, including decision-making within service delivery, involvement in case planning and in service evaluation, as discussed at various junctures in this book. Many excellent examples of engaging the public, service users and carers in social work education have already been discussed. Our focus here is specifically on how we may advance the involvement and leadership of service users, carers and the public in the actual production of the research and theory itself, as Beresford (2000: 489) argues, calling for an 'inclusive approach to social work theorizing'. In this call, we should also support the development of independent strands of knowledge development, as Beresford asserted two decades ago, but which remain a minority feature of social work theory and knowledge: 'While highlighting the importance of service users and their organizations being effectively included in social work theorizing, it also argues the need for them to have support and opportunities to develop their own prior and separate discussions about theory, including social work theory' (2000: 489).

A co-production approach is important to understand in order to value its purpose as one potential approach. Co-production is typically enabled by many differing professionals and across a range of individual familial and community contexts. For example, in working with people living with an intellectual disability, a co-production model is seen as rights-based, and typically phrased in a mantra of 'Nothing about us without us' (or a similar slogan), whereby upholding the personhood is key to care planning and so on. Similarly, in terms of town planning and community development, the inclusion of citizens as partners with architects has been found to co-produce better housing and improved social capital.

There are some features in social work practice, such as family group conferences (FGCs), which already provide a very promising structure around which such practice–public collaboration in relation to social work knowledge co-production could be built. FGCs have long existed as a progressive model for interventions with children, young people and families in social work (Connolly and Masson, 2014). As a model, they provide a framework where the social worker enables service users, in collaboration with their social support network of family, friends and other positive supporters, to self-develop solutions and contingencies to problems. Although this solution-focused model is age-old and can be traced historically to the Māori tradition in New Zealand, its resurgence in social work practice in the Western world over the last 20 years has been notable (Connolly and Masson, 2014). The FGC model, underpinned by partnership, has the potential to be advanced and used for the co-production of knowledge and theories for practice alongside planned 'solutions' or 'responses' to case-specific issues with service users, carers and the public. One could argue that the FGC model has been the forerunner to newer models for social work practice and social research that are emancipatory and democratic in nature. Their structure and ethos have much to contribute to the development of specific projects based on knowledge testing, analysis and production.

Another possibility for co-production we illustrate here relates to a model of engagement of young people specifically in research and knowledge production, called the model of Youth As Researchers (YAR) (Dolan et al, 2017; Kennan and Dolan, 2017). The YAR co-production model is targeted at young people who are marginalised, disadvantaged, disenfranchised and negatively labelled in research. Support and training is provided for them to become researchers and to create knowledge. The process is simple, yet effective. Youth are invited to come together and identify an issue in their lives that they are passionate about. They receive 'YAR training' from an academic research team from the UNESCO Child and Family Research Centre at NUI Galway, Ireland. This includes training on issues such as developing a research question, quantitative and qualitative methods, sampling, ethics and survey design. The participants, with university ethical approval and supervised by adult researchers from the Centre, go on to complete a specific research study. Rather than produce a written report, they compile a summary with a short video for dissemination to other youth educators, professionals, policy-makers and the public. Irish actor Cillian Murphy supports the project through narrating the videos and supporting many of the youth at the production phase. Examples of projects completed to date include youth in care researching other care leavers on their care experience; LGBTI youth and coping with discrimination; and supporting youth mental health (see 'Recommended resources' for links to these videos).

Importantly from a social work perspective, the YAR approach is both educative and emancipatory, and sits well with a social justice model. At a time when neoliberalism has been having a long-standing impact on children and young people (Satka et al, 2007), and efforts to engage young people in participatory practices continue to exclude, for the most part, those who are most marginalised (Chaskin et al, 2018), this example of youth-led research offers an excellent counterbalance to demonstrate the transformative impact of greater inclusion in research and knowledge production. The ongoing challenge is to continue to develop the programme to ensure it reaches those who are deemed the most marginalised due to societal inequalities. This is just a brief illustration, and using an enquiry-based approach you are encouraged to seek out and identify further examples, with an emphasis on the principles of civic engagement, where transformative processes are in place, to democratise knowledge development and support practitioners and ultimately service users from excellent examples worldwide.

Generally, initiatives such as patient and public involvement (PPI) can be used to advance specifically developed and proved shared knowledge through testing and production. However, this can also be constrained by processes including power and power relations, organisational barriers, inadequate resources or lack of capacity for cooperation, or more simply not engaging with those most marginalised. There is a need to extend, through a civic engagement perspective, greater emphasis on the public, engaging, collaboratively, in testing, critiquing and developing theories that are deemed relevant for supporting people in their environments. Overall, the ideal scenario for the future is where social work practice research and knowledge is characterised as a meeting point for knowledge production between practitioners, members of the public, professional agents, academics, policy-makers and researchers.

Social work as a discipline is well placed to be a leader in relation to advancing co-production approaches. In practice settings, the principles of co-production align well with those of social work in terms of partnership, redressing power imbalances and value-based practice. In academic settings, where greater emphasis is being placed on public engagement with communities to show the impact of research and knowledge production, the social work discipline has much to contribute and lead on, given this ethos. For example, by nature of the work, much research carried out in social work is directly intended to inform practice and policy that aligns our work well with aspirations of making positive impacts in our communities.

However, even though we are well placed to lead on this approach, there are challenges and barriers. One of these barriers is where there is a rift (whether actual or perceived) in the relationship between frontline social workers and service users and the accrued impact of perceived and actual power imbalances in the relationship. The reputation and public perception of social work will enable and constrain the scope of such partnership working, as relations of trust and mutual respect are key. Because social work has the core role and duty of care and control, experiences of the public of social work are always likely be mixed, especially where social work has had to engage families who have not asked for intervention, to regulate as well as support and protect. There is no easy answer to this challenge, although greater public awareness and engagement to articulate the complex, but not incomprehensible, nature of social work seems one critical requirement going forward.

Summary

Theories, paradigms and practice learning alluded to here are core expert subjects in themselves, warranting a number of modules within a social work course. Through to the end, we have sought to complement these resources. We have thought it particularly important to situate our framework and approach within the wider domain of social work theory, knowledge formation, production and application, as part of our intention is to provide an overarching framework for students that can help bind these together in a holistic way. We have also highlighted the urgent need for ongoing expansion and democratisation of knowledge in and for social work. We share the same urgency in our own domain, and consider this ongoing work. Our emphasis has been on the need to expand and dramatically change how we engage with 'knowledge' in and for social work. This is not to denigrate the ongoing value of academic and theoretical knowledge. Conversely, this is essential to uphold evidence-based practice and professional accountability vis-à-vis related disciplines. In the spirit of partnership, where every partner has an equally valuable but different contribution and responsibility, it is the duty of us, within academia, to continue to study, research, critique and distil knowledge for social work practice, just as it is the duty of those in practice to speak back to theories and methods with authority, to ensure they are doing as intended with regard to enabling best practice. We have argued that to achieve greater equality, we need transformation in terms of the power balances between academic, practitioner and public knowledge in and for social work. This is on the basis that all parties have a valued contribution to make, rather than it being seen as hierarchical tokenism in some way.

Recommended resources

Caroline McGregor's 'A paradigm framework for social work theory for 21st century practice' (2019) is freely available and provides a full overview of the 'paradigms' of social work as they have developed historically and how they continue to be relevant – or not – to present-day practice.

Marguerita McGovern's book series, *Social Work Placements: New Approaches. New Thinking*, is recommended as an excellent overview of a range of themes, specifically for practice learning. Access Book 1 at: https://books.apple. com/ie/book/social-work-placement-new-approaches-new-thinking-1/ id1102290962?mt=13 and Books 2–7 at: http://hdl.handle.net/10379/10018

For 'The Salisbury Statement' on practice research, see: https://ejournals.bib. uni-wuppertal.de/index.php/sws/article/view/2

For Youth As Researcher videos, see: www.childandfamilyresearch.ie/cfrc/ youth-as-researchers/youthresearchervideos.

Tips for critical ART in practice

Scaffolding to position our framework within the wider context of social work theory

Review Caroline McGregor's three tables in her 2019 article, showing the development of the paradigms for social work. Draw your own paradigm of practice. How can the framework be used as a constant to frame your critical ART in practice?

Consider the following updated constants for Table 3 in McGregor (2019); remember that it is freely available online to consult, at https://academic.oup. com/bjsw/article/49/8/2112/5368144.

Updated constants (McGregor, 2019):
• Bio-ecological context – PPCT
• Lifecourse
• Values, ethics, human rights, social justice, anti-oppressive practice, anti-racist practice.

Framework constants:
• Support and protection
• Lifecourse and transitions
• Intergenerational relations

- Partnership and civic engagement
- Health and wellbeing.

Key messages to inform learning exercises in class or in supervision on using theory well and developing your own perspective

These are some general points, summarised from this book, that could be used in PowerPoint slides, posters or as postcard reminders:

- Reflect back on the ethics of professional life and your notes on this from Part I.
- Remember, all methods offer 'model solutions for model problems' that need to be activated and delivered by professionals using their expertise in mediation in the social.
- Consider how theories help workers express their orientation to help with reflexive and critical reflection in practice.
- To guide practice and assumptions, ask:
  - What do I think the problem is here?
  - What is the cause?
  - What part has society played?
  - What part has the person played?
  - Where am I in the mix?
- Use paradigm frameworks to explain and justify choices of theory and intervention to other disciplines and service users and groups, but be critical of applying them in too deterministic a way, and be aware of the critiques from literature, such as McGregor's article (2019).
- Critically interrogate collaborative and partnership practice:
  - Who is involved?
  - How do people get involved?
  - Are those with the most power and resources most likely to be present?
  - How do we reach marginalised voices who are most affected by social work?
  - How do we reach out internationally to ensure we don't confine ourselves just to local knowledge?
  - How do we challenge the colonial nature of knowledge? And the Western domination of learning?
- Discuss the theories and methods you are using with people in accessible, not jargon-filled, language.
- Remember that theories will always be insufficient in themselves to guide practice or thinking; your professional judgement, skills and values will activate theories into action.
- Reject simple theoretical solutions – they are not realistic.
- Reject complex practice guidance – it is not implementable.
- Use your professional judgement, knowledge, values and skills acquired through professional training and education.

- See yourself as 'inside', not 'outside', the equation (show empathy).
- Locate yourself and the person, group or community in the environment in a way that recognises fluidity, the moment in time, the diversity and the potential.
- Use mapping and visuals for your own critical understanding and your conversations with those you are working with.
- Distil theory into actionable practice: theory does not drive practice; your practice drives you towards theory using enquiry-based learning and critical ART.
- Acquire and apply the skills of enquiry-based learning to take ownership of your responsibility for lifelong learning.

10

Binding our learning together and looking forward

Introduction

In this book, we offer a framework as one 'constant' in terms of a frame for critical ART to:

- recognise social work as a *duality of support and protection* that should be at the forefront, irrespective of the method or practice approach used;
- emphasise the important temporality of *life events and transitions*;
- commit to an ultimate goal of achieving *health and wellbeing* for individuals, families, groups and communities;
- automatically consider *intergenerational relations* at individual, family, community and social levels in our interventions;
- take an approach based on *civic engagement and partnership*, which assumes that whatever work is being done is carried out by co-citizens, each with a part to play in the process.

To bind together the learning from this book, and to identify ways forward, we begin this chapter with a commentary under the theme of 'critical ART'. We then reflect back on the framework to provide signposts of how to develop our framework, and how social workers can be leaders in this regard. We end with final reflections and acknowledgements, setting out some signposts as to the direction for our own future learning.

Critical ART

We have put forward the idea of critical ART to bring together the core practices of analysis, reflection and thinking to make connections between your practice context and the knowledge that informs this. The following sections provide some final illustrative commentary. In sum, we have argued that critical analysis will allow a balanced appraisal, using a defined approach to collecting evidence to support this. It also helps to weigh up the potential and limits of different approaches in line with the aims and objectives of service delivery and support. Critical reflection is best done with a clear set of scaffolds provided by the different perspectives to identify and embrace critical understandings about social justice and inequality from community and social development theory, for example. This can be applied in every assessment process, with either individuals, groups or communities. In doing this, the focus is on the 'subject', even when attempting to address objective processes and contexts. To illustrate this, we reflect on values below. The next section focuses on why critical thinking is needed on an ongoing basis to question this application, to ask questions about merits and limits, and to consider others' debates about the balance between individual and collective practices. Support and supervision to help continue to develop this thinking as a lifelong expectation of the professionally qualified social work practitioner is essential, and by way of illustration we focus on the use of enquiry-based learning.

Critical analysis

In this book, we have argued for the need for clear and systematic approaches to informing practice that begins with a practice issue or theme and builds back, up and across to seek relevant knowledge, understanding and evidence to help address a question or problem arising from that practice issue or dilemma. Learning from the specific to the general is essential, as it is through the application and insight that we gain sufficient understanding to appreciate depth, complexity and critique. As it is impossible to cover all scenarios, it is necessary to learn through illustration and specific case examples. This gives us the ability to dig deep into an issue, with a well-informed and ethical critical lens that can be adapted and applied to other contexts.

Returning to the discussion on theory in Chapter 9, we encourage you to critically analyse the approaches used in social work, and the wider social theories that underpin them. We mentioned Bloom's taxonomy in the Introduction as a framework for organising the stages of engagement with knowledge. While we emphasise that practice leads theory, at the same time, you also have to know what theory you are looking for. Understanding theory is essential before we consider how it can inform and be applied to practice in real-life scenarios on placement or in a work context. Bloom's taxonomy can be used to identify the 'essential ingredients' for critical knowledge development leading to better practice. Using it in this way can be a form of quality assurance for social work practice. Going through the process of steps, from knowledge to evaluation, ensures and demonstrates that the connecting of practice to theory has been considered, evidenced and well thought out. This is particularly necessary given the lead role social workers have in relation to professional judgement, and being able to evidence and defend this.

Another dimension of critical analysis is to look out for international perspectives as core to practice. While we have sought to consider practice from a range of global dimensions, we have also declared our own limits from the outset in terms of our Western positioning and the limits of scope of any one book. We rely heavily on the enquiry-based learning approach to encourage readers to identify relevant examples in their own contexts that resonate with the themes discussed in this book. With the expansion of digital technology, accelerated during the COVID-19 pandemic from 2019 onwards, it has become more accessible for practitioners, students and members of the public to engage in international conferences, seminars and events, unconstrained by the prohibitive costs of international travel, which remains disproportionately the privilege of academics from developed nations. Going 'online' has had the unintended positive consequence of levelling this field and enabling a more diverse level of participation no longer blocked by economic inequalities. This does not, of course, equal out the playing field sufficiently, because of the reality of digital inequalities too, but it has certainly opened up the scope for more inclusive, international collaboration. We need to build on this to work towards an approach to social work education that does not just include 'international perspectives' as a component of learning or a module but also considers it core to the underpinning basic learning for all social work students and practitioners. This enables students and practitioners to better recognise and understand how the plethora of social forces that affect social work globally impact on practice and on people's day-to-day lives (see Sewpaul, 2013). We also need to find ways to collaborate and share learning (Palattiyil et al, 2019). Transnational social work (Bartley and Beddoe, 2018) offers opportunities and challenges, and the scope for international social work (Lyons et al, 2017) to promote more sharing of learning about methods, approaches and practices between jurisdictions is immense.

Critical reflection: the importance of values

Following on from critical analysis, the extent to which you embrace this quest for knowledge and commitment to an inclusive global perspective will be influenced by your own values, commitments and passion about rights and justice. Indeed, values are core to critical reflection, as we discuss in this section by way of illustration. Whether working from the perspective of being a student, qualified social work practitioner, senior staff manager or educator in the field, there are commonalities for all involved. We have discussed how social work is value-laden in its quest to balance people's rights to both protection and support. To honour social justice and human rights in social work practice we need to have critical connection with our own values and attitudes. One way of achieving this is to consider the role of social empathy and its relationship with social work. Empathy is almost a beguiling aspect of social work practice but this does not mean it is present in practice. A way of ensuring social work practice underwrites empathetic responses is found in our own lives as people outside our work existence. If we consider how we wish to be treated with respect and recognition (Houston and Dolan, 2008), and with those who know the difference between caring about and caring for another person, we can quickly gauge how social work should function as a person–to–person human interaction. This may seem overly simple, but we would argue strongly here that it needs to be. This is part of the social work connection towards ethically binding together our personal life and our professional life. As Howe (2005) has pointed out, our personal attachments to others mirrors our professional capacity to engage and care. The drive for best practice programmes in social work, services that are constantly measured for outcome achievement, albeit for good reasons, can unintentionally undermine or lessen the significance of the core basics of social work values. Relationships are not just important in working with and for others, as discussed at various points during this book; they are the central station from which good social work practice can and does emerge (Ruch et al, 2017). And, as Golightley and Holloway (2020: 304) argue: 'Social work as a profession, as much as individual social workers, must learn to be kind to itself' too.

This view is simple, consistent and long-standing. For example, from his early important publication in the mid-1990s, Ross Thompson (1995) has advocated that social support is the key to preventing familial abuse, including harm to children. He posits the view that social support, with warmth from practitioners through direct work, acts as a core support function that leads to better protection. As far back as the 1930s this 'warmth model' for social work, which includes the capacity to positively admonish service users when needed, but in an inclusive and respectful way, was advocated for by the famous US pioneers of social work, sisters Edith and Grace Abbott (Editors of Encyclopaedia Britannica, 2020). Edith Abbott in particular suggested that such was the importance of person-to-person human connectivity in social work that it was the only route to enable practice that could engage with both advancing personal betterment and also social justice. This connects back to Banks and the idea of the 'ethics of professional life' and the importance of emotional intelligence in social work practice contexts (McGovern, 2016, 2018).

Critical thinking: using enquiry-based learning

An enquiry-based learning approach was promoted in this book as an aid to critical thinking. It has many advantages to defend its prioritisation in social work education. It encourages questioning rather than seeking answers that aid critical thinking, and has been found to enhance harmony and solidarity, leading to tolerance, even among young children (Wahid et al, 2018). An enquiry-based learning approach can be used in a range of learning approaches, from face-to-face, blended learning and fully online. It also supports the use of mobile activities in learning, such as blending visual and audio tools to report on learning, and combining research and discovery as an integ-rated part of the learning process. When fully engaged in such an approach, a module in college or a supervision plan on placement becomes less of a static weekly scheduled process for a period of time, and more a dynamic learning process. A well-developed and implemented enquiry-based learning approach can provide learners with a mechanism for learning that is transferable to other contexts, something to be extended into lifelong learning processes. It is as much a set of principles and beliefs about knowledge and power as it is a set of actions of questioning, investigating, discovering, analysing and applying. It also builds the skills required for practice-led and service user-engaged research. In addition, it can be used to develop practice, such as community walks and mobile activities that enhance spatial practices and networking, as discussed in Chapter 8.

In this book, we have encouraged a pragmatic approach to critical thinking and enquiry, as envisaged by Dewey (1929, 1938). We have encouraged learners to read it with a mindset based on ethics, values, social justice and human rights. We have proffered a framework to scaffold your thinking around five core themes, set within an ecological and lifecourse perspective, with an emphasis on interactions and networking. We have utilised Kolb's model of reflective practice (1984), which complements enquiry-based learning and brings together the core reflective practice tool of 'thinking in action coupled with thinking on action'. Just as a good carpenter knows to 'measure twice and then cut once', it ensures an approach that is not just focused on the outcome of the intervention, but also on the process to ensure good ethical practices were observed. Perhaps even more importantly, using this knowledge distillation and growth model for reflective practice (Dolan et al, 2006; Frost and Dolan, 2021) is more likely to lead to better outcomes for service users. It can also act as a better way of explaining the bona fide intentions on the part of the social worker, who may not necessarily be 'best at all times' but is doing their best.

Return to the framework

It is clear from Chapter 9 that there is much more that could and should be developed in the context of wider social work theories and methods, other possible international perspectives and more emphasis on the connections between values, skills, practice and knowledge co-production. It is also essential in using the framework that we connect it to our own lifecourse as well as using it to engage with others. In this way, we develop our skills of self-reflection and our capacity for empathy and our emotional intelligence. We also experience vulnerability – for example, in presenting how the framework connects to our lifecourse, as we ask students to do on our course – and the opportunity to learn the fascinating ways individuals interpret and respond to the framework as applied to their own lifecourse. We see multiple variations of the lifecourse map we ask students to draw, and are reminded that, notwithstanding all of the 'general knowledge' we acquire about attachment, loss, power, presence and so on, the essence of social work is the capacity to apply that general (objective) knowledge to the specific individual (subjective) context, be that a person, family, group or community. As Philp argues, 'the social worker cannot help but try to create people, subjects, where everyone else is seeing cold, hard, objective fact' (1979: 99).

The framework now needs to continue to be used as a scaffold for critical ART as a way to inform practice. It also needs to be developed and critiqued. For example, we have emphasised the focus on *support and protection* as an important duality that has to be extended to take cognisance of the complexities inherent in practice, from the mediation of informal community supports to sociolegal interventions. The ecological model and networking theory, as developed from McGregor and Devaney (2020b), give concrete suggestions for practical application, but more work is needed to continue to apply, test and evaluate practice to build on this critical framework.

It has been made very clear throughout this book that social work intervenes at key points of people's *lifecourses and trajectories*. This is often at times of transition or disruption. Thinking about practices at these junctures requires wide lenses that capture the social ecology, either through Bronfenbrenner's model or alternative social ecology perspectives (see, for example, Pinkerton, 2011). Reflecting on the lifecourse, and challenging normative assumptions, can go far to address issues of misframing and misrecognition. This fits well with a human rights and social justice approach aimed at getting the balance between recognition, redistribution, representation and parity of participation, as Boone et al (2019 argue.

Intrinsically linked to this commitment to Fraser's parity of participation at multiple levels of justice (social, economic, political and cultural) is a third element of the framework: *civic engagement and partnership*, and the promotion of citizenship. A stronger practice connection between social work and citizenship outlined by Lister (1998) has transformative potential as it enables a discussion about power, equality, parity of participation and citizenship rights. This is more likely to bring the levels of partnership with service users, discussed by Beresford (2000), to the fore. Moreover, in advancing this work, as McLaughlin (2010) argued, we have to ensure we are applying the same rigorous standards of 'scrutiny and critique' in this research and knowledge production through civic and public partnership as we would in any other domain (McLaughlin et al, 2020).

Reflecting on *health and wellbeing*, we need to pay further critical attention to health inequality and health justice. The impact of health and social inequality manifests itself in multiple ways. The need for enhanced multidisciplinary working with healthcare as well as social welfare and policy stakeholders is key (Bywaters, 2009). Wang et al (2020) discuss the health inequality relating to the 'left behind children' in Mainland China. Friedman and Merrick (2016) present a special edition on health inequalities and social work based on the work of the Social Work and Health Inequalities Network (established in 2004) with an emphasis on practices in South America examining the crucial role of social work in tackling health, and associated income, and inequality at micro, meso and macro levels.

We have shown throughout this book how *intergenerational relations* can be both a support and protective factor as well as a cause for disruption and difficulties in transitions. Another dimension of intergenerational relations we have not yet mentioned is in relation to the profession itself. As well as engaging internationally, among other disciplines and groups, we also need to think about how we enhance collaboration between the generations of social work. Experienced (not necessarily older) practitioners offer 'walking histories', and new (not necessarily younger) practitioners offer 'ready access to new ideas' and much more. It is important to reflect back on history to track and discuss some of the core debates that have shaped and influenced social work practice, as suggested in Part I. The potential for leadership from students and newly qualified social workers is also important. New graduates have great potential to exercise leadership as they come into the profession at a time of great challenges and opportunities. As we conclude, we devote the penultimate section to some thoughts of critical actions for social work leadership inspired by some of the discussions in this book.

Critical actions for social work leadership

Writing about social work in Ireland in the late 20th century, Skehill argued that:

> We need to ask questions about how social workers are equipped to manage this grey area in the ever more complex space of the social. It appears that the challenge for social work practitioners and educators is not just one of bringing the social back into social work (Howe, 1996) but also one of bringing social workers back into the social, where mediating appears to represent a unique and defining characteristic and function of the profession. (2003: 154)

This implies a leadership role in asserting the profession within its wider context to establish this position and communicate more clearly the unique role and purpose of social work for mediation in the social. Hyslop argues that it is 'regrettable that social work is not better understood and valued within the policy realm' (2013: 225). Throughout the book, there have been multiple examples of how social work is often perceived to be compromised between the goals and intentions of empowerment and transformation for an individual and the rational, technocratic, bureaucratic and managerialist, organisational, political forces. For example, regarding the principals of personalisation (relating to more autonomy), Ferguson argues that:

> ... given its acceptance of the marketization of social work and social care, its neglect of issues of poverty and inequality, its flawed conception of the people who use social work services, its potentially stigmatizing view of welfare dependency and its potential for promoting, rather than challenging, the deprofessionalization of social work, the philosophy of personalization is not one that social workers should accept uncritically. (2007: 387)

Leadership in social work is something we need to cultivate from the beginning of training, as Colby Peters (2018) argues. She discusses leadership in terms of organisational (this may also link to management, but not necessarily so), relational and individual leadership. While difficult to define, Colby Peters identifies two identifiable features: 'first, that the purpose of leadership is change, or some alteration of the status quo; second, that this change requires the actions of one or more individuals (aside from the "leader")' (2018: 40). It is remarkable when you review the literature on leadership how many of the skills and qualities align with those found within social work influenced by the core values of respect, working in partnership, addressing inequity and challenging stigma and discrimination. Preston-Shoot (2011), for example, discusses ethics-informed leadership in social work. In addition, as Cullen (2013) shows in her study of leadership within a hospice setting, social workers draw from a range of discipline-specific theories and methods to influence the practices of others as well as enhancing their own practice. In relation to the discussion here, the potential for leadership in terms of applying, testing and critiquing theoretical and academic frameworks for practice – including that presented in this book – is immense. While there are great examples of social work transformational leadership within organisations, with service users and in relation to policy, there is a need to continue to advance practitioner and service user-led critical engagement to inform social work theories, methods and knowledge, as discussed in Chapter 9. We have highlighted many such examples of collaborative practice and research in this book, and with the advancement of digital technology, a greater scope for collaboration and access to knowledge and information, the scope to mainstream and make commonplace such partnership practices exists.

As mentioned, the value of working from an international perspective helps us to view the issues and responses not just from within our own context but also looking to the wider international field and building networks and relationships. In our communication about social work, we need to highlight:

- the unique purpose and role of social work mediating in the ever-complex context of the 'person-in-environment';
- its constructive alignment with other social professions;
- its role in enhancing interdisciplinary and multidisciplinary working across all realms of practice (medical, psychiatric, criminal justice, law, social care, education, psychology and so on);
- learning collectively, through enquiry and evidence-based approaches;
- the diversity that is social work, from experts in in-depth therapeutic work to experts in politicised and policy-level practice.

The same recognition of superdiversity applies to those with whom we work. Greater mutual respect, collaboration, sharing of knowledge and using the power of this shared knowledge proactively has the potential to strengthen the overall profession. We are not so naive as to suggest this will 'solve' the seemingly 'unsolvable' problem of greed, discrimination, lack of empathy, abuse of power and persistence of capitalism and inequality that features across nations. Poverty and neoliberalism are just two examples of conditions that prevent best practice, as discussed in Chapter 9. We acknowledge social workers globally who have to practise under oppressive political regimes, in contexts of conflict, violence, sectarianism, apartheid, human rights abuses, discrimination and oppression. None of these situations are 'conditions to perform best practice', but somehow practitioners worldwide strive to do just that. We need to keep working together to figure out how we can do that better for the people we work with, our families and our communities, and for the profession. This requires an understanding of management and leadership from the outset, so that we can understand and critique organisational processes in service users' interests. This can include what may seem like routine tasks such as sharing complaints forms, accurate recording, reporting unmet need, evidencing the impact of cuts to resources, reporting systematically on the impact on rights being denied and so on. We also need to have the skills to 'influence up' (to bring issues to our educators, supervisors and managers) and 'across' (in our networks and with our peers across disciplines and occupations).

Summary

The ethos of learning and assumptions underpinning the framework presented here is aimed at helping students and practitioners to find ways to:

- exert their power through the profession, networks, knowledge, relationships and communities;
- use power positively and well to push back, using the power of law, policy, knowledge and critique;
- use their powers to promote rights and justice in partnership with citizen stakeholders, including those who use services in the present, past or in the future.

Enquiry-based learning requires a collaborative approach. We wish to acknowledge and sincerely thank our students in Galway who have attended our module for inspiring and sparking debates we have rehearsed in the book. The themes and issues illustrated are ones that engaged and connected for us in our collaborative learning. We have emphasised for our students and readers the importance of empathy that leads to self-reflection, emotional intelligence, awareness and a call to action. We have also emphasised the importance of in-depth understanding of power and power relations. In exercising our knowledge power in practice, for example, the 'moments' of intervention matter. Social workers, especially trainees and new graduates, have relatively the greatest power in their direct interactions with the people they are working with. Moments spent in this time have huge potential, to either reinforce inequality (by locating interactions at too micro a level, when the exo and macro factors are so impactful on a situation) or promote social justice (by using their mediation to identify, target and enact interactions with the wider exo and macro systems). Social work students and practitioners have certain powers to decide what to learn and what to apply to their work that impacts directly on the type of service a person gets. The student who has critically engaged, reviewed and sought to understand the breadth of knowledge surrounding their work will deliver a far better service to the people they work with than the student who has passively learned without fully engaging with the debates and dilemmas, and done the minimum (rather than the maximum) with regard to looking up, across and around for knowledge to inform their practice to gain a qualification. In other words, commitment to learning about and for social work is core to the ethics of professional life, underpinned by a moral imperative to be as well equipped as possible to empower, use power positively and challenge negative uses and forces of power.

To do this work, we need to promote resilience within social work while addressing the structural and organisational factors that can make the job difficult to deliver. As colleagues in an Irish study found in a longitudinal study on retention and social work (Burns et al, 2020), the 'staying power' that emerged from the findings was attributed to people feeling a sense of congruence and control over their work. We need to educate and train social workers to have staying power by equipping them personally, professionally and politically to mediate within the social.

As we finish, we see that our work continues to be one 'in progress'. We have sought to offer this framework as a practical approach to social work. This needs to be further activated through ongoing critical engagement within our ecological frame with a diverse range of stakeholders, ensuring those who use services, have used a service and may use services in the future – our citizen stakeholders – are at the centre. We need to continue to work within our own ecological system to develop partnerships in our micro–meso and exo–macro relationships with students, practitioners, their organisations, service user groups and advocates, policy-makers and regulators. We need to identify network points to engage, to promote and to challenge, to advance social work education and enable full participation of a wider range of stakeholders. We need to continue to engage critically and constructively in dialogue and exchange about the range of scaffolding we use to contribute to the lifelong learning process that being a professional social worker demands. From our vantage point, we remain humbly aware of that which enables and constrains us as educators and academics in this regard.

Recommended resources

At this point, your main resource should be your enquiry-based learning skills and abilities. We are conscious that in this book there are many areas of practice that are not covered, and practice within many countries that has not been mentioned. We have encouraged you throughout to develop your own enquiry-based approach, inspired by the illustrative discussions provided. For example, based on how we approached this book:

- Bring in your own experience and knowledge.
- Use the guidance provided in this book or from other sources on how to build evidence, knowledge and understanding (see, for example, Bloom, 1956).
- Find some 'foundational' examples of the theme you are interested in and identify the main authors within the field. Often, finding core textbooks in the relevant subject is the best entry point to this new knowledge.
- Decide on the scope of your enquiry based on what you are seeking to discover. Select your target sources.
- Create an organised system for saving and recording your searches and materials.
- Do 'grey searches' for relevant reports, policy documents and discussion papers.
- Select relevant websites, such as the sites of international social work bodies.
- Discuss the issues you are exploring with peers and colleagues.
- Apply critical ART throughout.
- Apply your material with your code of professional ethics in mind. Be aware of diversity, gender, age, representation, multidisciplinarity and balance in selecting your materials.

Tips for critical ART in practice

This is the final chapter. We are aware of so much more that could be covered, and so many more aspects of social work to reflect on that are beyond our scope. Our final tip for critical ART in practice is to develop this framework for your own context and perspective. It was not intended to be prescriptive, and we have used it in different ways throughout. The underpinning theme is a lifecourse-based ecological perspective within a framework of support and protection. We present support and protection as having four associated themes and have developed these throughout the book. We have emphasised the importance of attention to culture as something that influences the person from the micro through to the macro and chrono, in the past, present and future lifecourse. We have argued that thinking about our work as being underpinned by networking activates and connects our person-in-environment work. We have encouraged an approach that is non-linear, that embraces intersectionality and superdiversity. However, in doing this, we need to ensure that this framework is not so 'busy' that it becomes unworkable or overly complicated. Our message throughout is that you should adapt it for your context and your specific practice.

Figure 10.1 provides a summary overview of the framework that captures the core components you can adapt.

Figure 10.1: Summary overview of core components of the support and protection framework as a practical guide for social work

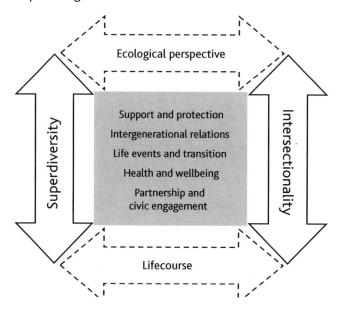

References

Ainsworth, M.D. (1964) 'Patterns of attachment behaviour shown by an infant in interaction with his mother', *Merrill-Palmer Quarterly*, 10: 51–8.

Ainsworth, M.D. and Bell, S.M. (1970) 'Attachment, exploration, and separation: Illustrated by the behaviour of one-year-olds in a strange situation', *Child Development*, 41: 49–67.

Anghel, R. and Beckett, C. (2007) 'Skateboarding behind the EU lorry: The experience of Romanian professionals struggling to cope with transitions while assisting care leavers', *European Journal of Social Work*, 10(1): 3–19.

Áras Attracta Swinford Review Group (2016) *Independent Report of the Áras Attracta (McCoy) Independent Review Group*, Dublin: Health Service Executive (HSE).

Arnett, J. (2001) *Adolescence and Emerging Adulthood: A Cultural Approach*, Auckland, New Zealand: Pearson Education.

Arnold, K. (2013) *State Sanctioned Child Poverty and Exclusion: The Case of Children in State Accommodation for Asylum Seekers*, Dublin: Irish Refugee Council.

Atkinson, C. and Hyde, R. (2019) 'Care leavers' views about transition: A literature review', *Journal of Children's Services*, 14(1): 42–58.

Atwool, N. (2019) 'Challenges of operationalizing trauma-informed practice in child protection services in New Zealand', *Child & Family Social Work*, 24(1): 25–32.

Azzopardi, C. (2020) 'Cross-cultural social work: A critical approach to teaching and learning to work effectively across intersectional identities', *The British Journal of Social Work*, 50(2): 464–82.

Azzopardi, C. and McNeill, T. (2016) 'From cultural competence to cultural consciousness: Transitioning to a critical approach to working across differences in social work', *Journal of Ethnic & Cultural Diversity in Social Work*, 25(4): 282–99.

Baart, A.J. (2002) *The Presence Approach: An Introductory Sketch of a Practice*, Utrecht, the Netherlands: Actioma/Catholic Theological University. Available at: www.presentie.nl/publicaties/item/download/246

Backwith, D. and Mantle, G. (2009) 'Inequalities in health and community-oriented social work: Lessons from Cuba?', *International Social Work*, 52(4): 499–511. doi:10.1177/0020872809104253.

Bailey, R. and Brake, M. (eds) (1975) *Radical Social Work*, London: Hodder & Stoughton Educational.

Ballard-Kang, J.L. (2020) 'Using culturally appropriate, trauma-informed support to promote bicultural self-efficacy among resettled refugees: A conceptual model', *Journal of Ethnic & Cultural Diversity in Social Work*, 29(1–3): 23–42.

Banks, S. (2010) 'From Professional Ethics to Ethics in Professional Life', in D. Zavirsek, B. Rommelspacher and S. Satub-Bernasconi (eds) *Ethical Dilemmas in Social Work: International Perspectives*, Ljubljana: Faculty of Social Work, University of Ljubljana, pp 119–32.

Barroso, N.E., Mendez, L., Graziano, P.A. and Bagner, D.M. (2018) 'Parenting stress through the lens of different clinical groups: A systematic review and meta-analysis', *Journal of Abnormal Child Psychology*, 46: 449–61.

Bartlett, T.S. (2019) 'Supporting incarcerated fathers: An exploration of research and practice in Victoria, Australia', *Probation Journal*, 66(2): 201–18.

Bartley, A. and Beddoe, L. (2018) *Transnational Social Work: Opportunities and Challenges of a Global Profession*, Chicago, IL: The University of Chicago Press.

Beck, U. (1992) *Risk Society: Towards a New Modernity*, London: SAGE Publications Ltd.

Bell, M. (1999) 'Working in partnership in child protection: The conflicts', *The British Journal of Social Work*, 29(3): 437–55.

Bellis, M.A., Hughes, K., Leckenby, N., Hardcastle, K.A., Perkins, C. and Lowey, H. (2014) 'Measuring mortality and the burden of adult disease associated with Adverse Childhood Experiences in England: A national survey', *Journal of Public Health*, 37(3): 445–54.

Belsky, J. (2009) 'Quality, Quantity and Type of Childcare: Effects on Child Development in the US', in G. Bentley and R. Mace (eds) *Substitute Parents: Biological and Social Perspectives on Alloparenting in Human Societies*, pp 302–22.

Beresford, P. (2000) 'Service users' knowledges and social work theory: Conflict or collaboration?', *The British Journal of Social Work*, 30(4): 489–503.

Beresford, P. (2009) *Whose Personalisation?*, London: Compass.

Beresford, P. and Croft, S. (2001) 'Service users' knowledges and the social construction of social work', *Journal of Social Work*, 1(3): 295–316.

Beresford, P. and Croft, S. (2019) 'Reprioritising Social Work Practice: Towards a Critical Reconnection of the Personal and the Social', in S.A. Webb (ed) *The Routledge Handbook of Critical Social Work*, Abingdon: Routledge, pp 511–22.

Bilson, A., Featherstone, B. and Martin, K. (2017) 'How child protection's "investigative turn" impacts on poor and deprived communities', *Family Law*, 47: 316–19.

Blom-Cooper, L. (1985) *A Child in Trust: Report of the Panel of Inquiry into the Circumstances Surrounding the Death of Jasmine Beckford*, Wembley: London Borough of Brent.

Bloom, B.S. (1956) *Taxonomy of Educational Objectives: The Classification of Educational Goals, Handbook 1: The Cognitive Domain*, London: Longmans, Green and Co Ltd.

Bolger, N. and Amarel, D. (2007) 'Effects of social support visibility on adjustment to stress: Experimental evidence', *Journal of Personality and Social Psychology*, 92(3): 458–75.

Boone, K., Roets, G. and Roose, R. (2019) 'Social work, participation, and poverty', *Journal of Social Work*, 19(3): 309–26.

Bowlby, J. (1969) *Attachment and Loss, vol 1: Attachment* (2nd edn), New York: Basic Books.

Bowlby, J. (1973) *Attachment and Loss, vol 2: Separation: Anxiety and Anger*, London: Hogarth Press.

Bowlby, J. (1980) *Attachment and Loss, vol 3: Loss: Sadness and Depression*, London: Hogarth Press.

Bowlby, J. (1988) *A Secure Base: Parent–Child Attachment and Healthy Human Development*, London: Routledge.

Brady, B., Dolan, P. and Canavan, J. (2004) *Working for Children and Families: Exploring Good Practice*, Galway: Child & Family Research and Policy Unit, WHB/National University of Ireland, Galway.

Brady, B., Dolan, P. and McGregor, C. (2020) *Mentoring for Young People in Care and Leaving Care*, London: Routledge.

Braye, S., Orr, D. and Preston-Shoot, M. (2012) 'The governance of adult safeguarding: Findings from research', *The Journal of Adult Protection*, 14(2): 55–72.

Braye, S., Orr, D. and Preston-Shoot, M. (2017) 'Autonomy and protection in self-neglect work: The ethical complexity of decision-making', *Ethics and Social Welfare*, 11(4): 320–35.

Bredewold, F., Hermus, M. and Trappenburg, M. (2020) '"Living in the community" the pros and cons: A systematic literature review of the impact of deinstitutionalisation on people with intellectual and psychiatric disabilities', *Journal of Social Work*, 20(1): 83–116.

Bridges, W. (2002) *Managing Transitions: Making the Most of Change*, London: Nicholas Brealey Publishing.

Bronfenbrenner, U. (1979) *The Ecology of Human Development: Experiments by Nature and Design*, Cambridge, MA: Harvard University Press.

Bronfenbrenner, U. (1988) 'Interacting Systems in Human Development: Research Paradigms: Present and Future', in N. Bolger, A. Caspi, G. Downey and M. Moorehouse (eds) *Persons in Context: Developmental Processes. Human Development in Cultural and Historical Contexts*, Cambridge: Cambridge University Press, pp 25–49.

Bronfenbrenner, U. (1995) 'Developmental Ecology Through Space and Time: A Future Perspective', in P. Moen, G.H. Elder and K. Lüscher (eds) *Examining Lives in Context: Perspectives on the Ecology of Human Development*, Washington, DC: American Psychological Association, pp 619–47.

Bronfenbrenner, U. (2005) *Making Human Beings Human: Bio-Ecological Perspectives on Human Development*, London: SAGE Publications Ltd.

Bronfenbrenner, U. and Ceci, S.J. (1994) 'Nature–nurture reconceptualized in developmental perspective: A bioecological model', *Psychological Review*, 101(4): 568.

Bronfenbrenner, U. and Morris, P.A. (1998) 'The Ecology of Developmental Processes', in W. Damon and R.M. Lerner (eds) *Handbook of Child Psychology, Vol 1: Theoretical Models of Human Development* (5th edn), New York: Wiley, pp 993–1028.

Bronfenbrenner, U. and Morris, P.A. (2006) 'The Bioecological Model of Human Development', in W. Damon and R.M. Lerner (eds) *Handbook of Child Psychology, Vol 1: Theoretical Models of Human Development* (6th edn), New York: Wiley, pp 793–828.

Brown, M.E. and Dustman, P.A. (2019) 'Identifying a project's greatest "hits": Meaningful use of Facebook in an underserved community's development and mobilisation effort', *Journal of Social Work Practice*, 33(2): 185–200.

Bryan, A., Hingley-Jones, H. and Ruch, G. (2016) 'Relationship-based practice revisited', *Journal of Social Work Practice*, 30(3): 229–33.

Buckley, H., Carr, N. and Whelan, S. (2011) '"Like walking on eggshells": Service user views and expectations of the child protection system', *Child & Family Social Work*, 16: 101–10.

Buckley, H., McArthur, M., Moore, T., Russ, E. and Withington, T. (2019) 'Stakeholder's Experiences of the Forensic Child Protection Paradigm', in B. Lonne, D. Scott, D. Higgins and T.I. Herrenkohl (eds) *Re-Visioning Public Health Approaches for Protecting Children*, Cham, Switzerland: Springer, pp 19–33.

Bugajska, B. (2017) 'The ninth stage in the cycle of life – Reflections on E.H. Erikson's theory', *Ageing & Society*, 37(6): 1095–110.

Bullen, P. and Onyx, J. (2005) *Measuring Social Capital in Five Communities in NSW: A Practitioner's Guide* (2nd edn), Coogee, NSW: Management Alternatives.

Burns, K. and McGregor, C. (2019) 'Child Protection and Welfare Systems in Ireland: Continuities and Discontinuities of the Present', in L. Merkel-Holguin, J.D. Fluke and R. Krugman (eds) *National Systems of Child Protection: Understanding the International Variability and Context for Developing Policy and Practice*, Dordrecht: Springer, pp 115–38.

Burns, K., Christie, A. and O'Sullivan, S. (2020) 'Findings from a longitudinal qualitative study of child protection social workers' retention: Job embeddedness, professional confidence and staying narratives', *The British Journal of Social Work*, 50(5): 1363–81.

Burrell, G. and Morgan, G. (1979) *Sociological Paradigms and Organisational Analysis*, London: Heinemann.

Butler, L. and Manthorpe, J. (2016) 'Putting people at the centre: Facilitating making safeguarding personal approaches in the context of the Care Act 2014', *The Journal of Adult Protection*, 18(4): 204–13.

Butler, S. (1995) 'Mental Health Social Work in Ireland: Missed Opportunities', in N. Kearney and C. Skehill (eds) *Social Work in Ireland: Historical Perspectives*, Dublin: Institute of Public Administration, pp 33–50.

Butler-Sloss, E. (1988) *Report of the Inquiry into Child Abuse in Cleveland 1987*, Cm 412, London: HMSO.

Bywaters, P. (2009) 'Tackling inequalities in health: A global challenge for social work', *The British Journal of Social Work*, 39(2): 353–67.

Bywaters, P., Brady, G., Bunting, L., Daniel, B., Featherstone, B., Jones, C., Morris, K., Scourfield, J., Sparks, T. and Webb, C. (2018) 'Inequalities in English child protection practice under austerity: A universal challenge?', *Child & Family Social Work*, 23(1): 53–61.

Cacciatore, J. and DeFrain, J. (2015) *The World of Bereavement: Cultural Perspectives on Death in Families*, Cham, Switzerland: Springer International Publishing.

Cairney, P. (2012) *Understanding Public Policy: Theories and Issues* (2nd edn), London: Red Globe Press

Campbell, J. and Pinkerton, J. (2020) 'Social Work, Social Justice and Sectarianism in Post-Conflict Northern Ireland', in G. Singh and S. Masocha (eds) *Anti-Racist Social Work: International Perspectives*, London: Red Globe Press, pp 113–28.

Campbell, J., Duffy, J., Traynor, C., Reilly, I. and Pinkerton, J. (2013) 'Social work education and political conflict: Preparing students to address the needs of victims and survivors of the Troubles in Northern Ireland', *European Journal of Social Work*, 16(4): 506–20.

Canavan, J., Dolan, P. and Pinkerton, J. (eds) (2000) *Family Support: Direction from Diversity*, London: Jessica Kingsley Publishers.

Canavan, J., Pinkerton, J. and Dolan, P. (2016) *Understanding Family Support: Policy, Practice and Theory*, London: Jessica Kingsley Publishers.

Capous-Desyllas, M., Perez, N., Cisneros, T. and Missari, S. (2020) 'Unexpected caregiving in later life: Illuminating the narratives of resilience of grandmothers and relative caregivers through photovoice methodology', *Journal of Gerontological Social Work*, 63(4): 262–94.

Carr, N. (2020) 'A new decade, some old debates', *Probation Journal*, 67(1): 3–5.

Carr, S., Hafford-Letchfield, T., Faulkner, A., Megele, C., Gould, D., Khisa, C., Cohen, R. and Holley, J. (2019) '"Keeping control": A user-led exploratory study of mental health service user experiences of targeted violence and abuse in the context of adult safeguarding in England', *Health & Social Care in the Community*, 27(5): e781–e92.

Cassel, J.C. (1976) 'The contribution of the social environment to host resistance', *American Journal of Epidemiology*, 104(2): 107–23.

Chambon, A.S., Irving, A. and Epstein, L. (1999) *Reading Foucault for Social Work*, New York: Columbia University Press.

Chan, C. and Ngai, S.S. (2019) 'Utilizing social media for social work: Insights from clients in online youth services', *Journal of Social Work Practice*, 33(2): 157–72.

Chaskin, R.J., McGregor, C. and Brady, B. (2018) *Engaging Urban Youth: Community Citizenship, and Democracy*, Galway: UNESCO Child and Family Research Centre, National University of Ireland Galway.

Cheetham, J. and Hill, M.J. (1973) 'Community work: Social realities and ethical dilemmas', *The British Journal of Social Work*, 3(3): 331–48.

Chon, Y. (2019) 'The marketization of childcare and elderly care, and its results in South Korea', *International Social Work*, 62(4): 1260–73.

Chow, E.O.W. and Yau, K.K.W. (2018) 'An assessment of social networking intervention with older Chinese adults in Hong Kong', *Research on Social Work Practice*, 28(8): 907–19.

Churchill, H. and Sen, R. (eds) (2016) 'Themed section: Intensive family support services: Politics, policy and practice across contexts', *Social Policy and Society*, 15(2): 251–336.

Cohen, S. (1985) *Visions of Social Control*, Cambridge: Polity Press.

Colby Peters, S. (2018) 'Defining social work leadership: A theoretical and conceptual review and analysis', *Journal of Social Work Practice*, 32(1): 31–44. doi:10.1080/02650533.2017.1300877.

Coleman, J.C. (1974) *Relationships in Adolescence*, London: Routledge & Kegan Paul.

Coleman, J.C. and Hendry, L.B. (1999) *The Nature of Adolescence* (3rd edn), London: Routledge.

Collins, P.H. and Bilge, S. (2016) *Intersectionality*, Malden, MA: Polity.

Colvin, M.L. and Miller, S.E. (2018) 'Serving clients and the community better: A mixed methods analysis of benefits experienced when organizations collaborate in child welfare', *Child & Family Social Work*, 23(4): 666–75.

Commission of Investigation into Mother and Baby Homes and certain related matters (2020) *Mother and Baby Homes Commission of Investigation Final Report*, Dublin: Department of Children, Equality, Disability, Integration and Youth, Government of Ireland.

Commission to Inquire into Child Abuse (2009) *The Report of the Commission to Inquire into Child Abuse (The Ryan Report)*, Dublin: Stationery Office.

Compas, B.E., Wagner, B.M., Slavin, L.A. and Vannatta, K. (1986) 'A prospective study of life events, social support, and psychological symptomatology during the transition from high school to college', *American Journal of Community Psychology*, 14(3): 241–57.

Connolly, M. and Masson, J. (2014) 'Private and public voices: Does family group conferencing privilege the voice of children and families in child welfare?', *Journal of Social Welfare and Family Law*, 36(4): 403–14.

Coogan, D. (2017) *Child to Parent Violence and Abuse*, London: Jessica Kingsley Publishers.

Corby, B., Millar, M. and Young, L. (1996) 'Parental participation in child protection work: Rethinking the rhetoric', *The British Journal of Social Work*, 26(4): 475–92.

Coulter, C. (2015) *Final Report of the Child Care Law Reporting Project*, Dublin: Child Care Law Reporting Project.

Coulter, C. (2018) *An Examination of Lengthy, Contested and Complex Child Protection Cases in the District Court*, Dublin: Child Care Law Reporting Project.

Coulter, S. (2014) '(Re)Introducing Themes of Religion and Spirituality to Professional Social Work Training in the Land of "Saints and Scholars"', in C. Readdick (ed) *Irish Families and Globalization: Conversations about Belonging and Identity across Space and Time*, Ann Arbor, MI: Michigan Publishing, pp 85–109.

Cox, D., Cleak, H., Bhathal, A. and Brophy, L. (2021) 'Theoretical frameworks in social work education: A scoping review', *Social Work Education*, 40(1): 18–43.

Cramer, S. (2019) 'Intergenerational narrative practice in response to intergenerational trauma', *The International Journal of Narrative Therapy and Community Work*, 1: 1–6.

Cree, V. (2011) *Social Work: A Reader*, London: Routledge.

Cree, V., Jain, S. and Hillen, D.P. (2019) 'Evaluating effectiveness in social work: Sharing dilemmas in practice', *European Journal of Social Work*, 22(4): 599–610.

Cullen, A.F. (2013) '"Leaders in our own lives": Suggested indications for social work leadership from a study of social work practice in a palliative care setting', *The British Journal of Social Work*, 43(8), 1527–44.

Cummins, I. (2020) 'Using Fraser's model of "progressive neoliberalism" to analyse deinstitutionalisation and community care', *Critical and Radical Social Work*, 8(1): 77–93.

Cury, S.P., Astray, A.A. and Gómez, J.L.P. (2019) 'Design of *ISD-1*: An instrument for social diagnosis in care homes for older persons', *European Journal of Social Work*, 22(3): 511–25.

Cutrona, C.E. (2000) 'Social Support Principles for Strengthening Families', in J. Canavan, P. Dolan and J. Pinkerton (eds) *Family Support: Direction from Diversity*, London: Jessica Kingsley Publishers, pp 103–22.

Daly, M., Bray, R., Bruckauf, Z., Byrne, J., Margaria, A., Pećnik, N. and Samms-Vaughan, M. (2015) *Family and Parenting Support: Policy and Provision in a Global Context*, Florence: Innocenti Insight, UNICEF Office of Research – Innocenti.

Daniel, B. and Wassell, S. (2002) *The School Years: Assessing and Promoting Resilience in Vulnerable Children* (vol 2), London: Jessica Kingsley Publishers.

Daro, D. (2016) 'Early family support interventions: Creating context for success', *Global Social Welfare*, 3(2): 91–6.

Daro, D. (2019) 'A shift in perspective: A universal approach to child protection', *The Future of Children*, 29(1): 17–40.

Davies, M. (1994) *The Essential Social Worker*, London: Routledge.

Davis, J.M. and Smith, M. (2012) *Working in Multi-Professional Contexts: A Practical Guide for Professionals in Children's Services*, London: SAGE Publications Ltd.

Davis, J.M. and Smith, M. (2020) 'Children's Rights, Social Justice and Family Support: Developing Inclusive, Socially Just and Participatory Practice', in P. Dolan and N. Frost (eds) *The Routledge Handbook of Global Child Welfare*, London: Routledge, pp 137–50.

De Montigny, G. (2011) 'Beyond anti-oppressive practice: Investigating reflexive social relations', *Journal of Progressive Human Services*, 22(1): 8–30.

Devaney, C. and Dolan, P. (2014) 'Voice and meaning: The wisdom of family support veterans', *Child & Family Social Work*, 22(S3): 10–20. doi:10.1111/cfs.12200.

Devaney, C. and McGregor, C. (2017) 'Child protection and family support practice in Ireland: A contribution to present debates from a historical perspective', *Child & Family Social Work*, 22(3): 1–9.

Devaney, C., McGregor, C. and Moran, L. (2019) 'Outcomes for permanence and stability for children in care in Ireland: Implications for practice', *The British Journal of Social Work*, 49(3): 633–52.

Dewey, J. (1929) *Experience and Nature* (2nd edn), LaSalle, IL: Open Court Publishing.

Dewey, J. (1938) *Logic: The Theory of Inquiry*, New York: Henry Holt.

Dima, G. and Bucata, M.D. (2015) 'The process of transition from public care to independent living: A resilience based approach', *Revesta de Cercetare si Interventie Sociala*, 50: 53–65.

Dima, G. and Pinkerton, J. (2016) 'The Role of Informal Leaving Care Peer Support Networks in Romania', in P. Mendes and P. Snow (eds) *Young People Transitioning from Out-of-Home Care*, London: Palgrave Macmillan, pp 409–24.

Dima, G. and Skehill, C. (2011) 'Making sense of leaving care: The contribution of Bridges' model of transition to understanding the psycho-social process', *Children and Youth Services Review*, 33(12): 2532–9.

Dingwall, R., Eekelaar, J. and Murray, T. (1983) *The Protection of Children*, Oxford: Blackwell.

Dixon, J. and Stein, M. (2006) 'Editorial Special Issue on young people leaving care', *Child & Family Social Work*, 11(3): 189–90.

Doel, M. (2010) *Social Work Placements: A Traveller's Guide*, Abingdon: Routledge.

Doel, M. (2012) *Social Work: The Basics*, London: Routledge.

Doka, K. (ed) (1989) *Disenfranchised Grief: Recognizing Hidden Sorrow*, New York: Lexington Books.

Dolan, B. (2019) 'Principal Investigator Impact Orientation in Medical Device Public Research', Unpublished doctoral dissertation, Galway: National University of Ireland Galway.

Dolan, P. (2006) 'Assessment, Intervention and Self Appraisal Tools for Family Support', in P. Dolan, J. Canavan and J. Pinkerton (eds) *Family Support as Reflective Practice*, London: Jessica Kingsley Publishers, pp 196–213.

Dolan, P. (2012) 'Travelling through Social Support and Youth Civic Action on a Journey Towards Resilience', in M. Ungar (ed) *Social Ecology of Resilience: A Handbook of Theory and Practice*, New York: Springer, pp 357–66.

Dolan, P. and Brady, B. (2012) *A Guide to Youth Mentoring: Providing Effective Social Support*, London: Jessica Kingsley Publishers.

Dolan, P. and Brennan, M.A. (2016) 'An Overview of Youth Civic Engagement', in UN (United Nations) *World Youth Report – Youth Civic Engagement*, New York: UNDESA, pp 16–26.

Dolan, P. and Frost, N. (eds) (2017) *The Routledge Handbook of Global Child Welfare*, London: Routledge.

Dolan, P. and McGregor, C. (2019) 'Social Support, Empathy and Ecology: A Theoretical Underpinning for Working with Young People Who Have Suffered Child Sexual Abuse or Exploitation', in J. Pearce (ed) *Child Sexual Exploitation: Why Theory Matters*, Bristol: Policy Press, pp 173–92.

Dolan, P. and Pinkerton, J. (2007) 'Family support, social capital, resilience and adolescent coping', *Child & Family Social Work*, 12(3): 219–28.

Dolan, P., Canavan, J. and Pinkerton, J. (eds) (2006) *Family Support as Reflective Practice*, London: Jessica Kingsley Publishers.

Dolan, P., Kenny, J. and Kennan, D. (2017) 'Activated Empathy in Child Welfare and Youth Development: A Case for Consideration', in P. Dolan and N. Frost (eds) *The Handbook of Global Child Welfare*, London: Routledge, pp 358–78.

Dolan, P., Zegarac, N. and Arsic, J. (2020) 'Family support as a right of the child', *Social Work and Social Sciences Review*, 21(2): 8–26.

Dominelli, L. (2012) *Green Social Work: From Environmental Crises to Environmental Justice*, Cambridge: Polity Press.

Dominelli, L. (ed) (2020) *The Routledge Handbook of Green Social Work*, London: Routledge.

Dominelli, L., Harrikari, T., Mooney, J., Leskošek, V. and Kennedy Tsunoda, E. (2020) *COVID-19 and Social Work: A Collection of Country Reports*, International Association of Schools of Social Work (IASSW). Available at: www.iassw-aiets.org/covid-19/5369-covid-19-and-social-work-a-collection-of-country-reports

Donnelly, S. (2019) 'Mandatory reporting and adult safeguarding: A rapid realist review', *The Journal of Adult Protection*, 21(5): 241–51.

Donnelly, S., Ní Raghallaigh, M. and Foreman, M. (2019) 'Reflections on the use of community based participatory research to affect social and political change: Examples from research with refugees and older people in Ireland', *European Journal of Social Work*, 22(5): 831–44.

Donzelot, J. (1979) *The Policing of Families* (translated by R. Hurley), New York: Pantheon Books.

Doughty, E.A. and Hoskins, W.J. (2011) 'Death education: An internationally relevant approach to grief counseling', *Journal for International Counselor Education*, 3: 25–38.

Duffy, J., Campbell, J. and Tosone, C. (2018) *Social Work Practice During the Troubles*, Belfast: BASW (British Association of Social Workers) (NI) and NISCC (Northern Ireland Social Care Council).

Duffy, J., Campbell, J. and Tosone, C. (eds) (2020) *International Perspectives on Social Work and Political Conflict*, London: Routledge.

Duffy, J., Gillen, P., Agnew, C., Casson, K., Davidson, G., McGlone, A. and McKeever, B. (2017) *Personal and Public Involvement and Its Impact – Monitoring, Measuring and Evaluating the Impact of Personal and Public Involvement (PPI) in Health and Social Care in Northern Ireland*, Belfast: Public Health Agency.

Editors of Encyclopaedia Britannica (2020) 'Edith Abbott, American social worker.' Available at: www.britannica.com/biography/Edith-Abbott

Elder, G.H., Kirkpatrick Johnson, M. and Crosnoe, R. (2003) 'The Emergence and Development of Life Course Theory', in J.T. Mortimer and M.J. Shanahan (eds) *Handbook of the Life Course*, Boston, MA: Springer, pp 3–19.

El-Lahib, Y. (2020) 'Social work at the intersection of disability and displacement: Rethinking our role', *Journal of Progressive Human Services*, 31(1): 1–20.

Engwall, K., Östberg, F., Andersson, G., Bons, T. and Bringlöv, Å. (2019) 'Children with disabilities in Swedish child welfare – A differentiating and disabling practice', *European Journal of Social Work*, 22(6): 1025–37.

Erikson, E.H. (1950) *Childhood and Society*, London: Penguin Books.

Erikson, E.H. (1974) *Dimensions of a New Identity: The 1973 Jefferson Lectures in the Humanities*, New York: W.W. Norton & Company.

Erikson, E.H. (1994) *Identity and the Life Cycle*, New York: W.W. Norton & Company.

Erikson, E.H. and Erikson, J.M. (1998) *The Life Cycle Completed* (extended version), New York: W.W. Norton & Company.

Fabian, K. and Korolczuk, E. (eds) (2017) *Rebellious Parents: Parental Movements in Central-Eastern Europe and Russia*, Bloomington, IN: Indiana University Press.

Featherstone, B., Gupta, A., Morris, K. and White, S. (2018) *Protecting Children: A Social Model*, Bristol: Policy Press.

Feely, M. (2016) 'Sexual surveillance and control in a community-based intellectual disability service', *Sexualities*, 19(5–6): 725–50.

Felitti, V.J., Anda, R.F., Nordenberg, D., Williamson, D.F., Spitz, A.M., Valerie, E., Koss, M. and Marks, J.S. (1998) 'Relationship of childhood abuse and household dysfunction to many of the leading causes of death in adults: The Adverse Childhood Experiences (ACE) Study', *American Journal of Preventative Medicine*, 14(4): 245–58.

Fenton, M. (2015) 'Transitions from residential care', *Relational Child & Youth Care Practice*, 28(1): 95–104.

Ferguson, H. (2004) *Protecting Children in Time: Child Abuse, Child Protection and the Consequences of Modernity*, Basingstoke: Palgrave Macmillan.

Ferguson, H. (2008a) 'The Theory and Practice of Critical Best Practice in Social Work', in K. Jones, B. Cooper and H. Ferguson (eds) *Best Practice in Social Work: Critical Perspectives*, Basingstoke: Palgrave Macmillan, pp 15–37.

Ferguson, H. (2008b) 'Liquid social work: Welfare interventions as mobile practices', *The British Journal of Social Work*, 38(3): 561–79.

Ferguson, H. (2018) 'Making home visits: Creativity and the embodied practices of home visiting in social work and child protection', *Qualitative Social Work*, 17(1): 65–80.

Ferguson, H., Warwick, L., Singh Cooner, T., Jadwiga, L., Beddoe, L., Disney, T. and Plumridge, G. (2020) 'The nature and culture of social work with children and families in long-term casework: Findings from a qualitative longitudinal study', *Child & Family Social Work*, 25(3): 694–703.

Ferguson, I. (2007) 'Increasing user choice or privatizing risk? The antinomies of personalization', *The British Journal of Social Work*, 37(3): 387–403.

Ferguson, I., Ioakimidis, V. and Lavlette, M. (2018) *Global Social Work in a Political Context: Radical Perspectives*, Bristol: Policy Press.

Filinson, R., McCreadie, C., Askham, J. and Mathew, D. (2008) 'Why should they be abused any more than children? Child abuse protection and the implementation of No Secrets', *The Journal of Adult Protection*, 10(2): 18–28.

Fitzpatrick, K. and Grace, M. (2019) 'Dementia patients' transition to residential aged care: Carers' and social workers' experiences', *Australian Social Work*, 72(3): 287–98.

Flynn, S. (2017) 'Social work practice in an economic downturn: Understanding austerity through an anti-oppressive framework', *Practice*, 29(3): 179–99. doi:1 0.1080/09503153.2016.1201467.

Flynn, S. (2019a) 'Making acquaintance: Compatibility of critical disability studies conventions with child protection and welfare social work practice in Ireland', *Practice*, 33(2): 137–48. doi:10.1080/09503153.2019.1699911.

Flynn, S. (2019b) 'Theorizing disability in child protection: Applying critical disability studies to the elevated risk of abuse for disabled children', *Disability & Society*, 35(3): 1–23. doi:10.1080/09687599.2019.1669433.

Flynn, S. (2019c) 'Social work intervention pathways within child protection: Responding to the needs of disabled children in Ireland', *Practice*, 33(1). doi:10.1080/09503153.2019.1704236.

Flynn, S. and McGregor, C. (2017) 'Disabled children and child protection: Learning from the literature through a non-tragedy lens', *Child Care in Practice*, 23(3): 258–76.

Foster, K., O'Brien, L. and Korhonen, T. (2012) 'Developing resilient children and families when parents have mental illness: A family-focused approach', *International Journal of Mental Health Nursing*, 21(1): 3–11.

Foucault, M. (1973) *The Birth of the Clinic: An Archaeology of Medical Perception* (translated by A.M. Sheridan Smith), New York: Pantheon Books.

Foucault, M. (1977) *Discipline and Punish* (translated by A.M. Sheridan Smith), Harmondsworth: Penguin.

Francis, M.W., Taylor, L.H. and Tracy, E.M. (2020) 'Choose who's in your circle: How women's relationship actions during and following residential treatment help create recovery-oriented networks', *Journal of Social Work Practice in the Addictions*, 20(2): 122–35.

Fraser, N. (2008) *Scales of Justice: Reimaging Political Space in a Globalising World*, Cambridge: Polity.

Fraser, N. (2019) *The Old Is Dying and the New Cannot Be Born*, London: Verso.

Friedman, B.D. and Merrick, J. (2016) 'Social work and health inequalities', *International Public Health Journal*, 8(2): 91–3.

Freire, P. (1968) *Pedagogy of the Oppressed*, New York: Seabury Press.

Frost, L. (2019) 'Why Psycho-Social Thinking is Critical', in S.A. Webb (ed) *The Routledge Handbook of Critical Social Work*, Abingdon: Routledge, pp 115–25.

Frost, N. (2017) 'From "silo" to "network" profession – A multi-professional future for social work', *Journal of Children's Services*, 12(2): 174–83.

Frost, N. (2021) *The Myth of Measurement: Inspection, Audit, Targets and the Public Sector*, London: SAGE Publications Ltd.

Frost, N. and Dolan, P. (2021) 'Theory, research and practice in child welfare: The current state of the art in social work', *Child & Family Social Work*. doi:10.1111/cfs.12824.

Frost, N., Abbott, S. and Race, T. (2015) *Family Support: Prevention, Early Intervention and Early Help*, London: Wiley.

Gardner, R. (2003) *Supporting Families: Child Protection in the Community*, Chichester: John Wiley & Sons.

Garrett, P.M. (2018) *Social Work and Social Theory: Making Connections* (2nd edn), Bristol: Policy Press.

Gavin, P. (2019) '"Prison is the worst place a Traveller could be": The experiences of Irish Travellers in prison in England and Wales', *Irish Probation Journal*, 16: 135–52.

Genova, A. and Barberis, B. (2019) 'Social workers and intercultural mediators: Challenges for collaboration and intercultural awareness', *European Journal of Social Work*, 22(6): 908–20. doi:10.1080/13691457.2018.1452196.

Gibbons, N. (2010) *Roscommon Child Care Case*, Dublin: Health Services Executive (HSE).

Gilbert, N., Parton, N. and Skivens, M. (eds) (2011) *Child Protection Systems: International Trends and Orientations*, New York: Oxford University Press.

Gillespie, P., O'Shea, E., Cullinan, J., Buchanan, J., Bobula, J., Lacey, L., Gallagher, D., Mhaolain, A.N. and Lawlor, B. (2015) 'Longitudinal costs of caring for people with Alzheimer's disease', *International Psychogeriatrics*, 27: 847–56.

Gilligan, R. (2000) 'Promoting Resilience in Children in Foster Care', in G. Kelly and R. Gilligan (eds) *Issues in Foster Care*, London: Jessica Kingsley Publishers, pp 107–26.

Gilligan, R. (2001) *Promoting Resilience: A Resource Guide on Working with Children in the Care System*, London: British Agencies for Adoption and Fostering.

Gilligan, R. (2009) *Promoting Resilience: Supporting Children and Young People Who Are in Care, Adopted or In Need*, London: British Agencies for Adoption and Fostering.

Gillingham, P. (2019) 'Decision support systems, social justice and algorithmic accountability in social work: A new challenge', *Practice*, 31(4): 277–90.

Golden, C., Killion, M.G. and McGregor, C. (2020) 'An evaluation of training for health and social care professionals when working with families where a parent has a mental illness', *Advances in Mental Health*, 18(3): 276–88. doi:10.1 080/18387357.2020.1829492.

Goldstein, J. (1973) *Social Work Practice: A Unitary Approach*, Columbia, SC: University of South Carolina Press.

Golightley, M. and Holloway, M. (2020) 'Editorial: Working on the front line: What war are we talking about?', *The British Journal of Social Work*, 50: 303–7.

Golightley, M. and Kirwan, G. (2017) *International Reflections on Approaches to Mental Health Social Work*, Oxford: Routledge.

Goodley, D. (2010) *Disability Studies: An Interdisciplinary Introduction*, Los Angeles, CA: SAGE Publications Ltd.

Gottlieb, M. (2020) 'The case for a cultural humility framework in social work practice', *Journal of Ethnic & Cultural Diversity in Social Work*. doi:10.1080/153 13204.2020.1753615.

Götzö, M. and McGregor, C. (2016) 'Special Issue: Exploring the work/welfare relationship: International perspectives on labour, migration and gender', *Swiss Journal of Social Work*, 17.

Granovetter, M. (1974) *Getting a Job: A Study of Contacts and Careers*, Cambridge, MA: Harvard University Press.

Grant, S., Allen, R., Nosowska G., Cree, V., Cullen, A., Holloway, M., Golightley, M., Higgins, M., Pinkerton, J., Unwin, P. and Ward, D. (2020) 'Editorial: Resilient, steadfast and forward-looking: The story of social work in the UK told through 50 years of *The British Journal of Social Work*', *The British Journal of Social Work*, bcaa137. Available at: https://doi.org/10.1093/bjsw/bcaa137

Gray, M. and Webb, C. (2009) *Social Work Theory and Methods*, London: SAGE Publications Ltd.

Gray, M., Coates, J. and Yellow Bird, M. (2008) *Indigenous Social Work Around the World: Towards Culturally Relevant Social Work Education and Practice*, London: Ashgate.

Gray, M., Coates, J., Yellow Bird, M. and Hetherington, T. (eds) (2013) *Decolonizing Social Work*, London: Ashgate Publishing.

Grotberg, E. (1995) *A Guide to Promoting Resilience in Children: Strengthening the Human Spirit*, the Hague: Bernard van Leer Foundation.

Grzymala-Kazlowska, A. and Phillimore, J. (2018) 'Introduction: Rethinking integration. New perspectives on adaptation and settlement in the era of super-diversity', *Journal of Ethnic and Migration Studies*, 44(2): 179–96.

Hagues, R.J., Cecil, D. and Stoltzfus, K. (2019) 'The experiences of German social workers working with refugees', *Journal of Social Work*, 21(1). doi:10.1177/1468017319860305.

Haight, W., Sugrue, E., Calhoun, M. and Black, J. (2017) '"Basically, I look at it like combat": Reflections on moral injury by parents involved with child protection services', *Children and Youth Services Review*, 82: 477–89.

Hall, E.L. and Jones, N.P. (2019) 'A deeper analysis of culturally competent practice: Delving beneath white privilege', *Journal of Ethnic & Cultural Diversity in Social Work*, 28(3): 282–96.

Halton, C., Harold, G., Murphy, A. and Walsh, E. (2018) *A Social and Economic Analysis of the Use of Legal Services (SEALS) in the Child and Family Agency (Tusla)*, Cork: University College Cork.

Hardiker, P. (1977) 'Social work ideologies in the Probation Service', *The British Journal of Social Work*, 7(2): 131–54.

Harrikari, T. and Pirkko-Liisa, R. (2019) *Towards Global Social Work in the Era of Compressed Modernity*, New York: Routledge.

Hart, R.A. (1992) *Children's Participation: From Tokenism to Citizenship*, Florence: UNICEF International Child Development Centre.

Haugaard, M. and Clegg, S.R. (2013) *The SAGE Handbook of Power*, London: SAGE Publications Ltd.

Hauss, G. and Schulte, D. (eds) (2009) *Amid Social Contradiction*, Opladen and Farmington Hills, MI: Barbara Budrich Publishers.

Hendrick, H. (2003) *Child Welfare: Historical Dimensions, Contemporary Debate*, Bristol: Bristol University Press.

Hendriks, P. and van Ewijk, H. (2019) 'Finding common ground: How superdiversity is unsettling social work education', *European Journal of Social Work*, 22(1): 158–70.

Hering, S. and Waaldijk, B. (2006) *Guardians of the Poor – Custodians of the Public: Welfare History in Eastern Europe 1900–1960*, Opladen and Farmington Hills, MI: Barbara Budrich Publishers.

Herrera-Pastor, D., Juárez, J. and Ruiz-Román, C. (2019) 'Collaborative leadership to subvert marginalisation: The workings of a socio-educational network in Los Asperones, Spain', *School Leadership & Management*, 40(2–3): 203–20.

Higgins, M. (2019) 'Contemporary debates in safeguarding children: National and international implications', *Practice*, 31(5): 349–58.

Hill, D.J. and Laredo, E. (2019) 'First and last and always: Streetwork as a methodology for radical community social work practice', *Critical and Radical Social Work*, 7(1): 25–9.

Hollington, K. and Jackson, S. (2016) 'Falling off the ladder: Using focal theory to understand and improve the educational experiences of young people in transition from public care', *Journal of Adolescence*, 52: 146–53.

Holman, R. (1973) 'Poverty: Consensus and alternatives', *The British Journal of Social Work*, 3(4): 431–46.

Holt, S., Overlien, C. and Devaney, J. (2017) *Responding to Domestic Violence: Emerging Challenges for Policy, Practice and Research in Europe*, London: Jessica Kingsley Publishers.

Hopkinson, P.J., Killick, M., Batish, A. and Simmons, L. (2015) '"Why didn't we do this before?" The development of making safeguarding personal in the London Borough of Sutton', *The Journal of Adult Protection*, 17(3): 181–94.

Horgan, D. and Ní Raghallaigh, M. (2019) 'The social care needs of unaccompanied minors: The Irish experience', *European Journal of Social Work*, 22(1): 95–106.

Hothersall, S. (2019) 'Epistemology and social work: Enhancing the integration of theory, practice and research through philosophical pragmatism', *European Journal of Social Work*, 22(5): 860–70.

Houston, S. (2010a) 'Beyond Homo Economicus: Recognition, self-realization and social work', *The British Journal of Social Work*, 40(3): 841–57.

Houston, S. (2010b) 'Further reflections on Habermas's contribution to discourse in child protection: An examination of power in social life', *The British Journal of Social Work*, 40(6): 1736–53.

Houston, S. (2015) *A Model for Supervision and Practice in Social Work*, Belfast: NISCC (Northern Ireland Social Care Council).

Houston, S. (2019) 'Extending Bourdieu for Critical Social Work', in S. Webb (ed) *The Routledge Handbook of Critical Social Work*, London: Routledge, Chapter 10.

Houston, S. and Butler, M. (2019) '"More than just a number": Meeting the needs of those with mental illness, learning difficulties and speech and language difficulties in the criminal justice system', *Irish Probation Journal*, 16: 22–41.

Houston, S. and Dolan, P. (2008) 'Conceptualising child and family support: The contribution on Honneth's theory of recognition', *Children and Society*, 22(6): 458–69.

Howe, D. (1987, 2008, 2017) *Introduction to Social Work* (1st, 2nd and 3rd edn), London: Routledge.

Howe, D. (1995) *Attachment Theory for Social Work Practice*, Basingstoke: Macmillan.

Howe, D. (1996) 'Surface and Depth in Social Work Practice', in N. Parton (ed) *Social Theory, Social Change and Social Work*, London: Routledge.

Howe, D. (2005) *Child Abuse and Neglect: Attachment, Development and Intervention*, Basingstoke: Macmillan.

Howe, D. (2011) *Attachment Across the Lifecourse: A Brief Introduction*, Basingstoke: Palgrave Macmillan.

HSE (Health Service Executive) (2014) *Safeguarding Vulnerable Persons at Risk of Abuse Policy – National Policy and Procedures*, Dublin: HSE.

Hubbard, R. (2018) 'Best interests assessor role: An opportunity or a "dead end" for adult social workers?', *Social Work in Action*, 30(2): 83–98.

Hurley, D. and Kirwan, G. (2020) 'Exploring resilience and mental health in services users and practitioners in Ireland and Canada', *European Journal of Social Work*, 23(2): 340–52.

Hutchinson, G.S. and Sandvin, J.T. (2019) 'Emergent voices. Exploring the lived experience of seniors with intellectual disability', *European Journal of Social Work*, 22(5): 738–48.

Hutchison, E.D. (2005) 'The life course perspective: A promising approach for bridging the micro and macro worlds for social workers', *Families in Society: The Journal of Contemporary Social Services*, 86(1): 143–52.

Hutchison, E.D. (2019) 'An update on the relevance of the life course perspective for social work', *Families in Society*, 100(4): 351–66.

Hyslop, I. (2013) 'Social Work Practice Knowledge: An Enquiry into the Nature of the Knowledge Generated and Applied in the Practice of Social Work', Doctoral dissertation, Albany Campus, Massey University, New Zealand.

Hyslop, I. and Keddell, E. (2018) 'Outing the elephants: A new paradigm for child protection social work', *Social Sciences*, 7(7): 105.

Ife, J. (2019) 'Foreword', in R. Munford and K. O'Donoghue (eds) *New Theories for Social Work Practice: Ethical Practice for Working with Individuals, Families and Communities*, London: Jessica Kingsley Publishers, pp 9–13.

IFSW (International Federation of Social Work) (2014) 'Global definition of social work.' Available at: www.ifsw.org/global-definition-of-social-work

Ingelby, D. (1985) 'Professionals as Socialisers: The Psy Complex', in A. Scull and S. Spitzer (eds) *Research in Law, Deviance and Social Control*, New York: Jai Press, pp 79–109.

IRC (Irish Refugee Council) (2013) *Direct Provision: Framing an Alternative Reception System for People Seeking International Protection*, Dublin: IRC.

Jack, G. (1997) 'An ecological approach to social work with children and families', *Child & Family Social Work*, 2(2): 109–20.

James, E., Harvey, M. and Mitchell, R. (2017) 'The Mental Capacity Act call to action: Online development of critical rights-based social work', *Practice*, 29(4): 279–92.

Johansson, S., Stefansen K., Bakketeig, E. and Kaldal, A. (eds) (2017) *Collaborating Against Child Abuse*, Basingstoke: Palgrave Macmillan.

Johnson, A.K. and Sloth-Nielsen, J. (2020) 'Safeguarding children in the developing world – Beyond intra-organisational policy and self-regulation', *Social Sciences*, 9(6): 1–19.

Jolly, A. (2018) '"You just have to work with what you've got": Practitioner research with precarious migrant families', *Practice*, 30(2): 99–116.

Joly, E. (2016) 'Integrating transition theory and bioecological theory: A theoretical perspective for nurses supporting the transition to adulthood for young people with medical complexity', *Journal of Advanced Nursing*, 72(6): 1251–62.

Jones, D.N. and Truell, R. (2012) 'The Global Agenda for Social Work and Social Development: A place to link together and be effective in a globalized world', *International Social Work*, 55(4): 454–72.

Jones, R. (2014) 'The best of times, the worst of times: Social work and its moment', *The British Journal of Social Work*, 44(3): 485–502.

Jönsson, J.H. (2019) 'Servants of a "sinking Titanic" or actors of change? Contested identities of social workers in Sweden', *European Journal of Social Work*, 22(2): 212–24.

Jordan, B. (2007) *Social Work and Well-Being*, Lyme Regis: Russell House.

Jordan, B. (2008) *Welfare and Well-Being: Social Value in Public Policy*, Bristol: Policy Press.

Joubert, L. and Webber, M. (eds) (2020) *The Routledge Handbook of Social Work Practice Research*, London: Routledge.

Kadushin, C. (2012) *Understanding Social Networks: Theories, Concepts, and Findings*, Oxford: Oxford University Press.

Käkelä, E. (2019) 'Narratives of power and powerlessness: Cultural competence in social work with asylum seekers and refugees', *European Journal of Social Work*, 23(3): 425–36. doi:10.1080/13691457.2019.1693337.

Kam, P.K. (2019) '"Social work is not just a job": The qualities of social workers from the perspectives of service users', *Journal of Social Work*, 20(6). doi:10.1177/1468017319848109.

Kamali, M. and Jönsson, J.H. (2019) 'Revolutionary social work: Promoting sustainable justice', *Critical and Radical Social Work*, 7(3): 293.

Kayama, M., Johnstone, C. and Limaye, S. (2019) 'The experiences of disability in sociocultural contexts of India: Stigmatization and resilience', *International Social Work*, 1–15. doi:10.1177/0020872819828878.

Keddell, E. (2014) 'Theorising the signs of safety approach to child protection social work: Positioning, codes and power', *Children and Youth Services Review*, 47(Pt 1): 70–7.

Keddell, E. (2019) 'Algorithmic justice in child protection: Statistical fairness, social justice and the implications for practice', *Social Sciences*, 8(10): 281.

Keddell, E. and Davie, G. (2018) 'Inequalities and child protection system contact in Aotearoa New Zealand: Developing a conceptual framework and research agenda', *Social Sciences*, 7(6): 1–14.

Keeling, A. (2017) '"Organising objects": Adult safeguarding practice and Article 16 of the United Nations Convention on the Rights of Persons with Disabilities', *International Journal of Law and Psychiatry*, 53: 77–87.

Kelly, B. and Byrne, B. (2015) 'Valuing disabled children and young people', *Child Care in Practice*, 21(1): 1–5.

Kelly, B., McShane, T., Davidson, G. and Pinkerton, J. (2014) *A Review of Literature on Disabled Care Leavers and Care Leavers with Mental Health Needs*, Belfast: Queen's University.

Kelly, B., Friel, S., McShane, T., Pinkerton, J. and Gilligan, E. (2020) '"I haven't read it, I've lived it!" The benefits and challenges of peer research with young people leaving care', *Qualitative Social Work*, 19(1): 108–24.

Kelly, C., Craig, S. and McConkey, R. (2019) 'Supporting family carers of children and adults with intellectual disability', *Journal of Social Work*, 20(5). doi:10.1177/1468017319860312.

Kelly-Irving, M. and Delpierre, C. (2019) 'A critique of the Adverse Childhood Experiences framework in epidemiology and public health: Uses and misuses', *Social Policy & Society*, 18(3): 445–56.

Kennan, D. and Dolan, P. (2017) 'Justifying children and young people's involvement in social research: Assessing harm and benefit', *Irish Journal of Sociology*, 25(3): 297–314.

Kennan, D., Brady, B. and Forkan, C. (2019) 'Space, voice, audience and influence: The Lundy model of participation (2007) in child welfare practice', *Practice*, 31(3), 205–18.

Kettle, M. and Jackson, S. (2017) 'Revisiting the rule of optimism', *The British Journal of Social Work*, 47(6): 1624–40.

Kilkelly, U. (2016) *Children's Rights in Ireland: Law, Policy and Practice* (2nd edn), Dublin: Bloomsbury Professional Limited.

Killick, C. and Taylor, B. (2020) *Assessment, Risk and Decision Making: An Introduction*, London: SAGE Publications Ltd.

Kirwan, G. (2019) 'Editorial: Networked relationships in the digital age – Messages for social work', *Journal of Social Work Practice*, 33(2): 123–26.

Kolb, D. (1984) *Experiential Learning as the Science of Learning and Development*, Englewood Cliffs, NJ: Prentice Hall.

Koppitz, A.L., Dreizler, J., Altherr, J., Bosshard, G., Naef, R. and Imhof, L. (2017) 'Relocation experiences with unplanned admission to a nursing home: A qualitative study', *International Psychogeriatrics*, 29(3): 517–27.

Kornbeck, J. (2019) 'Rebellious parents: Parental movements in Central-Eastern Europe and Russia', *European Journal of Social Work*, 22(4): 725–7.

Kubler-Ross, E. (1989) *On Death and Dying*, London: Routledge.

Kuis, E.E., Goossensen, A., van Dijke, J. and Baart, A.J. (2015) 'Self-report questionnaire for measuring presence: Development and initial validation', *Scandinavian Journal of Caring Sciences*, 29(1): 173–82.

LaMendola, W. (2019) 'Social work, social technologies, and sustainable community development', *Journal of Technology in Human Services*, 37(2–3): 79–92.

Larsen, A.K., Sewpaul, V. and Hole, G.O. (2013) 'Introduction', in A.K. Larsen, V. Sewpaul and G.O. Hole (eds) *Participation in Community Work: International Perspectives*, Abingdon: Routledge, pp 1–15.

Larson, G. (2008) 'Anti-oppressive practice in mental health', *Journal of Progressive Human Services*, 19(1), 39–54.

Lavalette, M., Ioakimidis, V. and Ferguson, I. (2020) *Social Work and the COVID-19 Pandemic – International Insights*, Bristol: Policy Press.

Lefevre, M., Hickle, K. and Luckock, B. (2019) '"Both/and" not "either/or": Reconciling rights to protection and participation in working with child sexual exploitation', *The British Journal of Social Work*, 49(7): 1837–55.

Leighninger, L. (1986) 'Bertha Reynolds and Edith Abbott: Contrasting images of professionalism in social work', *Smith College Studies in Social Work*, 56(2): 111–21. doi:10.1080/00377318609516610.

Lerner, R.M. (2005) *Promoting Positive Youth Development: Theoretical and Empirical Bases*, National Research Council/Institute of Medicine, National Academy of the Sciences.

Levitt, M.J. (2005) 'Social relations in childhood and adolescence: The convoy model perspective', *Human Development*, 48: 28–47.

Lister, R. (1998) 'Citizenship on the margins: Citizenship, social work and social action', *European Journal of Social Work*, 1(1): 5–18.

Lloyd, L. (2006) 'A caring profession? The ethics of care and social work with older people', *The British Journal of Social Work*, 36(7): 1171–85.

Lonne, B., Scott, D., Higgins, D. and Herrenkoh, T. (eds) (2019) *Re-Visioning Public Health Approaches for Protecting Children, vol 9*, Cham, Switzerland: Springer International Publishing.

Lonne, B., Russ, E., Harrison, C., Morley, L., Harries, M., Robertson, S., Pearce, T. and Smith, J. (2020) 'The "front door" to child protection – Issues and innovations', *International Journal on Child Maltreatment: Research, Policy and Practice*. doi:10.1007/s42448-020-00051-9.

Lorenz, W. (2007) 'Practicing history: Memory and professional contemporary practice', *International Social Work*, 50(5): 597–612.

Lorenz, W. and Shaw, I. (eds) (2019) *Private Troubles or Public Issues? Challenges for Social Work Research*, London: Routledge.

Lotty, M., Dunn-Galvin, A. and Bantry-White, E. (2020) 'Effectiveness of a trauma-informed care psychoeducational program for foster carers – Evaluation of the Fostering Connections program', *Child Abuse & Neglect*, 102: 104390.

Lulei, M. (2010) 'Current developments of probation and social work in Slovakia – Theoretical enthusiasm and practical scepticism', *Revista de Asistenţ? Social?ă Socială*, 3: 59–68.

Lumos (2019) 'Our approach towards advocacy.' Available at: www.wearelumos. org/what-we-do/policy/approach-advocacy

Lundy, L. (2007) '"Voice" is not enough: Conceptualising Article 12 of the United Nations Convention on the Rights of the Child', *British Educational Research Journal*, 33(6): 927–42.

Lymbery, M. (2012) 'Social work and personalisation', *The British Journal of Social Work*, 42(4): 783–92.

Lymbery, M. (2014) 'Austerity, personalisation and older people: The prospects for creative social work practice in England', *European Journal of Social Work*, 17(3): 367–82.

Lynch, D. and Burns, K. (2012) *Children's Rights and Child Protection: Critical Times, Critical Issues in Ireland*, Manchester: Manchester University Press.

Lyons, K., Manion, K. and Carlsen, M. (2017) *International Perspectives on Social Work: Global Conditions and Local Practice*, London: Red Globe Press.

MacDermott, D. and Harkin-MacDermott, C. (2020) 'Co-producing a shared stories narrative model for social work education with experts by experience', *Practice*, 32(2): 89–108.

Mackay, K. and Notman, M. (2017) 'Adult Support and Protection (Scotland) Act 2007: Reflections on developing practice and present-day challenges', *The Journal of Adult Protection*, 19(4): 187–98.

Mafile'o, T. (2019) 'Social Work with Pacific Communities', in R. Munford and K. O'Donoghue (eds) *New Theories for Social Work Practice: Ethical Practices for Working with Individuals, Families and Communities*, London: Jessica Kingsley Publishers, pp 212–30.

Malone, P. and Canavan, J. (2018) *Systems Change: Final Evaluation Report on Tusla's Prevention, Partnership and Family Support Programme*, Galway: UNESCO Child and Family Research Centre, National University of Ireland Galway.

Malone, P., Canavan, J., Devaney, C. and McGregor, C. (2018) *Comparing Areas of Commonality and Distinction Between the National Practice Models of Meitheal and Signs of Safety*, Galway: UNESCO Child and Family Research Centre, National University of Ireland Galway.

Manthorpe, J. (2014) *Adult Social Care Safeguarding Survey*, Leeds: Health and Social Care Information Centre.

Marder, I.D. (2019) 'Restorative justice as the new default in Irish criminal justice', *Irish Probation Journal*, 16: 60–82.

Marthinsen, E. (2019) 'Neoliberalisation, the social investment state and social work', *European Journal of Social Work*, 22(2): 350–61.

Marthinsen, E. and Julkunen, I. (eds) (2012) *Practice Research in Nordic Social Work: Knowledge Production in Transition*, London: Whiting & Birch.

Martin, A.J. and Marsh, H.W. (2006) 'Academic resilience and its psychological and educational correlates: A construct validity approach', *Psychology in the Schools*, 43(3): 267–81. Available at: https://doi.org/10.1002/pits.20149

Martin, J. and Allagia, R. (2013) 'Sexual abuse images in cyberspace: Expanding the ecology of the child', *Journal of Child Sexual Abuse*, 22(4): 398–415.

Masten, A.S. (2001) 'Ordinary magic: Resilience process in development', *American Psychologist*, 56(3): 227–38.

Mathebane, M.S. (2020) 'Quizzing the "social" in social work: Social work in Africa as a system of colonial social control', *Journal of Progressive Human Services*, 31(2): 77–92.

Mattsson, T. (2013) 'Intersectionality as a useful tool: Anti-oppressive social work and critical reflection', *Affilia*, 29(1): 8–17. doi:10.1177/0886109913510659.

Maylea, C. (2020) 'The end of social work', *The British Journal of Social Work*, 51(2): 772–89.

McCafferty, P. and Taylor, B. (2020) 'Risk, decision-making and assessment in child welfare', *Child Care in Practice*, 26: 107–10.

McCartan, C., Morrison, A., Bunting, L., Davidson, G. and McIlroy, J. (2018) 'Stripping the wallpaper of practice: Empowering social workers to tackle poverty', *Social Sciences*, 7(193): 1–16.

McCauliffe, D. and Chenoweth, L. (2019) 'Repositioning Ethical Theory in Social Work Education', in R. Munford and K. O'Donoghue (eds) *New Theories for Social Work Practice: Ethical Practice for Working with Individuals, Families and Communities*, London: Jessica Kingsley Publishers, pp 289–306.

McCormack, C., Gibbons, M. and McGregor, C. (2020) 'An ecological framework for understanding and improving decision making in child protection and welfare intake (duty) practices in the Republic of Ireland', *Child Care in Practice*, 26(2): 146–62.

McCubbin, H.I. and McCubbin, M.A. (1992) 'Research Utilization in Social Work Practice of Family Treatment', in A.J. Grasso and I. Epstein (eds) *Research Utilization in the Social Sciences: Innovations for Practice and Administration*, New York: Haworth, pp 149–92.

McDonald, A. (2010) 'The impact of the 2005 Mental Capacity Act on social workers' decision making and approaches to the assessment of risk', *The British Journal of Social Work*, 40(4): 1229–46.

McGovern, M. (2016) *Social Work Placement: New Approaches. New Thinking. No 1: Language – Professional Identity – Expectations and Beginnings*. Available at: https://books.apple.com/ie/book/social-work-placement-new-approaches-new-thinking-1/id1102290962

McGovern, M. (2018) *Social Work Placement: New Approaches. New Thinking. No 4: Reflective Practice Influenced by Emotional Intelligence*, Book 4, Galway: NUI Galway. Available at: https://aran.library.nuigalway.ie/handle/10379/10021

McGregor, C. (2014) 'Why is history important at moments of transition? The case of "transformation" of Irish child welfare via the new Child and Family Agency', *European Journal of Social Work*, 17(5): 771–83.

McGregor, C. (2015) 'History as a resource for the future: A response to "Best of times, worst of times: Social work and its moment"', *The British Journal of Social Work*, 45(5): 1630–44.

McGregor, C. (2016) 'Balancing regulation and support in child protection: Using theories of power to develop reflective tools for practice', *Irish Social Worker*, Spring, 11–16. Available at: http://hdl.handle.net/10147/617865

McGregor, C. (2019) 'A paradigm framework for social work theory for 21st century practice', *The British Journal of Social Work*, 49(8): 2112–29. Available at: https://academic.oup.com/bjsw/article/49/8/2112/5368144

McGregor, C. and Devaney, C. (2020a) 'Protective support and supportive protection for families "in the middle": Learning from the Irish context', *Child & Family Social Work*, 25(2): 277–85.

McGregor, C. and Devaney, C. (2020b) 'A framework to inform protective support and supportive protection in child protection and welfare practice and supervision', *Social Sciences*, 9(4): 43. Available at: www.mdpi.com/2076-0760/9/4/43

McGregor, C. and Millar, M. (2020) 'A systemic lifecycle approach to social policy practice in social work: Illustrations from Irish child welfare and parenting research and practice', *The British Journal of Social Work*, 50(8): 2335–53. Available at: https://doi.org/10.1093/bjsw/bcaa194

McGregor, C., Brady, B. and Chaskin, R.J. (2020) 'The potential for civic and political engagement practice in social work as a means of achieving greater rights and justice for marginalised youth', *European Journal of Social Work*, 23(6): 958–68. doi:10.1080/13691457.2020.1793109.

McGregor, C., Devaney, C. and Moran, L. (2019) 'A critical overview of the significance of power and power relations in practice with children in foster care: Evidence from an Irish study', *Child Care in Practice*, 1–15. doi:10.1080/13575279.2018.1555135.

McGuinness, C. (1993) *Kilkenny Incest Investigation: Report Presented to Mr Brendan Howlin, TD, Minister for Health*, Dublin: Stationery Office.

McIntosh, P. (1988) *White Privilege and Male Privilege: A Personal Account of Coming to See Correspondences Through Work in Women's Studies*, Working Paper No 189, Wellesley, MA: Wellesley College, Center for Research on Women.

McKenna, D. and Staniforth, B. (2017) 'Older people moving to residential care in Aotearoa New Zealand: Considerations for social work at practice and policy levels', *Aotearoa New Zealand Social Work*, 29(1): 28–40.

McLaughlin, H. (2010) 'Keeping service user involvement in research honest', *The British Journal of Social Work*, 40(5): 1591–608.

McLaughlin, H., Beresford, P., Cameron, C., Casey, H. and Duffy, J. (2020) *Routledge International Handbook of Service User Involvement in Human Services Research and Education*, New York: Routledge.

McPherson, L. and MacNamara, N. (2017) *Supervising Child Protection Practice: What Works?*, Cham, Switzerland: Springer International Publishing.

Meagher, G., Lundström, T., Sallnäs, M. and Wiklund, S. (2016) 'Big business in a thin market: Understanding the privatization of residential care for children and youth in Sweden', *Social Policy & Administration*, 50(7): 805–23.

Meleis, A.I., Sawyer L.M., Im, E.O., Messias, D.K.H. and Schumacher, K. (2000) 'Experiencing transitions: An emerging middle-range theory', *Advances in Nursing Science*, 23(1): 12–28.

Mendes, P. and Snow, P. (eds) (2016) *Young People Transitioning from Out-of-Home Care: International Research, Policy and Practice*, London: Palgrave Macmillan.

Merkel-Holguin, L., Fluke, J.D. and Krugman, R. (eds) (2019) *Child Maltreatment Series, Vol 8: National Systems of Child Protection*, New York: Springer.

Molgaard, V. and Spoth, R. (2001) 'The Strengthening Families Program for young adolescents: Overview and outcomes', *Residential Treatment for Children & Youth*, 18(3): 15–29.

Montgomery, L. and McKee, J. (2017) 'Adult safeguarding in Northern Ireland: Prevention, protection, partnership', *The Journal of Adult Protection*, 19(4): 199–208.

Montgomery, L., Hanlon, D. and Armstrong, C. (2017) '10,000 voices: Service users' experience of adult safeguarding', *The Journal of Adult Protection*, 19(5): 236–46.

Montgomery, L., Anand, J., McKay, K., Taylor, B., Pearson, K.C. and Harper, C.M. (2016) 'Implications of divergences in adult protection legislation', *The Journal of Adult Protection*, 18(3): 149–60.

Mooney, J. (2018) 'Adult disclosures of childhood sexual abuse and Section 3 of the Child Care Act 1991: Past offences, current risk', *Child Care in Practice*, 24: 245–57.

Mooney, J. and McGregor, C. (2021) 'The importance of teaching social work practice from a socio-legal perspective', *Journal of Social Work Education*.

Moore, S.E., Jones-Eversley, S.D., Tolliver, W.F., Wilson, B. and Harmon, D.K. (2020) 'Cultural responses to loss and grief among Black Americans: Theory and practice implications for clinicians', *Death Studies*, 1–11. doi:10.1080/074 81187.2020.1725930.

Moran, L., McGregor, C. and Devaney, C. (2017) *Outcomes for Permanence and Stability for Children in Long-Term Care*, Galway: UNESCO Child and Family Research Centre, National University of Ireland Galway.

Morrison, A., McCartan, C., Davidson, G. and Bunting, L. (2018) *Anti-Poverty Practice Framework for Social Work in Northern Ireland*, Belfast: Department of Health.

Morrison, T. (2005) *Staff Supervision in Social Care* (3rd edn), Brighton: Pavilion Publishing.

Morriss, L. (2016) 'AMHP work: Dirty or prestigious? Dirty work designations and the approved mental health professional', *The British Journal of Social Work*, 46(3): 703–18.

Mossberg, L. (2019) 'Construction of service users in strategic collaboration including mental health and social services, and service user organisations', *European Journal of Social Work*, 23(4): 594–605. doi:10.1080/13691457.2019.1589426.

Mulally, R. (1993) *Structural Social Work: Ideology, Theory and Practice*, Oxford: Oxford University Press.

Mulally, R. (2007) *The New Structural Social Work*, Don Mills, ON: Oxford University Press.

Mullineux, J.C., Taylor, B.J. and Giles, M.L. (2019) 'Probation officers' judgements: A study using personal construct theory', *Journal of Social Work*, 19(1): 41–59.

Mullineux, J.C., Taylor, B.J. and Giles, M.L. (2020) 'Professional judgement about re-offending: Factorial survey', *Journal of Social Work*, 20(6): 797–816.

Mulvihill, A. and Walsh, T. (2014) 'Pregnancy loss in rural Ireland: An experience of disenfranchised grief', *The British Journal of Social Work*, 44(8): 2290–306.

Munford, R. and O'Donoghue, K. (eds) (2019) *New Theories for Social Work Practice: Ethical Practice for Working with Individuals, Families and Communities*, London: Jessica Kingsley Publishers.

Munro, E. (2004) 'The impact of audit on social work practice', *The British Journal of Social Work*, 34(8): 1073–4.

Munro, E. (2011) *The Munro Review of Child Protection: Final Report. A Child-Centred System*, vol 8062, London: The Stationery Office.

Munro, E. and Stein, M. (2008) 'Introduction: Comparative Exploration of Care Leavers' Transitions to Adulthood', in M. Stein and E. Munro (eds) *Young People's Transitions from Care to Adulthood: International Research and Practice*, London: Jessica Kingsley Publishers, pp 11–20.

Murphy, K. and Bantry-White, E. (2020) 'Behind closed doors: Human rights in residential care for people with an intellectual disability in Ireland', *Disability & Society*. doi:10.1080/09687599.2020.1768052.

Muurinen, H. and Satka, M. (2020) 'Pragmatist Knowledge Production in Practice Research', in L. Joubert and M. Webber (eds) *The Routledge Handbook of Social Work Practice Research*, London: Routledge, Chapter 11.

Narey, M. (2014) *Making the Education of Social Workers Consistently Effective*, London: Department for Education.

Naseh, M., MacGowan, M.J., Wagner, E.F., Abtahi, Z., Potocky, M. and Stuart, P.H. (2019) 'Cultural adaptations in psychosocial interventions for posttraumatic stress disorder among refugees: A systematic review', *Journal of Ethnic & Cultural Diversity in Social Work*, 28(1): 76–97.

Näslund, H., Sjöström, S. and Markström, U. (2019) 'Service user entrepreneurs and claims to authority – A case study in the mental health area', *European Journal of Social Work*, 1–13. doi:10.1080/13691457.2019.1580249.

Negroni, L.K., Medina, C.K., Rivera Díaz, M. and Paniccia, M. (2020) 'Perceptions of mental health and utilization of mental health services in Puerto Rico', *Social Work in Mental Health*, 18(2): 149–69.

Ní Léime, A. and Street, D. (2016) 'Gender and age implications of extended working life policies in the US and Ireland', *Critical Social Policy*, 3(3): 464–83.

Nilsson, L. and Westlund, O. (2007) *Våld Mot Personer med Funktionshinder* [*Violence Against People with Disabilities*], Report 2007:26, Stockholm: Swedish National Council for Crime Prevention.

Ní Raghallaigh, M. (2011) 'Religion in the lives of unaccompanied minors: An available and compelling coping resource', *The British Journal of Social Work*, 41(3): 539–56.

Ní Raghallaigh, M. (2013) 'The causes of mistrust amongst asylum seekers and refugees: Insights from research with unaccompanied asylum-seeking minors living in the Republic of Ireland', *Journal of Refugee Studies*, 27(1): 82–100.

Ní Raghallaigh, M. and Thornton, L. (2017) 'Vulnerable childhood, vulnerable adulthood: Direct provision as aftercare for aged-out separated children seeking asylum in Ireland', *Critical Social Policy*, 37(3): 386–404.

Nistor, G.C. (2019) 'Social media and domestic violence', *Scientific Annals of the 'Al I Cuza' University, Iasi Sociology and Social Work/Analele Stiintifice ale Universitatii 'Al I Cuza' Iasi Sociologie si Asistenta Sociala*, 12(1): 95–103.

Norris, D., Fancey, P., Power, E. and Ross, P. (2013) 'The critical-ecological framework: Advancing knowledge, practice, and policy on older adult abuse', *Journal of Elder Abuse & Neglect*, 25(1): 40–55.

O'Donnell, M., Taplin, S., Marriott, R., Lima, F. and Stanley, F.J. (2019) 'Infant removals: The need to address the over-representation of Aboriginal infants and community concerns of another "stolen generation"', *Child Abuse & Neglect*, 90: 88–98.

O'Hare, T., Shen, C. and Sherrer, M.V. (2019) 'Racial differences in response to trauma: Comparing African-American, White, and Hispanic people with severe mental illness', *Journal of Ethnic & Cultural Diversity in Social Work*, 28(2): 151–64.

O'Malley, S. and Devaney, C. (2016) 'Supporting incarcerated mothers in Ireland with their familial relationships: A case for the revival of the social work role', *Probation Journal*, 63(3): 293–309.

Office of the Minister for Children (2007) *The Agenda for Children's Services: A Policy Handbook*, Dublin: Stationery Office.

Owens, J., Mladenov, T. and Cribb, A. (2017) 'What justice, what autonomy? The ethical constraints upon personalisation', *Ethics and Social Welfare*, 11(1): 3–18.

Palattiyil, G., Sidhva, D., Pawar, M., Shajahan, P.K., Cox, J. and Anand, J.C. (2019) 'Reclaiming international social work in the context of the Global Agenda for Social Work and Social Development: Some critical reflections', *International Social Work*, 62(3): 1043–54.

Papalia, N.L., Luebbers, S. and Ogloff, J.R.P. (2020) 'A Developmental Lifecourse Approach to the Study of Offending and Victimisation Following Child Sexual Abuse', in I. Bryce and W. Petherick (eds) *Child Sexual Abuse*, London: Academic Press, pp 293–323.

Parker, J. and Ashencaen Crabtree, S. (eds) (2020a) *Human Growth and Development in Children and Young People*, Bristol: Policy Press.

Parker, J. and Ashencaen Crabtree, S. (eds) (2020b) *Human Growth and Development in Adults*, Bristol: Policy Press.

Parton, N. (1991) *Governing the Family*, London: Macmillan Education.

Parton, N. (1997) *Child Protection and Family Support: Tensions, Contradictions and Possibilities*, London: Routledge.

Parton, N. (2014a) *The Politics of Child Protection*, Basingstoke: Palgrave Macmillan.

Parton, N. (2014b) 'Social work, child protection and politics: Some critical and constructive reflections', *The British Journal of Social Work*, 44(7): 2042–56.

Patton, K.A., Ware, R., McPherson, L., Emerson, E. and Lennox, N. (2018) 'Parent-related stress of male and female carers of adolescents with intellectual disabilities and carers of children within the general population: A cross-sectional comparison', *Journal of Applied Research in Intellectual Disabilities*, 31(1): 51–61.

Payne, M. (2016) *Modern Social Work Theory*, Oxford: Oxford University Press.

Payne, M. and Reith-Hall, E. (2019) *The Routledge Handbook of Social Work Theory*, London: Routledge.

Pearce, J. (2019) *Child Sexual Exploitation: Why Theory Matters*, Bristol: Policy Press.

Perlman, H. (1979) *Relationships: The Heart of Helping People*, Chicago, IL: The University of Chicago Press.

Phillimore, J. (ed) (2019) 'Special issue on rethinking integration: New perspectives on adaptation and settlement in an era of super-diversity', *Journal of Ethnic and Migration Studies*.

Philp, M. (1979) 'Notes on the form of knowledge in social work', *The Sociological Review*, 27(1): 83–111.

Pincus, A. and Minahan, A. (1973) *Social Work Practice: Model and Method*, Itasca, IL: Peacock.

Pinkerton, J. (2008) 'States of Care Leaving: Towards International Exchange as a Global Resource', in M. Stein and E. Munro (eds) *Young People's Transitions from Care to Adulthood: International Research and Practice*, London: Jessica Kingsley Publishers, pp 241–57.

Pinkerton, J. (2011) 'Constructing a global understanding of the social ecology of leaving out of home care', *Children and Youth Services Review*, 33(12): 2412–16.

Pinkerton, J. (2021) 'Exploring history in the social ecology of care leaving: Northern Ireland as illustration', *Child & Family Social Work*, 26(2): 270–9.

Pinkerton, J. and Rooney, C. (2014) 'Care leavers' experiences of transition and turning points: Findings from a biographical narrative study', *Social Work & Society*, 12(1): 1–12.

Pinkerton, J., Canavan, J. and Dolan, P. (2019) 'Family Support and Social Work Practice', in R. Munford and K. O'Donoghue (eds) *New Theories for Social Work Practice: Ethical Practice for Working with Individuals, Families and Communities*, London: Jessica Kingsley Publishers, pp 44–62.

Pon, G. (2009) 'Cultural competency as new racism: An ontology of forgetting', *Journal of Progressive Human Services*, 20(1): 59–71.

Portes, A. (1998) 'Social capital: Its origins and applications in modern sociology', *Annual Review of Sociology*, 24(1): 1–24.

Powell, J.L. (2018) *Life Course and Society*, New York: Nova Science Publishing.

Preston-Shoot, M. (2011) 'On administrative evil-doing within social work policy and services: Law, ethics and practice', *European Journal of Social Work*, 14(2): 177–94. doi:10.1080/13691450903471229.

Preston-Shoot, M. and Cornish, S. (2014) 'Paternalism or proportionality? Experiences and outcomes of the Adult Support and Protection (Scotland) Act 2007', *The Journal of Adult Protection*, 16(1): 5–16.

Price, J. (2020) 'The experience of young people transitioning between youth offending services to probation services', *Probation Journal*, 67(3): 246–63.

Raftery, M. and O'Sullivan, E. (1999) *Suffer the Children: The Inside Story of Ireland's Industrial Schools*, Dublin: New Island.

Rasmussen, T. (2012) 'Knowledge Production and Social Work: Forming Knowledge Production', in E. Marthinsen and I. Julkunen (eds) *Practice Research in Nordic Social Work: Knowledge Production in Transition*, London: Whiting & Birch, pp 43–66.

Raynor, P. and Vanstone, M. (2016) 'Moving away from social work and halfway back again: New research on skills in probation', *The British Journal of Social Work*, 46(4): 1131–47.

Redmond, S. and Dolan, P. (2016) 'Towards a conceptual model of youth leadership development', *Child & Family Social Work*, 21(3): 261–71.

Reupert, A. (2017) 'A socio-ecological framework for mental health and well-being', *Advances in Mental Health*, 15(2): 105–7.

Reupert, A., Maybery, D., Nicholson, J., Göpfert, M. and Seeman, M. (eds) (2015) *Parental Psychiatric Disorder: Distressed Parents and their Families* (3rd edn), Cambridge: Cambridge University Press.

Richmond, M. (1917) *Social Diagnosis*, New York: Russell Sage Foundation.

Risley, A. (2014) 'Protecting children and adolescents in Uruguay: Civil society's role in policy reform', *Social Sciences*, 3(4): 705–25.

Rodriguez, L., Cassidy, A. and Devaney, C. (2018) *Meitheal Process and Outcomes Study*, Galway: UNESCO Child and Family Research Centre, National University of Ireland Galway.

Roets, G., van Beveren, L., Saar-Heiman, Y., Degerickx, H., Vandekinderen, C., Krumer-Nevo, M., Rutten, K. and Roose, R. (2020) 'Developing a poverty-aware pedagogy: From paradigm to reflexive practice in post-academic social work education', *The British Journal of Social Work*, 50(5): 1495–512.

Rogowski, S. (2015) 'From child welfare to child protection/safeguarding: A critical practitioner's view of changing conceptions, policies and practice', *Practice*, 27(2): 97–112.

Rojek, C. (1986) 'The subject in social work', *The British Journal of Social Work*, 16(1): 65–77.

Rojek, C., Peacock, G. and Collins, S. (1988) *Social Work and Received Ideas*, Abingdon: Routledge.

Rose, N. (1985) *The Psychological Complex: Psychology, Politics and Society in England 1869–1939*, London: Routledge.

Ruch, G., Winter, K., Cree, V., Hallet, S., Morrisson, F. and Hadfield, M. (2017) 'Making meaningful connections: Using insights from social pedagogy in statutory child and family social work practice', *Child & Family Social Work*, 22(2): 1015–23.

Ruiz-Román, C., Molina, L. and Alcaide, R. (2019) '"We have a common goal": Support networks for the educational and social development of children in disadvantaged areas', *The British Journal of Social Work*, 49(6): 1658–76.

Rutter, M. (2012) 'Resilience: Causal Pathways and Social Ecology', in M. Ungar (ed) *The Social Ecology of Resilience: A Handbook of Theory and Practice*, New York: Springer, pp 33–42.

Rutter, M., Giller, H. and Hagell, A. (1998) *Antisocial Behaviour by Young People*, Cambridge: Cambridge University Press.

Ruwhiu, P. (2019) 'Te Whakapakari Ake I te Mahi: Mana-Enhancing Practice: Engagement with Social Work Students and Practitioners', in R. Munford and K. O'Donoghue (eds) *New Theories for Social Work Practice: Ethical Practices for Working with Individuals, Families and Communities*, London: Jessica Kingsley Publishers, pp 195–211.

Sabatini, F. (2006) *Social Capital and Economic Development*, SPES Development Studies Discussion Paper No 1.2006. Available at: https://papers.ssrn.com/sol3/papers.cfm?abstract_id=901362

Saleebey, D. (1996) 'The strengths perspective in social work practice: Extensions and cautions', *Social Work*, 41(3): 296–305.

Salisbury Forum Group (2011) 'The Salisbury Statement', *Social Work and Society, Special Issue: 'Practice Research'*, 4–9.

Satka, M. (2013) 'Practice research in Nordic social work: Knowledge production in transition', *Nordic Social Work Research*, 3(1): 96–8.

Satka, M. (2014) 'Looking to the Past for the Sustainable Social Work of the Future', in T. Harrikari, R. Pirkko-Liisa and E. Virokannas (eds) *Social Change and Social Work: The Changing Societal Conditions of Social Work in Time and Place*, London: Routledge, pp 193–202.

Satka, M. and Skehill, C. (2012) 'Michel Foucault and Dorothy Smith in case file research: Strange bed-fellows or complementary thinkers?', *Qualitative Social Work: Research and Practice*, 11(2): 191–205.

Satka, M., Harrikari, T., Hoikkala, S. and Pekkarinen, E. (2007) 'The diverse impacts of the neoliberal social policies on children's welfare and social work with young people: The Finnish perspective', *Social Work & Society*, 5(3): 125–35.

Schäfer, G. (2020a) 'An Introduction to the Principles of Attachment Theory', in J. Parker and S. Ashencaen (eds) *Human Growth and Development in Children and Young People*, Bristol: Policy Press, pp 133–46.

Schäfer, G. (2020b) 'Critical Aspects of Attachment Theory: Empirical Research Findings and Current Applications', in J. Parker and S. Ashencaen (eds) *Human Growth and Development in Adults*, Bristol: Policy Press, pp 103–15.

Scheibl, F., Fleming, J., Buck, J., Barclay, S., Brayne, C. and Farquhar, M. (2019) 'The experience of transitions in care in very old age: Implications for general practice', *Family Practice*, 36(6): 778–84.

Schilde, K. and Schulte, D. (2005) *Need and Care – Glimpses into the Beginnings of Eastern Europe's Professional Welfare*, Opladen and Farmington Hills, MI: Barbara Budrich Publishers.

SCIE (Social Care Institute for Excellence) (2011) *User Involvement in Adult Safeguarding*, Report No 47, London: SCIE.

Scourfield, P. (2005) 'Social care and the modern citizen: Client, consumer, service user, manager and entrepreneur', *The British Journal of Social Work*, 37: 107–22.

Segal, E.A. (2011) 'Social empathy: A model built on empathy, contextual understanding, and social responsibility that promotes social justice', *Journal of Social Service Research*, 37(3): 266–77.

Serbati, S., Moe, A., Halton, C. and Harold, G. (2019) 'Pathways for practitioners' participation in creating the practice–research encounter', *European Journal of Social Work*, 22(5): 791–804.

Sewpaul, V. (2013) 'Community Work and the Challenges of Neoliberalism and New Managerialism', in A.K. Larsen, V. Sewpaul and G.O. Hole (eds) *Participation in Community Work: International Perspectives*, Abingdon: Routledge, pp 217–29.

Sewpaul, V. (2021) *The Tension Between Culture and Human Rights*, Calgary: University of Calgary Press.

Sewpaul, V. and Larsen, A.K. (2013) 'Community Development: Towards an Integrated Emancipatory Framework', in A.K. Larsen, V. Sewpaul and G.O. Hole (eds) *Participation in Community Work: International Perspectives*, Abingdon: Routledge, pp 230–46.

Shanahan, M.J., Mortimer, J.L. and Kirkpatrick Johnson, M. (2016) *Handbook of the Life Course, Vol II*, New York: Springer.

Sharkey, P. (1989) 'Social networks and social service workers', *The British Journal of Social Work*, 19: 387–405.

Shaw, I. (2020) 'Practice Research as a Collective Enterprise', in L. Joubert and M. Webber (eds) *The Routledge Handbook of Social Work Practice Research*, London: Routledge, Chapter 6.

Shemmings, D., Shemmings, Y. and Cook, A. (2012) 'Gaining the trust of "highly resistant" families: Insights from attachment theory and research', *Child & Family Social Work*, 17(2): 130–7.

Sheppard, M. (2009) 'Social support use as a parental coping strategy: Its impact on outcome of child and parenting problems – A six-month follow-up', *The British Journal of Social Work*, 39(8): 1427–46.

Shier, M., Sinclair, C. and Gault, L. (2011) 'Challenging "ableism" and teaching about disability in a social work classroom', *Critical Social Work*, 12(1): 47–64.

Shokane, A.L. and Masoga, M.A. (2019) 'Social work as protest: Conversations with selected first black social work women in South Africa', *Critical and Radical Social Work*, 7(3): 435–45.

Siagian, C., Arifiani, S., Amanda, P. and Kusumaningrum, S. (2019) 'Supporting children, blaming parents: Frontline providers' perception of childhood's adversity and parenthood in Indonesia', *Social Sciences*, 8(2): 64. doi.org/10.3390/socsci8020064.

Silke, C., Brady, B., Boylan, C. and Dolan, P. (2018) 'Factors influencing the development of empathy and pro-social behaviour among adolescents: A systematic review', *Children and Youth Services Review*, 94(3): 421–36.

Silke, C., Brady, B., Dolan, P. and Boylan, C. (2019) 'Social values and civic behaviour among youth in Ireland: The influence of social contexts', *Irish Journal of Sociology*, 28(1). doi:10.1177/0791603519863295.

Simpson, G. and Murr, A. (2014) 'Reconceptualising well-being', *Culture Unbound*, 6(4): 891–904.

Skehill, C. (1999) *History of Social Work in the Republic of Ireland*, Lampeter: Edwin Mellen Press.

Skehill, C. (2000) 'An examination of the transition from philanthropy to professional social work in Ireland', *Research on Social Work Practice*, 10(6): 688–704.

Skehill, C. (2003) 'Social work in the Republic of Ireland: A history of the present', *Journal of Social Work*, 3(2): 141–59.

Skehill, C. (2004) *History of the Present of Child Protection and Welfare Social Work in Ireland*, Lampeter: Edwin Mellen Press.

Skehill, C. (2007) 'Researching the history of social work: Exposition of a history of the present approach', *European Journal of Social Work*, 10(4): 449–63.

Skehill, C. (2008) 'Editorial: Looking back while moving forward: Historical perspectives in social work', *The British Journal of Social Work*, 38(4): 619–24.

Slettebø, T. (2013) 'Partnership with parents of children in care: A study of collective user participation in child protection services', *The British Journal of Social Work*, 43: 579–95.

Sloth-Nielsen, J. (2014) 'Regional frameworks for safeguarding children: The role of the African Committee of Experts on the rights and welfare of the child', *Social Sciences*, 3(4): 948–61.

Smart, C. (1989) *Feminism and the Power of Law*, New York: Routledge.

Smith, D. (2005) 'Probation and social work', *The British Journal of Social Work*, 35(5): 621–37.

Smith, R. (2008) *Social Work and Power*, Basingstoke: Palgrave Macmillan.

Somerville, L. and Brady, E. (2019) 'Young people and social networking sites: Exploring the views and training opportunities of CAMHS social workers in Ireland', *Journal of Social Work Practice*, 33(2): 141–55.

Southall, C., Lonbay, S.P. and Brandon, T. (2019) 'Social workers' negotiation of the liminal space between personalisation policy and practice', *European Journal of Social Work*, 24(3): 1–13. doi:10.1080/13691457.2019.1633624.

Spicker, P. (2013) 'Personalisation falls short', *The British Journal of Social Work*, 43(7): 1259–75.

Spira, M., Perkins, N.H. and Gilman, A.H. (2020) 'Trauma from physical and emotional sibling violence as a potential risk factor for elder abuse', *Journal of Gerontological Social Work*, 63(3): 162–73.

Spratt, T. (2012) 'Why multiples matter: Reconceptualising the population referred to child and family social workers', *The British Journal of Social Work*, 42(8): 1574–91.

Spratt, T., Devaney, J. and Frederick, J. (2019) 'Adverse Childhood Experiences: Beyond signs of safety; Reimagining the organisation and practice of social work with children and families', *The British Journal of Social Work*, 49(8): 2042–58.

Starns, B. (2018) 'Moving to a systems approach to safeguard adults in residential care', *Practice*, 30(3): 157–61.

Stein, M. (2005a) 'Young People Leaving Care: Poverty Across the Life Course', in G. Preston (ed) *At Greatest Risk: The Children Most Likely to Be Poor*, London: Child Poverty Action Group, pp 166–78.

Stein, M. (2005b) *Resilience and Young People Leaving Care: Overcoming the Odds*, York: Joseph Rowntree Foundation.

Stein, M. (2006) 'Young people aging out of care: The poverty of theory', *Children and Youth Services Review*, 28(4): 422–34.

Stein, M. (2008) 'Transitions from Care to Adulthood: Messages from Research for Policy and Practice', in M. Stein and E. Munro (eds) *Young People's Transitions from Care to Adulthood: International Research and Practice*, London: Jessica Kingsley Publishers, pp 289–306.

Stein, M., Pinkerton, J. and Kelleher, P. (2009) 'Young People Leaving Care in England, Northern Ireland and Ireland', in J. Thoburn and M. Courtney (eds) *Children in State Care*, London: Routledge, pp 423–34.

Stein, M., Ward, H. and Courtney, M. (2011) 'International perspectives on young people's transitions from care to adulthood', *Children and Youth Services Review*, 33(12): 2409–11.

Stevens, M., Manthrope, J., Martineau, S. and Norrie, C. (2020) 'Practice perspectives and theoretical debates about social workers' legal power to protect adults', *Journal of Social Work*, 20(1): 3–22.

Stevenson, O. (1971) 'Knowledge for social work', *The British Journal of Social Work*, 1(2): 225–38.

Stevenson, O. (1986) 'Guest Editorial on the Jasmine Beckford Inquiry', *The British Journal of Social Work*, 16(5): 501–10.

Stone, K. (2019) 'Approved mental health professionals and detention: An exploration of professional differences and similarities', *Practice*, 31(3): 83–96.

Storø, J. (2017) 'Which transition concept is useful for describing the process of young people leaving state care? A reflection on research and language', *European Journal of Social Work*, 20(5): 770–81.

Stroebe, M. and Schut, H. (1999) 'The dual process of coping with bereavement', *Death Studies*, 23: 197–224.

Sudbery, J. (2010) 'Human growth and development: An introduction for social work', *Journal of Social Work*, 12(1): 101–2.

Sudbery, J. and Whittaker, A. (2019) *Human Growth and Development: An Introduction for Social Workers* (2nd edn), London: Routledge.

Sulimani-Aidan, Y. and Paldi, Y. (2020) 'Youth perspectives on parents' involvement in residential care in Israel', *Journal of Social Work*, 21(1): 64–82.

Szasz, T. (1975) *The Age of Madness: The History of Involuntary Mental Hospitalization Presented in Selected Texts*, Abingdon: Routledge & Kegan Paul.

Talpin, S. (2020) 'Loss and Bereavement in Childhood', in J. Parker, J. and S. Ashencaen (eds) *Human Growth and Development in Children and Young People*, Bristol: Policy Press, pp 191–202.

Talpur, A.A., Ryan, T., Ali, P. and Hinchcliff, S. (2018) 'Elder mistreatment in South Asian communities: A review of the literature', *The Journal of Adult Protection*, 20(5/6): 193–206.

Tanner, D., Littlechild, R., Duffy, J. and Hayes, D. (2017) '"Making it real": Evaluating the impact of service user and carer involvement in social work education', *The British Journal of Social Work*, 47(2): 467–8.

Taylor, B.J. (2017) 'Heuristics in professional judgement: A psycho-social rationality model', *The British Journal of Social Work*, 47(4): 1043–60.

Tembo, M.J., Studsrød, I. and Young, S. (2020) 'Governing the family: Immigrant parents' perceptions of the controlling power of the Norwegian welfare system', *European Journal of Social Work*. doi:10.1080/13691457.2020.1738349.

Tew, J. (2006) 'Power and powerlessness: Towards a framework for emancipatory practice in social work', *Journal of Social Work*, 6(1): 33–51.

Thompson, N. (2020) *Anti-Discriminatory Practice: Equality, Diversity and Social Justice* (7th edn), London: Red Globe Press.

Thompson, R. (1995) *Preventing Child Maltreatment Through Social Support – A Critical Analysis*, London: SAGE Publications Ltd.

Thyer, B.A., Dulmus, C.N. and Sowers, K.M. (2012) *Human Behaviour in the Social Environment: Theories for Social Work Practice*, Hoboken, NJ: Wiley.

Tierney, E., Kennan, D., Forkan, C., Brady, B. and Jackson, R. (2018) *Children's Participation Work Package Final Report: Tusla's Programme for Prevention, Partnership and Family Support*, Galway: UNESCO Child and Family Research Centre, National University of Ireland Galway.

Timms, E. (1990) 'Social networks and social service workers: A comment on Sharkey', *The British Journal of Social Work*, 20: 627–31.

Timonen, V. (2019) *Grandparenting Practices Around the World*, Chicago, IL: The University of Chicago Press.

Tomiţă, M. and Goian, C. (2009) 'Romanian probation system and the effect of semantics in social work', *Revista de Cercetare şi Intervenţie Socială*, 27(1): 99–111.

Tracy, E.M. and Whittaker, J.K. (1990) 'The social network map: Assessing social support in clinical practice', *Families in Society*, 71(8): 461–70.

Trevithick, P. (2012) *Social Work Skills and Knowledge: A Practice Handbook*, Milton Keynes: Open University Press.

Tudge, J.R., Payir, A., Merçon-Vargas, E., Cao, H., Liang, Y., Li, J. and O'Brien, L. (2016) 'Still misused after all these years? A re-evaluation of the uses of Bronfenbrenner's bioecological theory of human development', *Journal of Family Theory & Review*, 8(4): 427–45.

Turba, H., Breimo, J.P. and Lo, C. (2019) 'Professional and organizational power intertwined: Barriers to networking?', *Children and Youth Services Review*, 107: 104527.

Turnell, A. and Murphy, T. (2017) *The Signs of Safety: A Comprehensive Briefing Paper* (4th edn), Perth, WA: Resolutions Consultancy Pty Ltd.

Tysnes, I.B. and Kiik, R. (2019) 'Support on the way to adulthood: Challenges in the transition between social welfare systems', *European Journal of Social Work*, 24(2): 201–11. doi:10.1080/13691457.2019.1602512.

Uggerhoj, L. (2012) 'Theorising Practice Research in Social Work', in E. Marthinsen and I. Julkunen (eds) *Practice Research in Nordic Social Work: Knowledge Production in Transition*, London: Whiting & Birch, pp 67–94.

Ungar, M. (ed) (2005) *Handbook for Working with Children and Youth: Pathways to Resilience Across Cultures and Contexts*, London: SAGE Publications Ltd.

Ungar, M. (2012a) *The Social Ecology of Resilience*, New York: Springer.

Ungar, M. (2012b) 'Social Ecologies and Their Contribution to Resilience', in M. Ungar (ed) *The Social Ecology of Resilience: A Handbook of Theory and Practice*, New York: Springer, pp 13–31.

UNICEF (2020) *UNICEF's Global Social Protection Programme Framework*, New York.

Van Breda, A.D.P. and Pinkerton, J. (2020) 'Raising African voices in the global dialogue on care-leaving and emerging adulthood', *Emerging Adulthood*, 8(1): 6–15.

Van Ryzin, M.J., Mills, D., Kelban, S., Vars, M.R. and Chamberlain, P. (2011) 'Using Bridges' transition framework for youth in foster care: Measurement development and preliminary outcomes', *Children and Youth Services Review*, 33(11): 2267–72.

Wahid, A., Sugiharto, D.Y.P., Samsudi, S. and Haryono, H. (2018) 'Tolerance in inquiry-based learning: Building harmony and solidarity in students', *Walisongo Jurnal Penelitian Sosial Keagamaan*, 26(1): 147–70.

Walker, J. and Horner, N. (2020) *Social Work and Human Development* (6th edn), Exeter: Learning Matters.

Wang, M., Victor, B.G., Hong, J.S., Wu, S., Huang, J., Luan, H. and Perron, B.E. (2020) 'A scoping review of interventions to promote health and well-being of left-behind children in Mainland China', *The British Journal of Social Work*, 50(5): 1419–39.

Ward, H., Courtney, M., Del Valle, J.F., McDermid, S. and Zeira, A. (2009) 'Improving outcomes for children and young people in care', *Vulnerable Children and Youth Studies*, 4(2): 101–6.

Webb, P., Davidson, G., Edge, R., Keenan, F., McLaughlin, A., Montgomery, L., Mulvenna, C., Norris, B., Owens, A. and Shea Irvine, R. (2020) 'Service users' experiences and views of support for decision making', *Health & Social Care in the Community*, 28(4): 1282–91.

Webb, S. (2019) *Routledge Handbook of Critical Social Work*, London: Routledge.

Webber, M., Morris, D., Howarth, S., Fendt-Newlin, M., Treacy, S. and McCrone, P. (2019) 'Effect of the connecting people intervention on social capital: A pilot study', *Research on Social Work Practice*, 29(5): 483–94.

Weedon, C. (1996) *Feminist Practice and Poststructuralist Theory* (2nd edn), Hoboken, NJ: Wiley-Blackwell.

Westoby, P., Lathouras, A. and Shevellar, L. (2019) 'Radicalising community development within social work through popular education – A participatory action research project', *The British Journal of Social Work*, 49(8): 2207–25. Available at: https://doi-org.libgate.library.nuigalway.ie/10.1093/bjsw/bcz022

Wilberforce, M., Abendstern, M., Batool, S., Boland, J., Challis, D., Christian, J., Hughes, J., Kinder, P., Lake-Jones, P., Mistry, M. and Pitts, R. (2020) 'What do service users want from mental health social work? A best–worst scaling analysis', *The British Journal of Social Work*, 50(5): 1324–44.

Williams, C. (2020) 'Politics, preoccupations, pragmatics: A race/ethnicity redux for social work research', *European Journal of Social Work*, 23(6): 1057–68. doi: 10.1080/13691457.2020.1751590.

Willoughby, M. (2019) 'A review of the risks associated with children and young people's social media use and the implications for social work practice', *Journal of Social Work Practice*, 33(2): 127–40.

Wilson, S., Hean, S., Abebe, T. and Heaslip, V. (2020) 'Children's experiences with child protection services: A synthesis of qualitative evidence', *Children and Youth Services Review*, 113: 1–14.

Winter, B. and Burholt, V. (2018) 'The Welsh Welsh – Y Cymry Cymreig: A study of cultural exclusion among rural dwelling older people using a critical human ecological framework', *International Journal of Ageing and Later Life*, 12(2): 119–51.

Winter, K. and Cree, V.E. (2016) 'Social work home visits to children and families in the UK: A Foucauldian perspective', *The British Journal of Social Work*, 46(5): 1175–90.

Witkin, S. (2017) *Transforming Social Work: Social Constructionist Reflections on Contemporary and Enduring Issues*, London: Palgrave.

Woolcock, M. and Narayan, D. (2000) 'Social capital: Implications for development theory', *Research, and Policy, The World Bank Research Observer*, 15(2): 225–49. Available at: https://doi.org/10.1093/wbro/15.2.225

Worden, J.W. (2003) *Grief Counselling and Grief Therapy: A Handbook for the Mental Health Practitioner*, Philadelphia, PA: Routledge.

Xiang, X. and Han, M. (2020) 'The link between family violence in childhood and internalizing and externalizing problems in later life among college students in China: Attachment as a mediator', *Social Work in Mental Health*, 18(1): 39–54.

Yates, S. and Gatsou, L. (2020) 'Undertaking family-focused interventions when a parent has a mental illness – Possibilities and challenges', *Practice*, 33(2): 103–18. doi:10.1080/09503153.2020.1760814.

Yellow Bird, M.J. and Chenault, V. (1999) 'The Role of Social Work in Advancing the Practice of Indigenous Education: Obstacles and Promises in Empowerment-Oriented Social Work Practice', in K.G. Swisher and J.W. Tippeconnic (eds) *Next Steps: Research and Practice to Advance Indian Education*, Charlestown, NH: Eric Clearing House.

Yi-Bing, X., Quan-Cai, L. and Meng, C. (2020) 'Snapshot of social work in China: Outcomes of stakeholder competition', *The British Journal of Social Work*, bcaa236. Available at: https://academic.oup.com/bjsw/advance-article-abstract/doi/10.1093/bjsw/bcaa236/6050075

Zamanzadeh, V., Rahmani, A., Pakpour, V., Chenoweth, L.L. and Mohammadi, E. (2017) 'Psychosocial changes following transition to an aged care home: Qualitative findings from Iran', *International Journal of Older People Nursing*, 12(2): e12130. doi: 10.1111/opn.12130.

Zavirsek, D., Rommelspacher, B. and Satub-Bernasconi, S. (2010) *Ethical Dilemmas in Social Work: International Perspectives*, Ljubljana: Faculty of Social Work, University of Ljubljana.

Zimba, Z.F. (2020) 'Cultural complexity thinking by social workers in their address of Sustainable Development Goals in a culturally diverse South Africa', *Journal of Progressive Human Services*, 31(2): 93–106. doi:10.1080/10428232.2020.1732270.

Index

References to tables and figures appear in *italic* type